Teaching in Mind:
How Teacher Thinking Shapes Education

Teaching in Mind:
How Teacher Thinking Shapes Education

Judith Lloyd Yero, MA

Acknowledgments

As I read or listen to someone speak, my mind often grabs hold of an idea and runs with it. By the time I stop to catch my breath, I am often so far from where I began that I can no longer remember the idea that triggered my mental journey. Because I've done this for so many years—well before I ever considered writing this book, I can't even guess at the number (or identity) of all the people to whom I owe my thanks. I can only say "Thank you."

My thanks also go to the many men and women whose works I have quoted. They laid the groundwork of ideas on which this book is built.

Teaching in Mind would never have been written if it were not for the comments of teachers who attended my workshops and awakened me to the fascinating world of teacher thinking, as well as my students who, in their own unique ways, forced me to question my own behaviors and beliefs.

Special thanks go to the following:

The trainers from NLP Comprehensive, NLP of Chicago, and Anchor Point Training for giving me choices, making me aware of the power of beliefs, and literally "changing my mind."

Peggy Rubin for asking the question that started me on my journey and Jean Houston for sharing a passion for the possible.

Marianne Matthews, a classroom teacher in the finest tradition, who contributed her valuable time, energy, and expertise reading and commenting on the earliest (extremely long) version. She will recognize her touch in many places.

James Lawley, for his wonderfully gentle and diplomatic way of pointing out my own inconsistencies and limiting beliefs. Every author should be blessed with such thought-provoking comments.

My son, Rich, for his confidence in me and for keeping me "on task" whenever I was tempted to stray. "Write it and they will come."

Finally, to my parents, Whitten Lloyd and Julia Perry Lloyd, who taught me that nothing was impossible. Dream big and work hard. This is for you.

Table of Contents

Preface

When I imagine young children engaged in learning, the scene is dynamic. The faces of those children are alight with wonder, with puzzlement, with interest, and yes, with joy. When I picture students in many of today's classrooms, the image is often static. Locked into a prescribed system of learning, the faces of many young people register boredom, disinterest, or resignation..

Early in my teaching career, I recognized my need to guide the educational development of young people in ways that didn't, at the same time, take the joy out of their lives. I reasoned that my classroom environment must effectively support the natural ways in which children learn. Through postgraduate courses in the neurosciences, I worked to bridge the gap between emerging knowledge of the brain and the practices of education. I then shared these ideas with other teachers through workshops entitled *"Learning from the Inside Out."*

At the close of each workshop, participants were asked to comment on the ideas they had found the most valuable. To my surprise, rather than focusing on what they had learned about students, most of the teachers commented on how much they had learned about *themselves!*

Their comments made me realize the extent to which teachers are ignored in educational planning. Yet the beliefs and values that provide the unconscious foundation for teacher behavior, the metaphors that set the stage of their classrooms and the mental models of the world through which they conceptualize their work are highly individualistic. Rather than the constants they are often assumed to be, *the teacher may well be the most influential variable in the educational equation!*

Substantive change in education is unlikely to occur until educators understand how each teacher's thinking influences everything that occurs in the classroom. This book examines those issues and more. In its pages, you will be encouraged to probe the realms of *subjective* experience—the beliefs, values, presuppositions, and metaphors that shape your personal world.

The word *subjective* makes many educational researchers cringe. Recommendations for reform must be supported by "hard data"—research studies scrupulously conducted using the scientific method.

Because messy subjective concepts such as beliefs and values don't lend themselves to statistical manipulation, they were largely ignored.

In the past several decades, theorists have begun to recognize the importance of teacher thinking. Many research studies have explored the effects of teacher beliefs, the metaphors a teacher uses to describe his or her work, and the values a teacher assigns to a particular practice or concept. The studies have found that these thought processes have a profound influence on educational choices, but the results of those studies have been largely limited to academia. It is time for practicing teachers to have access to these ideas. It is the minds and actions of *those* teachers that make education what it is today.

My conclusions are my own, but I've attempted to include support from as many different disciplines as possible. The references are there for those who want or need them. However, many teachers are less interested in research studies than in practical ways to improve their teaching experience. The main thrust, therefore, is about what you can do today to be the teacher who matters to students.

You may be astounded at how differently teachers think—even about something as basic as the meanings of the words *teach, learn,* or *understand.* I invite you to let your own experiences verify the validity of these ideas. Take the ideas you can use and leave the rest for others who may have different perceptions and different experiences.

I invite you to imagine what our schools might be like if they became places where students and teachers alike shared the joyous and innate love of learning with which infants comes into the world. A handful of reflective teachers have it within their power to literally "change the face of education." Let us begin.

Introduction

"You may feel like a voice in the wilderness, but it is
your voice we are waiting to hear. Yours is the
crucial vote. You are the determining factor.
We reach Critical Mass when we reach you—
and you choose to reach others…."
~ Neale Donald Walsch[1]

In the wealth of rhetoric on school improvement and educational reform, one critical factor is consistently ignored. There is a pervasive lack of attention to teachers in educational planning. Frequently, teachers are perceived as constants, much like the books, desks, and other inanimate objects in the educational environment. More attention is paid to the attractive design and packaging of knowledge than on the one factor that may well be the most influential variable in the educational equation—the teacher!

Peter Temes, president of the Great Books Foundation, reminds us,

"Once the classroom door closes, once the lesson begins, once the student steps toward the teacher asking for help, it is all up to the teacher, not the school. Good schools help; great schools help more; but great teachers are the far more precious commodity."[2]

Recent studies reaffirm that "the most important factor that affects student learning is quality teaching."[3] Theorists have attempted to define and describe the characteristics of "quality teaching," focusing largely on observable behaviors. Yet the unconscious ways in which teachers perceive the world—create their mental models of "reality"—are highly individualistic. Identifying what makes one teacher effective is helpful,

---

1 Walsch, N.D. (1998). Quoted by Thom Hartmann in The Last Hours of Ancient Sunlight. Northfield, VT: Mythical Books.
2 Temes, P. (2001, April 4). The End of School Reform. Education Week, 36
3 Tell, C. (2000, April 20). Fostering High performance and Respectability. ASCD Infobrief. URL: http://www.ascd.org/readingroom/infobrief/0008.html

but that teachers' behaviors cannot be directly transferred to others. This is why no two classrooms are, or can be, the same.

Hundreds of books offer answers to questions teachers have asked since the beginning of organized education. What should we teach? How should we teach? How should we assess learning? Many books imply that, if only teachers would behave in the prescribed manner, education would miraculously improve. Yet despite this wealth of available answers, why is education still plagued with problems? Why?

Individual teachers neither understand nor implement the "answers" in the same way. The ways in which those answers fit into teachers' existing realities vary tremendously, resulting in widely differing behaviors. What does it mean to teach, to learn, to understand? Does it mean the same to others? And if not, what are the implications?

Teaching in Mind begins with questions rather than answers. What can educators gain by focusing on what teachers already do and why they do it rather than on generic ideas about how everyone should teach? Why does one teacher wait patiently as students think about a question while another pops in with the answer if one is not quickly forthcoming? Why is one teacher able to maintain discipline with no overt effort while another constantly reprimands students with little lasting effect? What sets *Dead Poet's Society's* John Keating or Jaime Escalante of *Stand and Deliver* apart from their peers? Examining why teachers make the choices they do offers significant insights into what occurs in classrooms.

What can be gained by asking those questions? As you'll discover, *your* answers to these questions are the ones that really count. When you understand the unique ways in which you represent teaching and learning in your own inner reality, you have the opportunity to make reasoned choices. You can accept things as they are or change the only thing that is within your power to directly change—yourself.

Teachers have always had the power to determine the tone and direction of a school, to create exemplary worlds within the classroom, and to scuttle reform movements that failed to fit their mental models. For too long, those actions have taken place without conscious thought or choice. It's time for teachers to recognize and accept their responsibility in shaping education, to begin mindfully applying stress where the system is dysfunctional, and to take their rightful place as wise and compassionate experts and decision makers. I invite you to my paradigm playground. Have fun!

Chapter 1 ~ The Power of Teachers

"There's power in how we think about things."
~Thom Hartmann[1]

Mention the topic of education in almost any group of people and nearly everyone will offer a solution to the perceived problems of the institution. Imagine how those same people would respond if someone made the following suggestion.

- From now on, individual teachers will decide the goals and indeed, the very meaning of education.
- Each teacher will define the purposes of education as he or she sees fit.
- Each teacher will modify the official curriculum according to personal preferences, interests, and teaching strengths and weaknesses.
- Each teacher will teach his or her personal beliefs and values.

Heresy! How could anyone suggest teachers should be free to choose what and how their students should learn? How could schools possibly ensure students would develop into educated and successful members of society with that kind of variability in the classroom?

Individual teacher control of classroom practice has existed from the earliest days of formal schooling, exists now, and will continue to exist. Many studies have shown that the individual beliefs and values of teachers play a vital role in shaping the objectives, goals, curriculum, and instructional methods of schools. Those same beliefs and values can spell success or failure for any reform efforts imposed by a school or district.[2] A school may publish its goals, objectives, and standards to represent its intended purposes and subject matter coverage. However, any uniformity outside of those published lists is largely mythical.

Even when there is surface agreement on what should be done, variations in the way teachers perceive the task create huge differences in implementation. Here's what happened when four teachers tried to collaborate on a unit dealing with the Great Depression.

1

- One teacher wanted students to read *The Grapes of Wrath* in order to understand the profound impact of the Depression on people's lives.
- The second teacher contended that material on dust storms and droughts must be included to illustrate the impact on the land.
- A third was certain economic and political issues were the most important aspects of the Depression for students to understand.
- The fourth insisted the other three had totally missed the point. Students needed to understand how the Great Depression was relevant to them personally—how it affected their lives.

All four teachers had master's degrees in education and secondary school teaching certificates in social studies. All agreed that the Great Depression should be taught. It was, however, their personal interests and values that determined the content they believed should be included. [3]

There is a comforting myth that the curriculum, as set down neatly in a school's handbook, defines what is going on in the school. Reform efforts focus on how the curriculum can be modified or improved, how the curriculum can be more effectively transmitted to students, and how acquisition of the curriculum's content can be assessed. It is clear that curriculum developers recognize a teacher's influence on even the most scrupulously designed and detailed curriculum. They have even attempted to design "teacher proof" curricula to prevent teachers from contaminating the purity of the design. "In the current reform, teachers are expected to play a key role in the reform effort, but their views of teaching and learning are thought to be a major impediment in that effort."[4]

Content is not the only thing that differs from classroom to classroom. Teachers' beliefs and values shape the *atmosphere* of the classroom itself. Within that atmosphere, from the interactions among teachers and students, students learn their most pervasive lessons. These are lessons about respect, values, the nature of knowledge, thought processes, self-worth, and expectations. "…Pedagogy, the art and science of teaching, is crucial to what students learn. *How we teach becomes what we teach.*"[5]

Distinctions such as those described in box 1.1 demonstrate that curriculum is significantly more than a simple list of what students should learn!

1.1 The Four Curriculums

Educational theorist Larry Cuban questions the myth that a well-defined curriculum determines what is taught (and learned) in a school. He has proposed there are actually four different curriculums in use in our schools.

"The *official* curriculum is what state and district officials set forth in curricular frameworks and courses of study. They expect teachers to teach it; they assume students will learn it."

The *taught* curriculum is what teachers, working alone in their rooms, actually choose to teach. "Their choices derive from their knowledge of the subject, their experiences in teaching the content, their affection or dislike for topics, and their attitudes toward the students they face daily."

The *learned* curriculum. Beyond what test scores reveal about content learning, students also learn many unspecified lessons embedded in the environment of the classroom. Depending on what the teacher models, the student will learn to process information in particular ways and not in others. They will learn when and when not to ask questions and how to act attentive. They may imitate their teacher's attitudes. They learn about respect for others from the teacher's own demonstration of respect or lack thereof. The learned curriculum is much more inclusive than the overtly taught curriculum.

The *tested* curriculum. "What is tested is a limited part of what is intended by policy makers, taught by teachers, and learned by students." The farther removed teachers are from the actual construction of the tests, the worse the fit between the other curriculums and what is tested. Standardized tests often represent the poorest assessment of the other curriculums.

Cuban, L. (1995). The Hidden Variable: How Organizations Influence Teacher Responses to Secondary Science Curriculum Reform. *Theory into Practice, Vol.34, No.1*, 4-11.

In recent years, individual differences among students have emerged as an important factor in designing learning materials and instructional methods. However, professional development seminars and "how-to" books continue to assume that every teacher will use the material presented in the same way and imply that success would be assured if only teachers would apply these lessons.

Despite recognizing that teachers can and do influence the success or failure of reform efforts[6], they are largely ignored in designing those efforts. Why? Clark and Peterson[7] explain that the process of teaching involves two major domains: 1) teachers' thought processes and 2) teachers' actions and their observable effects. Thought processes occur inside teachers' heads. They are unobservable and resist traditional experimental methods. Worse, individuals report their processes differently—subjectively. It's all so messy—unlike the measurable "objective" data with which researchers are accustomed to dealing.

Researchers have generally bypassed teachers' thought processes in favor of the teacher action domain. Teacher behavior, student behavior, and student achievement scores are much easier to observe and measure. They are subject to empirical research.[8] Yet one of history's greatest scientists, Albert Einstein, reminds us, "Not everything that can be counted counts, and not everything that counts can be counted."

Are teachers really that important? Isn't a well-designed and organized curriculum, accompanied by detailed suggestions for teaching the material, likely to produce similar results regardless of the teacher using it? If not, what are the implications of teacher variability?

The Autonomous Teacher

"It is what teachers think, what teachers believe, and what teachers do at the level of the classroom that ultimately shapes the kind of learning that young people get."
~Andy Hargreaves and Michael Fullan[9]

Why are educational leaders hesitant to acknowledge the influence of teachers? Do they find the idea disturbing? Perhaps. If, indeed, each teacher becomes a variable in the educational equation, how is top-down educational reform realistically possible? Such fears are justified. But ignoring it won't make it go away. It is time to explore that variability in an attempt to understand how it influences teaching and learning. It is even more important for you and other teachers to embark on this exploration for yourselves. Only you can decide what, if any, changes are necessary. Only you are capable of choosing to make those changes.

Teacher thinking about educational issues varies tremendously from individual to individual. Here are just a few of those differences.

1. Each teacher has a personal "definition" of education that shapes and limits what the teacher chooses to do and to not do. How would the emphasis a teacher places on content or process, student- vs. teacher-centered lessons, discipline, group work, standards, or assessment shift if that teacher believed each of the following definitions?

- Education is the efficient transmission of a body of knowledge that a culture values and that has historically produced progress.

- Education is the total development of a child.

- Education is the process of providing a rich, complex, and varied environment within which students can, through experience, develop effective thinking processes.

Do you agree or disagree with any of these "definitions"? How would you define education? Simply stated, *there is no agreed upon definition of education.* Is it any wonder there has been little success "fixing" the educational system when its primary *purpose* is still a matter of debate?

2. Each teacher has a set of beliefs about the nature of knowledge. Recently, there has been increased interest in how beliefs about the structure and certainty of knowledge affect learning and academic achievement. These include beliefs about the definition of knowledge, how it constructed and evaluated, where it resides, and how knowing occurs.[10] How does one uncover such beliefs? As mentioned earlier, most research on teaching has involved teacher's actions and their observable results. When observing another's behavior, one can only infer the beliefs that underlie the actions. These inferences are shaped by the beliefs and experiences of the observer. Therefore, they often reflect more about the beliefs that might drive the observer to the same behavior than about the beliefs of the research subject.

Another method of studying beliefs is self-reporting, but this too has its issues. Studies have found that teachers' beliefs change depending on context. A self-reporting questionnaire that taps a specific context may elicit one belief, while one that refers to knowledge in general produces different results.

Other facets of a responder's thinking will elicit very different responses to a general statement such as "Learning is a slow process of building knowledge." For example, some people tend to first notice statements with which they agree. One name for this tendencency is "matching." Others first pick out anything with which they disagree (mismatching). A *matcher* will read the statement and immediately think of ways in which learning has taken them a long time. A *mismatcher* will immediately think of exceptions to the statement—instances in which learning has been instantaneous. So how much does their response really tell the researcher about their beliefs?

3. Each teacher has a set of beliefs about how students acquire knowledge. For example, there are volumes of educational research on individual differences among students. Despite this, there is little evidence that the majority of American teachers consider those differences during lesson planning or actual instruction. Indeed, government policies, such as No Child Left Behind totally ignore these individual differences. Instead, traditional educational method focus on what Richard Prawat[11] calls the "Federal Express" approach, emphasizing the efficient packaging and rapid delivery of content.

4. Each teacher has a set of beliefs and assumptions about the nature of learning and about students in general. Jerry frequently disciplines students for making "too much noise." He *believes* "quiet" is a requirement for learning. In Carol's classroom, students are enthusiastically arguing about an issue. Does this mean no learning is taking place? If a teacher consistently acts on the belief that silence promotes learning, are there some cases in which learning is actually inhibited rather than supported?

5. Each teacher has a personal set of values that determines the priorities operating in the classroom. Which is more important—content or process, discipline or self-esteem, student respect for the teacher or mutual respect? How do you rank the most important factor from moment to moment? For example, if you notice a child sleeping in your class when you're in the middle of explaining something important, what do you do? Stop what you're doing and wake the child up so she won't miss the content, or continue the lecture? Would it matter which child it was? How would the interest level of the rest of the class influence your decision? In other words, what do you value most highly at that moment in time?

Because teachers profoundly influence students through their beliefs, attitudes, and values—their individual mental "maps"—isn't it time to bring those largely unconscious processes into consciousness? How many of your fellow teachers could put their most deeply held beliefs and values about education into words? How many are aware that other teachers, principals, or supervisors may not share those beliefs and values? Just because everyone uses words such as *understanding, learning,* or *thinking skills,* there is no guarantee those words have the same meaning for each person. In fact, they are generally very different!

Fortunately, you and your fellow teachers needn't wait for educational research to accept your importance. After all, it is your own beliefs and values that influence your work, not those of "*n*" teachers in a research study. Who better to explore the geography of your mental landscape than you?

An individual's beliefs, values, and metaphors, and the meaning people attach to words and actions generally exist outside of conscious awareness. Yet these factors drive our behavior automatically, without our attention. That's not all bad. Imagine what it would be like if you had to stop and consciously go through the decision-making process for every action in your life.

The point is a teacher's behaviors frequently spring, not from higher-level thinking processes, but from habit. One of the primary purposes of this book, then, is to assist you in identifying the habitual factors that unconsciously influence your behavior and thus, the influence you have on your students.

A Shift of Perspectives

In a 1995 *Phi Delta Kappan* article, Frank Smith suggests we "…declare education a disaster and get on with our lives."[12] Smith compares the current state of education with the state of the Titanic after it hit the iceberg. He points out that there was absolutely nothing the captain and crew could have done at that point to save the ship and its passengers. In Smith's words, "…you don't find solutions to disasters—you try to extricate yourself and others from them. The way to survive a disaster is to do something different."

Although some critics share Smith's view, there are still alternatives to "jumping ship." Shifting perspective away from the conventional wisdom that has traditionally driven reform efforts offers "something different" educators can do before the ship is irrevocably lost. What are some of those different perspectives?

A Shift from Things to People

One such shift is to move the focus of attention away from the factors that exist "out there"—the curriculum, the schedule, the arrangement of desks in the classroom, teaching methodologies, motivating students, assessing knowledge.... There is little agreement about what's wrong "out there." By shifting the focus inward—to the inner landscape of education from the perspective of each individual teacher—startling new insights emerge. Questions appear that people had never thought to ask.

Psychologist Arthur Combs suggests that one reason for the failure of reform is:

> "(It) concentrate(s) on things rather than people. Each effort...(focuses) on things—on gadgets, gimmicks, methods, subjects, ways of organizing or administering. But education is a people business made up of 100 million students and at least 10 million professional educators. Assuming that vital changes can be brought about in such a colossus by administrative fiat or by tinkering with methods and organization is flirting with futility. Truly effective change in so complex an institution can only be accomplished by effecting changes in people—especially through teachers, those men and women in closest touch with students." [13]

There is really only one thing people have the power to *directly* change—their own behavior. We bring about change in others (or in larger systems) only by changing ourselves. When you act differently, you force others around you to respond in different ways. For example, Diane criticizes her students for not taking more responsibility for their own learning. Yet Diane controls every aspect of that learning, from the content of lectures to the acceptable forms of classroom activity and assignments. What motivation will Diane's students have to take more responsibility unless she first relinquishes some of her control—changes her own behavior?

Just as students must "own" a problem before they exert any energy to solve it, so must teachers own the problems of education before they will feel the need to change their existing behaviors. Wally reads from his yellowed notes, following the detailed lesson plans he has used for the past ten years. He is oblivious to the disengagement of his students. Despite what others may think about Wally's teaching style, he is operating within his *beliefs* about the role of the teacher in transmitting knowledge. He is unlikely to enthusiastically embrace a new mandated program requiring him to change.

Only when Wally himself recognizes a problem *and* participates in the development of solutions will change become a priority for him. Any attempt to force him to use a new method, or to behave differently, without his participation makes him feel powerless, threatened, or overworked. He will unconsciously expend more energy avoiding the task than implementing it.

What's Good for the Goose...

The second shift of perspective applies research about students to teachers themselves. If, as research suggests, students have different "learning styles," different "intelligences," and different ways of processing information, what about teachers? As people age, do they become more alike? Hardly!

If you've spent any time browsing the World Wide Web, you've experienced the mental processes of many website designers. Some sites are straight text. Some force you to listen to music while they take an eternity to load elaborate graphics. Some feel friendly, intuitively guiding you exactly where you want to go. Others are like hacking your way through a jungle trying to locate the one tree that bears fruit. The design of a website reflects the mental processes, beliefs, and values of the designer. In the same way, the design and execution of what goes on in the classroom reflects the mental processes of the teacher.

Isn't it reasonable to spend at least as much effort understanding *teaching styles* as is spent studying learning styles? To admit teachers are as different as the students in their classes? Teachers are much more than simply robotic purveyors of the curriculum!

Examining the Foundation

After shifting our focus inward and exploring what individual teachers believe and value, the world of education "out there" remains. We must examine the beliefs and values of the system in which teachers operate for two important reasons.

First, differences between teachers' beliefs and values and those held by the people controlling the school environment produce a lot of discontent. Identifying those differences can shed light on the real problems and possible solutions.

Second, many educators go through their teaching careers accepting that what "the system" believes and values must be correct. They incorrectly assume the educational edifice is built on a solid foundation. This acceptance of the status quo places severe limits on thinking.

The very word *reform* embodies this limitation. Linguistically, to *re-form* means to change the form of *existing* parts. This presupposes that those parts must remain. Therefore, changes tend to be cosmetic rather than fundamental. Rearrange the existing facilities, reorganize the existing subject matter, present the existing curriculum in high-tech formats—in short, simply change the form of what is already there. Seldom do reformers begin by examining the foundation on which the structure is built. By digging into this foundation—checking the validity of some of the "truths" on which the educational edifice is built—educators may find that at least some of the old, rotted timbers and crumbling concrete needs to be replaced.

These new perspectives—shifting the focus from things to people and looking inward rather than outward for answers, and digging deeply into the foundations of educational practice—provoke many new questions about the problems confronting today's teachers and students. With new questions come new and potentially more useful answers.

Pre-Service and Prospective Teachers

As stated earlier, the purpose of this book is to encourage self-reflection among practicing teachers. What about pre-service teachers? They certainly don't enter teacher education as blank slates, eager and willing to be molded and shaped into effective teachers. Their beliefs about the nature of knowledge, learning, the role of the teacher, and many other aspects of classroom life are already firmly established. Studies have consistently shown that "…prospective teachers' prior beliefs influence what is learned during their teacher preparation program by acting as a filter through which teacher candidates acquire and interpret new knowledge."[14]

In a 2008 study, researchers attempted to discover the sources for the body of beliefs, termed "personal practical theories (PPTs)," of prospective teachers. PPTs encompass beliefs about all aspects of the educational process, including the role of the teacher, the potential and role of the student, the environment of the classroom, and instructional preferences. The study found that one-third of the prospective teachers' beliefs and attitudes about instruction arose from a combination of their religion (2%), family values (5%), and their K-12 instruction (28%).[15]

Beliefs formed early in life are among the most difficult to dislodge and are particularly influential. How easy will it be for a prospective teacher who has sat through 12 years of "teacher as source of knowledge and student as silent receptacle" to accept, much less embrace, constructivist theories of learning?

A good teacher education program can and does influence the thinking of prospective teachers. However, one can't ignore the PPTs of the professors themselves! Some interesting inconsistencies may be observed in teacher education classes. For example, in one three hour graduate education class, the professor spent the entire time lecturing. The topic of the lecture was, "Why teachers shouldn't lecture students." Despite all the valid arguments put forth in his lecture, what the professor modeled was loud and clear!

Students who are long accustomed to being "taught" by being lectured may not even recognize that other types of teaching are possible. Unless those other modes are effectively modeled, what are the chances that the students' belief in their role will change? Examining prior beliefs and values and their potential effect on teacher behavior during pre-service education can strengthen the foundation on which the new teacher's experience can build.

The characteristics that define an effective teacher have been the subject of an ongoing debate since NCATE added "dispositions" to their standards in 2000. A more complete discussion of arguments for and against assessing dispositions can be found in Appendix B.

৩•৵

Becoming a reflective teacher by looking inward entails examining teacher beliefs and values, the meanings teachers attach to words, and the metaphors they use to describe their work. More important, it means exploring *your* beliefs, *your* values, *your* meanings and metaphors. Theories are extremely useful, but if they are inconsistent with what is within the hearts and minds of individual teachers, they are little more than interesting ideas. Only through *self*-knowledge will practical approaches to meaningful change within the classroom become clear.

1 Hartmann, T. (1998) *The Last Hours of Ancient Sunlight*. Northfield, VT: Mythical Books.
2 For example, Battista, M. T.. (1994, February). Teacher Beliefs and the Reform Movement in Mathematics Education. *Phi Delta Kappan*, 462–470. Munby, H. (1990). Metaphorical Expressions of Teachers' Practical Curriculum Knowledge. *Journal of Curriculum and Supervision*, Vol. 6 No. 1, 18–30. Wilson, S. M.& Wineburg, S. S. (1988). Peering at History Through Different Lenses: the Role of Disciplinary Perspectives in Teaching History. *Teachers College Record*, Vol. 89, No. 4, 525–539. Specific findings of many research studies will be cited throughout the book.
3 Wilson, S. M.& Wineburg, S. S. (1988). Peering at History Through Different Lenses: the Role of Disciplinary Perspectives in Teaching History. *Teachers College Record*, Vol. 89, No. 4, 525–539.
4 Prawat, R. S. (1990, April). Changing Schools by Changing Teachers' Beliefs About Teaching and Learning. Elementary Subjects Series No. 19. (ERIC Document Reproduction Service No. ED 322 144).
5 Cuban, L. (1993, October). The Lure of Curricular Reform and its Pitiful History. Phi Delta Kappan, 182–185. Other more recent articles by Cuban elaborate on this issue.
6 For example, Cronin-Jones, L. L. (1991). Science Teacher Beliefs and Their Influence on Curriculum Implementation: Two Case Studies. *Journal of Research in Science Teaching*, Vol. 28, No.3, 235–250.
7 Clark, C. M.& Peterson, P. L. (1986). Teachers' Thought Processes. In M. C. Wittrock (Ed.). *Handbook of Research on Teaching* (pp. 255-296). New York: Macmillan.
8 Fang, Z. (1996). A Review of Research on Teacher Beliefs and Practices. *Educational Research*, Vol. 38, No. 1, 47–65.
9 Hargreaves, A.& Fullan, M. G. (Eds.) (1992). *Understanding Teacher Development*. New York: Teachers College Press. XI.

10 Debacker, Teresa K. et al. (2008) The challenge of measuring epistemic beliefs: an analyzis of three self-report instruments." *The Journal of Experimental Education* 76.3: 281+. General OneFile. Web, 14 June 2010.

11 Prawat, R. S. (1990, April). Changing Schools by Changing Teachers' Beliefs About Teaching and Learning. Elementary Subjects Series No. 19. (ERIC Document Reproduction Service No. ED 322 144). 15

12 Smith, F. (1995, April). Let's Declare Education a Disaster and Get On With Our Lives. *Phi Delta Kappan*, 584–590.

13 Combs, A. W. (1988, February). New Assumptions For Educational Reform. *Educational Leadership*, 38–40.

14 Richardson, V. (2003). Preservice teachers' beliefs. In J. Raths & A. McAninch (Eds.), Teacher beliefs and teacher education. *Advances in teacher education* (pp. 1-22.). Greenwich, CT: Information Age Publishers.

15 Levin, B. and Ye, He. (2008). Investigating the Content and Sources of Teacher Candidates' Personal Practice Theories (PPTs). *Journal of Teacher Education*, Vol. 59, No. 1, January/February 2008, 55-68.

Chapter 2 ~ The Reflective Teacher

"We don't see things as they are,
we see them as we are."
~Anaïs Nin

Teachers rarely appreciate how influential they are in shaping the lives of their students. I'm often amazed when a former student says, "Do you remember when you said...? That changed my life." At times, I don't even remember saying whatever it was that touched the student so profoundly. How often does something you say or do in passing have that sort of effect on a particular student?

As Carl Jung once said, "Children are educated by what the grown-up is and not by his talk." If teachers don't know who they are—if they are unaware of their beliefs about learning, teaching, and the nature of knowledge itself—then they are also unaware of what they are teaching by reason of those beliefs. That is why it is incumbent on teachers to become reflective—to understand what drives their behavior.

Teachers are role models for their students. Even more than what they "plan" to teach, their personal values and behaviors are part of the "taught" curriculum. In his study of *Extraordinary Minds*, Howard Gardner concluded, "Extraordinary individuals stand out in the extent to which they reflect—often explicitly—on the events in their lives, large as well as small."[1]

What thinking processes do you expect your students to learn? How, specifically, do you "teach" those processes? If you don't regularly use a particular thinking process in your life outside the classroom, how likely are you to use it while you're teaching? If you want students to "consider alternatives," to what alternative ideas or methods of teaching are you open? If you expect students to "analyze for bias," to what extent have you explored your own biases about student behavior, ability, ethnicity, or motivation?

What is a reflective teacher? Here's one example of a reflective approach to teaching. Consider a specific lesson plan you have used or are planning to use in your teaching. If it's not already on paper, jot down a few things you plan to do or to have your students do.

Now, examine the plan. Look at each step. Ask yourself why you included that step.

- Is it because you've always done it that way, because the teacher's guide said to do it that way, because you had a teacher who did it that way, or because you personally enjoy it or are good at it?

- What is it you expect to accomplish in that particular action? Is it worthwhile?

- How will you know the action has accomplished what you wanted? What, specifically, will you see, hear, or feel if your students accomplish the goal?

- What is it you value that drives you to use a particular method or to teach a particular concept?

- What beliefs about yourself and others are at the root of your planning?

Many teachers have never asked those questions—never reflected on *why* they teach as they do. When asked, it's easy to mouth the platitudes and educational jargon with which teachers are so familiar.

"The overwhelming majority of teachers…are unable to name or describe a theory of learning that underlies what they do in the classroom, but what they do—what any of us does— is no less informed by theoretical assumptions just because these assumptions are invisible. Behind the practice of presenting a colorful dinosaur sticker to a 1st grader who stays silent on command is a theory that embodies distinct assumptions about the nature of knowledge, the possibility of choice, and what it means to be a human being."[2]

What does it mean to be a teacher? What is *your* purpose? Have you become something of an automaton—cranking out lesson plans according to the list of objectives on the curriculum guide? Do you use the same activities you've used for years, or even those in which you engaged when you were a student?

Too often, once teachers have settled into their classrooms and found a rhythm that suits them, they become part of the educational mind. If not embraced, conventional wisdom is rarely questioned. *If* that "wisdom" is periodically reexamined in the light of new research, *if* it is based on a convincing body of supporting evidence, and *if* it is producing effective results, this behavior would be appropriate. However, if such "wisdom" is merely inertia, then to not question it is what Harvard psychologist Ellen Langer calls *mindlessness*.

Mindlessness is a pattern of action people consistently carry out without any real thought.[3] This story, a favorite of psychologist Abraham Maslow, is a wonderful example of mindlessness—or as we sometimes call it, tradition!

During WWII, the British Army hired an efficiency expert to help their artillery crews refine their procedures. The expert carefully watched as the crew used a truck to move the field cannon into position. They then went through their operations of loading and aiming the gun. Just before the crew fired the gun, two of the crewmembers moved to the rear of the gun and stood at attention. After firing, the two returned to the gun and helped to unload the used casing and reload the gun for firing. When the expert asked the men why they stood at attention during firing, they replied that this was part of the procedure they had been taught. They had never really thought about why they did it, but assumed that there must be a good reason if it was part of the procedure.

After extensive questioning up the chain of command, asking older and older officers why this was part of the procedure, the expert finally asked a veteran of the Boer War to explain what the two men were doing. The veteran laughed and replied, "They're holding the reins of the horses so they won't run away with the gun when it fires!"[4]

To what extent are educators still "holding the reins of the horses"? As educational theorist Marion Brady suggests, "Nothing evades our attention as persistently as that which we take for granted." Brady continues,

"In our schools, we teach what we think is important, and we think it is important because it is what we were taught. No one has bothered to point to the circularity of this type of thinking. What gets taught, with minor variations, is what was taught last year.... The decades roll on, without even a suggestion that perhaps the whole matter must be rethought."[5]

Self-reflection and introspection are ways to begin "rethinking the whole matter." They are ways to open up those mindless behaviors and choices to closer examination and to begin making intelligent and informed choices. Early behaviorists claimed introspection was not reliable because each person described his or her sensations uniquely. *Exactly!* That's the whole point! Each person's experience is unique, yet educational policy makers continue to behave as if each teacher experiences (or should experience) the world of the classroom in the same way.

What is that world like for you? In what metaphors do you represent that world? What happens if your internal world differs from a student's internal world? Whose fault is it if the student fails to respond to a teacher's world in the way the teacher expects? In *mindless* teaching, students are often accused of being lazy, unmotivated, or perhaps just "remedial" when, in fact, they simply process information differently.

Unless teachers become aware of how their internal worlds influence and constrain their perception and behavior, they will continue to act mindlessly. They will remain secure in the belief they are acting in the "right" way, because they have never considered an alternative.

What's Behind Your Choice?

Here's another example of how a teacher might reflect on behavior. Which choice would you make in answering the following question?

If I don't know the answer to a student's question, I would tend to:

1. Change the subject.
2. Tell the student you will "get to that later".
3. Tell the student you don't know.
4. Tell the student it is an interesting question you never thought of, but will find out about.
5. Tell the student to look up the answer for himself.
6. Other (specify)

Whatever choice you selected, think about what beliefs and values might be motivating—driving—that response. For example, a teacher may say she values student curiosity. This suggests that she would welcome student questions. However, the same teacher may also possess the following complex set of beliefs, meanings, and values.

- She values being a good teacher.

- She believes being a teacher means transmitting knowledge to her students. Therefore, to be a good teacher she must be an expert. For her, the word expert implies always knowing the right answer.

- She values having the respect of her students.

- She believes students will think less of her if she doesn't know an answer.

A teacher who holds this set of values and beliefs is unlikely to select choices 3 or 4—even though she values student curiosity. The values with personal meaning for the teacher take priority over her values regarding others. What does this mean for her students? What is this teacher teaching through her actions?

By not honoring the student's question at that point in time, she *is* teaching—that a student's question is of less value than what the teacher is doing or saying. If you were a student, for how long would you retain your curiosity if your questions were ignored or treated as if they weren't as important as covering the lesson plan for the day? And if you did retain your curiosity, how long would it take you to figure out that school—or at least this class—was not a place where your curiosity would be satisfied?

Teachers must become consciously aware of what they are doing and why. They must realize that much of their behavior is driven by what has always been and therefore, what they assume must be "right." Begin by examining your own beliefs about teaching and learning; about what you really value for yourself and your students. How, specifically, do your actions support those values, and how you will know when you have reached your goals. Being a reflective teacher means deliberately switching from *mindless* teaching to a *mindful* practice.

Know Thyself!

"Progress is impossible without change; and those who cannot change their minds cannot change anything."~ George Bernard Shaw

What is the most important subject of learning? Self! Some may believe this is a selfish perspective and that other concepts are more important. Think about it. The only *direct* experience you have with the acquisition of knowledge is your own. If you don't understand how you learn, what motivates you to seek out one type of information and not another, what values underlie your learning, and what beliefs about learning you hold, how can you even begin to understand the minds of your students?

Understanding your own beliefs, values, and biases, and the ways you process information about the world is an important first step in understanding your students. People are incredibly naïve if they assume all "reasonable" people think similarly. There is no right or wrong way to think—only more or less effective, efficient, or elegant ways. Without reflection that leads to self-awareness, many teachers become stuck in the rut of their habitual selves.

> "…Unless the teacher begins with an understanding of her
> or his particular way of learning, a way among several 'learning
> styles,' each of which is characteristic of some but not all
> people, each of which is legitimate in that it is productive for
> some learners, the teacher will be unable to grasp the different
> starting points of students, that is, flex to their individual
> styles."[6]

When teachers don't understand the vast range of learning strategies that can yield comparable results, the students are the ones who suffer. A student who can't or doesn't learn what is taught *in the way it is taught* is seen as flawed. How long would you continue to consult a doctor who blamed you when his or her treatment didn't work? For that matter, how long would you consult a doctor who considered a third of the people who came to him "remedial patients"—unwilling or unable to respond to the treatment he has chosen?

Personal Preferences

In addition to teaching from an unexamined set of beliefs, assumptions, metaphors, meanings, and values, teachers often teach in certain ways and not in others because of their own strengths and weaknesses. Here's an example.

When Ruth is teaching about elaboration in writing, she begins by interviewing a student about his job or some other interest. When the student responds with a one or two word answer, Ruth probes for more detail to demonstrate how elaboration increases interest. She asks other students what more they'd like to know, exemplifying the need for elaboration and demonstrating its value.

When four other teachers observed Ruth's class, they all remarked that this was a great teaching technique. The students were captivated and the lesson practically taught itself. *Yet not one of the teachers said they would personally use it*! Why? Because they would be too nervous or unsure of themselves!

Ruth is comfortable "thinking on her feet." She doesn't have to have every question and answer preplanned because her *beliefs* about teaching don't force her to be the expert at all times. Other teachers are less comfortable in a situation where they have to respond to something spontaneously. They carefully (and unconsciously) control their teaching to keep them in the expert position—or at least to avoid situations in which they might feel uncomfortable.

Think about several teaching methods you've seen used effectively by other teachers. Select one you'd be unlikely to use. Then ask yourself why! Do you have a sound educational reason or belief to support your decision? Or might your *reasons* more accurately be called *excuses* for not using an approach that would make you uncomfortable or that you simply didn't enjoy doing?

Everyone has preferences. There's nothing wrong with teaching from your strengths and avoiding methods or approaches you don't feel comfortable using or don't sufficiently understand. All teachers do it. Everyone realizes it, but few openly acknowledge the practice.

One example of failing to acknowledge and value the strengths of individual teachers is apparent in the scornful way in which many educators use the word "lecturing." Lecturing is, if we are to believe some research, a *bad* way to teach. Students are supposed to be *involved* in acquiring knowledge—not listening to some teacher talk about it. But this presupposes that every lecture equates to "boring teacher talk"!

This idea contains a fundamental flaw. The implication is that when a teacher is "talking," the students are not "involved." Have you ever walked by a classroom where the teacher was in the middle of a lecture and you could tell by the students' faces that they were paying rapt attention? Any teacher would envy that kind of involvement. Some people are brilliant lecturers—engaging their audience in ways "hands-on" activity might never do. People even pay money to hear them!

Yes, there are many teachers who could patent their droning as a cure for insomnia. They do their students a great disservice with their constant "teaching as telling" approach because they are simply not very good at it. They may, however, be brilliant at conducting "hands-on" activities. That's the whole point. What's wrong with teachers teaching from their strengths—*and acknowledging that this is what they're doing?*

This certainly doesn't mean they should teach that way to the exclusion of other potentially useful approaches. Or that they shouldn't attempt to strengthen their skills in other methodologies. But how much harm is done when research declares any approach, any methodology "less effective" than another? Less effective for whom? Under what circumstances? It is inappropriate and often inaccurate to make a blanket statement about the effectiveness of a teaching approach by comparing "average" test scores. Telling teachers they should always use approach A rather than approach B makes about as much sense as telling artists they should all work in the same medium and use the same brush strokes!

Are You Being Served?

That may seem like a strange question. Up to now, the subject has been how individual differences among teachers might affect their students. There is, however, another factor that profoundly influences how teachers feel about their work. How they feel, in turn, cannot help but be reflected in both their verbal and nonverbal interactions with their students.

Generations of adults were taught as children that doing anything for one's self was selfish. Let's use a metaphor to explore this idea. Many teachers find satisfaction in giving to their students—giving of themselves, their time, their knowledge and wisdom, and their love. Think of them as philanthropists to the young. How long can a philanthropist continue to give if there is no income, no replenishing of funds? Depending on how rich the philanthropist is to begin with, he might be able to give for a long time, but eventually his resources will be depleted. He will have nothing left to give.

Would we consider it selfish if this philanthropist continued to make money, to increase his resources, even as he gave to others? I doubt it. Why then is it selfish for teachers to think about how they maintain their own resources—in what ways they might replenish their emotional and psychological funds? A number of recent studies have focused on what teachers need for professional satisfaction. "For the benefit of the entire field, it is essential to continually collect and analyze the perceptions of teachers concerning their motivation, the ways they gauge success, and their explicit motivation to continue in the profession."[7] But again, you need not wait for formal research. What keeps you satisfied, motivated, and inspired in your role as a teacher?

Barry Farber[8] says a significant reason for teacher burnout is lack of reward. What reward do you need to keep you going—to replenish your resources and satisfy your needs? Is it money, respect, recognition, intellectual challenge, personal satisfaction? How, specifically, do you get what you need?

Some people thrive without external praise or reinforcement, nourished by their own internal sense of accomplishment. Some require at least a minimal amount of external reinforcement, while still others need constant external validation. External "reward" of any kind is rare in many school environments. Many teacher evaluators interpret their jobs as a "fault-finding" mission. It's easier to point out what is wrong than what is right. That can be a frustrating environment for a person who requires an occasional external boost to keep going.

Knowing and acknowledging what you need—what personal rewards you require to replenish your resources and maintain your motivation—is useful in several ways. First, you will have a greater understanding about potential feelings of content or discontent. Second, you can take steps to get more of what you need out of your environment.

Taking the First Steps

"If we don't change the direction we're going,
we're likely to end up where we are headed."
~Chinese proverb

The profession of teaching is unlikely to change in any meaningful way until the following conditions are met:

- Educators and policy makers recognize teaching for the complex and demanding profession it is.

- Teachers acknowledge and examine the influence of their own thinking on their behavioral choices.

- Each teacher feels important enough to the process of education that self-reflection becomes a necessity.

In his book, *The Predictable Failure of Educational Reform*, Seymour Sarason suggests that internal, unconscious values and beliefs about teaching and learning are at the heart of the failure of reform efforts. Speaking to reform advocates, he states,

"The problem is not technical. Nor is it motivational. Nor is it moral. The problem inheres in your unreflective acceptance of assumptions and axioms that seem so obviously right, natural, and proper that to question them is to question your reality. Therefore, faced with failure after failure, having tried this, that, and almost everything else, you don't examine your bedrock assumptions. Instead, you come up with variations on past themes—now with more desperation and anger, but less hope."[9]

I Don't Have Time

Commenting on the call for self-reflection among teachers, Geraldine Gilliss[10] argues that teachers simply don't have time. Gilliss admits teachers do sometimes reflect on what they're doing but claims "...they are not in a position to make these occasions their normal modus operandi." Gilliss concludes, "Life is too short to allow reflection on every occurrence."

No one is suggesting teachers should reflect on each and every behavior, each and every choice they make in the classroom. However, saying teachers don't have time to reflect on the fundamental beliefs, values, and attitudes that drive their behavior is like saying they don't have time to fill their cars with gas or build a solid foundation for their homes. Would you go to a mechanic who didn't have time to update his methods as automobile design changed? Who took a hammer and wrench to your brand new computerized vehicle in the same way he used to fix a 1940s Studebaker? When people deem something important enough, they find the time!

Seymour Sarason argues "...you cannot have students as continuous learners and effective collaborators, without teachers having these same characteristics."[11] Michael Fullan agrees, insisting "...it is simply not possible to realize the moral purpose of teaching—making a difference in the lives of students—without similar development for teachers."[12]

The present state of education is unlikely to change through externally mandated reform. But remarkable changes can arise from a reflective body of teachers who recognize the tremendous influence they have on the lives of their students. The historical perception of teachers as constants has, over the years, given them a sense of powerlessness. On the contrary, teachers have tremendous power. By bringing their thoughts into consciousness, teachers can mindfully create a transformative vision for education.

Reading or Doing?

"Skimming the surface" of any topic may provide a few new insights, but it's unlikely to influence you at any deep level. Because this book is about you, isn't exploring in depth worthy of your time and effort?

Teaching in Mind contains a lot of food for thought. Rather than nibbling around the edges, I urge you to commit yourself to *doing* the suggested processes. That is the only true way to digest the material—to make it a part of you. If you take that time, I think I can promise you that you'll know a lot more about yourself when you complete the book than you do now. If the reactions of some of my workshop participants are any indication, you will also be very surprised at some of the things you discover.

One of the most important processes is the Self-Inventory, found in Appendix A. By taking your time and honestly answering the questions, you'll give yourself a place to start in understanding material in the following chapters. You can, of course, choose to merely read the chapters without completing the inventory. But should you decide that some of the points made have merit, how will you know what you want to change if you don't have a sense of who you are now? Oh, you say, I'll just adopt the new ideas and that will be that.

Consider this. Some years ago, educators were tremendously excited about the work of Jean Piaget. Piaget's theory of internally generated knowledge made excellent sense, addressing obvious problems with teaching and learning. What educators failed to take into account was the pervasive belief that unconsciously permeates the educational establishment. That belief is that there exists a body of knowledge—

facts—truths—"out there" and that the goal of education involves teachers *giving* that objective knowledge to the students.

Without recognizing either the nature or the power of that underlying belief, educators tried to fit student-constructed knowledge into their existing practice. They were unaware they were attempting to apply Piaget's ideas *without also adopting his belief system*. How can one "internally generate" what is already "out there"? Consistent with their own beliefs, teachers would first *give* students the facts and then assign an activity, defined by the teacher, in which the students were supposed to "mess about" with those facts. Was this what Piaget meant? Where was the student given the opportunity to "internally generate" anything?

When Piaget's approach failed to bring about the expected changes in test scores—tests that were often the same as those used with the old paradigm—many teachers simply decided that the approach didn't work. Work to do what? What expectations did they have? Were those expectations valid in terms of the theory itself? How can any method based on the belief in internally constructed knowledge "work" if all knowledge is, ultimately, "out there"?

When teachers hold a fundamental belief that learning *means* accumulating knowledge objects, they may cognitively accept the wealth of research supporting internally generated knowledge, *but it will not significantly affect their practice*. It's difficult to build an effective rocket ship on the framework of a Model T Ford!

We see similar problems in many areas of our lives. We make up our minds to exercise, eat more nutritious foods, or watch less television. For a while, we follow through on our decisions and feel good about ourselves. But then, wham, we go right back to what we'd been doing before. Why? Because there is an unexamined subtext to the "old" lifestyle—a huge foundation of beliefs, values, and experience supporting it. This system of roots taps into many other facets of our unconscious mind, reaching all the way to the bedrock on which our lives are constructed. These roots are cultural, sociological, genetic, and are based on a collected lifetime of experience. They have grown over time into a formidable support system for our personal "plant."

Although a new behavior may seem desirable or beneficial to our conscious mind, it may conflict with or not be supported by something deeper—something out of our conscious awareness. Without examining those unconscious roots, people may cognitively accept something as true and consciously choose to implement new ideas, but in many cases, they will not "stick." That is why I urge you to explore your unconscious underpinnings through the Self-Inventory before reading on.

Everyone has choices. Subsequent chapters will investigate many alternative beliefs, metaphors, and myths related to education. The more you know and the more alternatives you explore, the more choices you will have. The more choices you have, the greater your flexibility. And in the increasingly complex and rapidly changing world of the twenty-first century, flexibility may be one of the most valuable characteristics you can possess.

1Gardner, H. (1997). *Extraordinary Minds: Portraits of Exceptional Individuals and an Examination of Our Extraordinariness*. New York: Basic Books, 15

2 Kohn, A. (1993). *Punished by Rewards*. Boston: Houghton Mifflin, 10.

3 Langer, E. J. (1989). *Mindfulness*. Reading, MA: Addison Wesley. 1-18.

4 Andreas, S. (1995). *Is There Life Before Death?* Moab, UT: Real People Press, 141.

5 Brady, M. (1996). Educating For Life As It Is Lived. *The Educational Forum, Vol. 60*, 249–255.

6 Sarason, S. B. (1991). *The Predictable Failure of Educational Reform: Can We Change Course Before It's Too Late?* San Francisco: Jossey-Bass, 180.

7Jenkins, Kathryn, and Amelia Hewitt. "A teacher's vision: a friendly teaching environment that supports growth and learning." *Childhood Education* 86.5 (2010): 316+. *General OneFile*. Web. 19 Aug. 2010.

8 Farber, B. A. (1991). *Crisis in Education: Stress and Burnout in the American Teacher*. San Francisco: Jossey-Bass.

9 Sarason, S. B. (1991). *Predictable Failure...*, 148.

10 Gilliss, G. (1988). Schön's Reflective Practitioner: A Model for Teachers? In P. P. Grimmett, & G. L. Erickson (Eds.). *Reflection in Teacher Education* (p. 52). New York: Teachers College Press.

11 Sarason, S. B. (1991). The Predictable...

12 Quoted in Fullan, *Change Forces*, 46.

Chapter 3 ~ Beliefs, Values, Meanings, and Worldviews: An Introduction

"The real difficulty in changing the course of any
enterprise lies not in developing new ideas
but in escaping from the old ones"
~John Maynard Keynes

I Know...or I Believe...?

Many of the statements made in the school environment or published in the literature are not statements of fact, but rather of belief. When people use those statements to justify behavior, "reasoning" may be adversely affected. What is a belief? How does it differ from a fact?

The chemical formula for water is H_2O. That is a fact—by definition and convention. Few people in the United States would question me if I stated that Chicago is west of New York. They would, however, balk if I stated that Chicago was east of New York. They accept the first statement as a fact because most people in the United States conceptualize direction in that way. Although it's unlikely, one could also get to Chicago by traveling east from New York. The point is, facts are often statements that *from a particular perspective* are part of "consensus" reality. There is little doubt connected to facts as long as one stays within that context. On a continuum, there is less doubt about facts than about beliefs.

Once you get past defined terms about concrete things—once the context shifts or there is the slightest bit of complexity—the statements made about a situation begin to enter the realm of belief, not fact. Take the word *accountability*. Many people, both in and out of education, agree that both students and teachers should be held accountable for learning. Beyond that simple agreement, any further discussion about what accountability entails resembles the action on the floor of the New York Stock Exchange! Each person is certain that his or her perception of accountability is "correct"—a fact, yet there is little or no consensus.

27

The more complex a situation gets—the more possible perspectives it may have—the more different people involved—the less likely one can state a "fact" about the situation on which everyone will agree. Thus, we enter the realm of beliefs.

People generally accept statements that are facts by definition or for which there is an overwhelming body of support and no contradictory evidence. People have choices when it comes to beliefs. The key, then, is to identify which statements frequently used in education are facts and which are beliefs.

What Are Beliefs?

"Belief is a moral act for which the believer
is to be held responsible." ~H. A. Hodges

People use the word *belief* in a variety of ways. In his insightful article on the problems of researching the role of teacher beliefs, Frank Pajares[1] says:

> "...Defining beliefs is at best a game of player's choice.
> They travel in disguise and often under alias—attitudes, values,
> judgments, axioms, opinions, ideology, perceptions,
> conceptions, conceptual systems, preconceptions, dispositions,
> implicit theories, explicit theories, personal theories, internal
> mental processes, action strategies, rules of practice, practical
> principles, perspectives, repertories of understanding, and
> social strategy, to name but a few that can be found in the
> literature."[2]

Rather than engaging in a technical discussion about what may or may not make something a belief rather than factual knowledge, I'll simply define the way in which I intend to use the term. Drawing on the work of Robert Dilts[3], I'll define *beliefs* as judgments and evaluations that we make about ourselves, about others, and about the world around us. Beliefs are *generalizations* about things such as causality or the meaning of specific actions. Here are a few examples of belief statements made in the educational environment.

• A quiet classroom is conducive to learning.

• Studying longer will improve a student's score on the test.

• I'm not very good in math.

28

- Grades encourage students to work harder.

Are any of these statements facts? Not in the sense that they are consistently true in all contexts. There are exceptions to each and every one of the statements.

Where do beliefs come from? All of the experiences in a person's life, particularly those from childhood, contribute to a person's beliefs. Educator Theodore Marchese states:

> "...The insight is simple enough: It begins with the innate need of humans to make meaning out of their experience of the world. So we develop, at quite early ages—as five-year-olds, for example—basic sets of ideas about how the world works, what's dangerous, who's friendly, about right and wrong, what to like and how to behave, and so on. The scary part is that these childhood versions of reality tend to get pretty hard-wired into the brain and prove quite resistant to change. Once we think we've figured out some corner of the world, we tend to see what we want to see and hear what we want to hear, bending subsequent experience into confirmation. I say 'scary' because the existence of prior beliefs can be a major impediment to subsequent learning. The beliefs, after all, may be objectively wrong, or bigoted, or dysfunctional, and block fair and open encounter with the new or different. Very significantly, prior beliefs turn out to be especially impervious to classroom-based instruction, and especially to teaching as telling."[4]

Marchese was writing about the effects of a child's beliefs on later learning, but what are teachers if not grownup versions of those children? When those in authority "tell" a teacher to use a particular methodology, to attend more to individual differences, to listen to what students have to say, it is often as effective as teachers "telling" their students the sun does not really rise—the earth rotates! It is often contrary to the teacher's established beliefs based on personal perception and experience. Personal experience generally wins!

For teachers, many beliefs about school come from their experiences as students. They have formed impressions about themselves and their abilities, about the nature of knowledge, and about how knowledge is acquired or "learned." Consider the young child "playing teacher." She lines her dolls up in neat rows and stands at the front of her class "lecturing" and admonishing her students to "pay attention." At this early age, she already has a strong sense of what school is "s'posed to be." Is it any wonder that when she grows up and becomes a teacher, it would not occur to her to teach in any other way?

If a person has an experience, even once or twice, he may produce a generalization about that type of event—a belief. Unfortunately, beliefs are often based on limited experience of the world. At their most harmful, beliefs can take the form of "one-trial learning" that is extremely difficult to dislodge because the person attaches personal significance to it. A bride jilted at the altar may develop the belief that men can't be trusted, but this one-trial learning will be as strongly held as a belief that the sun rises and sets each day.

Another clue to distinguishing between factual knowledge and belief is how a person responds to a challenge. If someone points out that you spelled a word wrong, you don't generally "defend" the misspelling. You merely change a bit of memory to "fix" the problem. When someone questions a person's beliefs, the person often responds as if it were a personal threat, emotionally defending their position.

Fixed Facts, Alternative Beliefs

You can't arbitrarily decide what time you'll hold your class or choose to teach that $12 - 5 = 17$ (at least not if you want to keep your job). By contrast, a belief represents one alternative among many rather than the one true fact or rule agreed upon by all. Because of this, people are *free to choose* among the alternatives. For example, not everyone agrees classrooms must be quiet for learning to take place. Some believe collaboration benefits learning. It's a bit difficult to collaborate without some level of conversation.

Because beliefs provide stability in our world, it stands to reason that they do not change easily. "Beliefs give consistency to our lives. Imagine waking up each morning believing something new—if you didn't drive yourself mad, you would drive all those around you bonkers."[5]

Some beliefs, such as those that organize our lives and make the world a predictable place in which to live, are very useful. Others, such as believing you are incapable of some behavior, or that there is only one way to accomplish a task, are limiting. The trick is to identify a belief and decide if it is justified, based on the best information available at the

30

time. Are there alternative beliefs based on better evidence that might serve you better? You can't "choose" the facts you accept. You *can* choose your beliefs!

Many people associate the word *belief* with religious ideas. There is real resistance to the suggestion that people can just change what they believe. For some, their "faith" includes a whole system of beliefs that are fundamentally intertwined with their values, perceptions, and behavior. Those beliefs give them a tremendous sense of security.

I'm not suggesting teachers change any beliefs. What I am suggesting is that, because a teacher's beliefs strongly influence students' development, it is critical for teachers to examine what those beliefs are. Are they based on solid foundations? What, if any, alternatives would be in the best interest of both the teacher and the students?

Beliefs and Perceptions

> "Whatever one believes to be true either is true or becomes true in one's mind." ~ John C. Lilly

Beliefs not only affect how people behave but what they perceive (or pay attention to) in their environment. Contrary to the old saying "seeing is believing," it is more likely that "believing is seeing." When people *believe* something is true, they *perceive* information supporting that belief. Beliefs alter expectations. People perceive what they expect.

If, for example, Stan believes Jamie is a "troublemaker," he will unconsciously interpret some of Jamie's behaviors as disruptive. Cheryl, who believes Jamie is "full of energy," may not even notice the behavior. The same thing is true of a teacher who has no prior belief, one way or the other, about Jamie. Think of the damage teachers do when they "help out" another teacher by telling him to "Watch out for that one. He's a real troublemaker." Sharing facts? Hardly.

If teachers believe a program they have been told to use is based on a solid foundation, and if the program is based on beliefs similar to their own, they will notice ways in which the program works. If they believe it is a waste of time, they will notice evidence supporting that belief. It's imperative to recognize that teachers are interpreting *the same events* in different ways. They assign different meanings to the event in order to support their prior beliefs.

What Should *Teachers Believe?*

> "One's personal predispositions are not only relevant
> but, in fact, stand at the core of
> becoming a teacher." ~ Dan Lortie

In reviewing the literature on beliefs, I came across one study in which a researcher concluded the beliefs of preservice teachers did, indeed, influence their teaching behaviors. This researcher then went on to suggest that, in teacher education classes, prospective teachers should be taught the correct beliefs. Sound reasonable? But where might we find such pearls of wisdom?

First, she assumes there *are* correct beliefs. Second, she assumes that by teaching (telling) people what they should believe, they will do so. If that were true, why are there still so many arguments about fundamental issues in education? Telling people that they *should* do or not do something is based on *our* beliefs, not theirs. How willing are you to change your own beliefs because someone tells you to?

If, after a long history of public education, educators can't even agree on the definition of education, what hope is there that they will agree on the "correct beliefs" all teachers should hold about it? If there is no correct set of beliefs, what might teachers gain by identifying their current beliefs? There are many benefits, including identifying sources of conflict and frustration, pinpointing beliefs based on outdated or erroneous information, and increasing behavioral flexibility. Perhaps the most compelling reason for teachers to explore the beliefs that shape the topography of their inner landscape is contained in these words by Parker Palmer:

> "When I do not know myself, I cannot know who my
> students are. I will see them through a glass darkly, in the
> shadows of my unexamined life—and when I cannot see them
> clearly, I cannot teach them well."[6]

Sources of Conflict

"Washing one's hands of the conflict between the powerful and the powerless means to side with the powerful, not to be neutral." ~ Paulo Freire

If you've been around the field of education for any length of time, you've probably grown accustomed to the parade of "revolutionary" ideas touted as "solutions" to the problems of education. Theorists roll into view on their new bandwagons, bullhorns blaring promises that would do any political candidate proud. Condemnations of previous reforms often accompany these promises. Recent examples include the push for more and more standards and the vilification of progressive education.

It should come as no surprise that experienced teachers respond with cynicism, having seen so many sound ideas disintegrate under the weight of oversimplification, overstatement, and administrative infighting. Why expend effort on something with the life expectancy of a blade of grass at a lawnmower exhibition?

Why are such well-intended efforts so often doomed to failure? There are, of course, many answers. The remainder of the chapter will address three factors that have received insufficient attention—the values that create conflicts within individuals, personal meaning, and the worldviews that generate conflict among larger segments of the educational system.

Values

Every individual has a personal hierarchy of values. Typical values include success, monetary comfort, love/companionship, a sense of accomplishment or achievement, and of course, survival. These same values—things people want or need for themselves—are often at the root of the values people hold with respect to others. When a teacher spends time after school to help a student, he may feel he has sacrificed his own needs to the needs of the student. At the same time, he is likely to have gained something for himself—perhaps a heightened sense of self-worth or the good feelings that come with the student's gratitude. Because values influence a person's behaviors and choices, they are worthy of exploration.

Robert Dilts[7] suggests that *values* are the words or phrases with which people respond when asked what motivates them. They are principles, qualities, or objects that, for a given individual, have intrinsic worth. When people possess what they value, they are contented. If they are deprived of what they value, they feel frustration or dissatisfaction. People, therefore, unconsciously behave in ways that move them *toward* what they value or *away from* anything counter to that value.

Beliefs support and reflect our values. For example, if Luis *believes* studying harder produces better grades, he is motivated to study harder. Why? Because he also *believes* getting better grades is a way to achieve success. Success is something Luis *values*. Through his beliefs, he has equated getting good grades with becoming successful.

Chances are Luis never made that decision consciously. Through his experience in school and what his parents and teachers have told him, Luis simply accepted a positive relationship between high grades in school and success. Is there actually a cause-effect relationship between high grades in school and success? That depends on how one defines success, but the lives of such people as Albert Einstein, Abraham Lincoln, Grandma Moses, and Thomas Edison attest to the fact that it is not always true. Because beliefs are generalizations, they "feel" true in some absolute sense. Luis experiences the sense that to achieve what he values—success—there is no other alternative but to get good grades.

It's often easier to identify the hierarchy of a person's values by his behavior than by what he says he values. For example, Ed says he values higher-level thinking skills. Yet his tests rarely require students to do anything more than simple recall or recognition—skills that machine graded multiple-choice questions can easily test. This doesn't mean Ed is lying. He simply has another value of which he is unaware—perhaps time spent with his family. Taking the time to grade essay tests that assess higher-level thinking would cut into his family time. He fails to notice that he's not "walking his talk" because he believes a good teacher values higher-level thinking skills and Ed perceives himself as a good teacher. Complicated, isn't it?

Conflicted Values

Teachers become frustrated when outside pressures force them to choose one value at the expense of another. For example, Raymond *believes* students learn most effectively in a stimulating and varied classroom environment. In his ideal classroom, individual students are actively engaged in activities appropriate to their interests, abilities, and preferred cognitive processes. They are excited about learning. Implementing that learning environment gives Raymond a tremendous *sense of accomplishment* (value 1). Because of his regard for individual students, he is *liked and respected* by those students (value 2). Raymond's beliefs and values march hand-in-hand and he feels good about himself and his job.

Along comes an in-service day. A well-known "motivational" speaker gives a forty-five-minute talk embracing all of the behaviors in which Raymond already engages. Wow! An expert has validated his beliefs and values. Raymond is elated!

At the end of the workshop, the principal makes an announcement. The district has selected a battery of tests that will assess student knowledge of the standards adopted by the district. The results of the tests will influence teacher evaluations. Oh, oh! Conflict of values!

In addition to valuing a sense of accomplishment and the good will of the students, Raymond values eating and keeping a roof over his head—survival! Although his curriculum includes the general content defined by the standards, Raymond's focus is more on in-depth understanding than on the acquisition of testable facts. If he continues to teach in his typical way, the students may not "learn" all of the specific bits of information covered by the standards and included in the tests. Their test scores will suffer. Raymond's evaluation will go down, negatively influencing his professional future. But if he changes the way he's teaching, he will lose the respect of the students. Worse, according to his belief system, he will fail to provide the most effective learning environment, so his self-concept suffers. Raymond's sense of accomplishment disappears.

At this point, whatever decision Raymond makes *must* deprive him of one or more of the things he values. Is it any wonder he feels conflicted—less than satisfied with whatever decision he makes?

Luisa strongly believes her responsibility as a teacher includes transmitting a specific body of knowledge to her students. For her, the test will be the ultimate indication of whether she is doing a good job. Luisa gets what she values—a sense of accomplishment and well-being—when her students get good grades on the test.

Along comes a new directive requiring Luisa to take fifteen minutes of each class to discuss current events as they relate to her subject or grade level. External pressures force her to make a decision that violates her beliefs and values. If she discusses current events during those fifteen minutes, she won't have time to teach the students everything she believes they really need. But if she closes her door and uses those fifteen minutes as she's always used them—to teach what she believes is important—the value she places on being a good employee and doing what she is told is violated. Thus, another teacher feels stress in her job.

Both of these teachers are confronted with situations that threaten their sense of self-respect—an important value for most people. Many teachers have experienced similar situations that result in frustration, stress, and dissatisfaction. Understanding where these conflicts in values and beliefs lie is the first step in resolving them.

Education as Enculturation

People often speak of "cultural" or "societal" values. Society and culture are constructs—not actual entities. Our language treats them as if they were living entities—beings with minds that can have beliefs and values. In the same way, we speak of *education* providing opportunities rather than address the complex issue of who, specifically, in education provides those opportunities.

Society is a group of individual people. The *culture* of a school is the set of complex relationships among the *people* in the school—the students, teachers, administrators, support staff, parents, and members of the school board. Each teacher within that culture has personal values, but it's difficult to avoid buying into values many others in the immediate environment possess.

Neil Postman suggests that the values that once formed the unspoken but pervasive foundation of society, and thus public education, have shifted. Earlier values of religion, democracy, and "opportunity for all" have all but disappeared in favor of economic utility and consumerism. Today, success is often defined as getting a well-paid job in a respectable profession so that one can buy a BMW or a big home in the suburbs—"he who dies with the most toys wins."

Postman argues that this is a feeble set of values on which to base a meaningful education. Because teachers are part of this society, many of them inadvertently accept those values and thus, teach them—

consciously or unconsciously. One need only read a few of the arguments for tougher standards to realize they clearly reflect those values and thus, reinforce them in the minds of both the school personnel and ultimately the students.[8]

Here is a statement from the New Jersey Mathematics Curriculum Framework: "…our students need to meet these standards in order for them *to be well prepared for careers in the 21st century, and in order for our state and country to have suitable employees in the 21st century.*"[9] [Author's emphasis] No mention is made of students becoming concerned and involved citizens. No mention is made of the psychological and moral development of the student. Careers and employment are the values named and thus, the values implicitly taught.

Parents would probably be the first to protest if their child's school announced that values were to become part of the curriculum. Sociologists, however, argue that one of the functions of education is the transmission of the culture, or enculturation. If there are *cultural values*, as our language implies, we must assume enculturation includes transmission of values.

Even if a list of cultural values existed, each teacher would possess his or her own "take" on those values. In every action, every decision, every interaction with students, teachers are teaching values. Values are part of the *learned* curriculum (See Cuban sidebar—Chapter 1) Shouldn't educators at least identify the more fundamental values they hold, and therefore, teach?

What Do You Mean by That?

"Oh, what tangled webs we weave
when first we practice to believe."
~Laurence J. Peter[10]

Macbeth's admonition about the confusion caused by deceit is no less true when applied to beliefs. It's confusing enough when *different* individuals hold conflicting beliefs and values about the same context, but one would at least expect the *same* individual to have consistent beliefs. Wrong! Because values and beliefs arise from and reside in so many different contexts within our lives, people are often unaware that, as they shift from context to context, they contradict themselves.

The same person who condemns abortion or murder ("Thou shalt not kill") may support the death penalty for capital crimes or without much soul-searching, take the life of someone who threatens a child. The same person who says "Absence makes the heart grow fonder" to one friend may say "Out of sight, out of mind" to another, in a different context. Truth—meaning—is a highly contextualized experience! Just when you think you have a person "figured out," he or she behaves in a completely unexpected way.

In a graduate education class, the professor frequently presented us with "value-laden" problems such as the following: Imagine you have a child who is dying from a rare disease for which no cure is readily available. A man has developed a cure but refuses to sell it or make it available for use. When you visit him to beg for the medication, you see a vial of the medicine on the man's desk. When the man again refuses to make the medication available, would you, if you had the opportunity, take the medication to save your child?

A woman in the class was adamant about any issue that she could interpret using the Ten Commandments. As expected, her answer to this problem was, "Absolutely not!" Her rationale: "Thou shalt not steal!"

Then, the professor changed the problem slightly. This time, when you visit the man, what you see on the desk is a paper with the formula for the medicine. The question becomes, "Would you memorize the formula and give it to the doctors to reproduce?"

My assumption was that, if you wouldn't do the first, you wouldn't do the second. The *meaning* I assign to *stealing* is taking something that belongs to another person without their permission. So I was amazed when the Ten Commandments lady said, "Oh, of course, I'd do that." She explained you couldn't steal with your eyes—only with your hands! For her, stealing *means* taking something that belongs to another person without their permission *with your hands!* This woman, who consistently defended the highest moral ground, was completely at home with the idea of taking the formula "with her eyes."

I later discovered there's a common perception that when one "takes" something without removing the physical object from a person's possession, it's not stealing. Isn't that what we do when we copy something from a book or make a photocopy of an article from a magazine? Is that stealing, or does one have to use the item for one's personal gain—be it health, an increased reputation, or monetary gain? If it's not stealing to photocopy a few pages for one's own reference, is it stealing to copy the entire book instead of buying one's own copy? What if the book is no longer in print?

Truth is not always easy to define. Each individual determines the truth—the meaning—of a situation based on personal beliefs, values, and experiences. People assume that when they use the same words, they've reached agreement. Yet, judging by the previous example, even words such as *steal* do not hold the same meaning for everyone.

Educators constantly toss around words such as *successful, effective, appropriate, respect, learn, understand,* and *teach.* What, specifically, does each of those words mean to you? What is your measure of *success?* Is it the same as that of a student? The student's parents? The experts writing educational standards? The people urging more individualized learning environments? When teachers try to motivate students to *succeed,* whose definition are they using?

Making Sense of the World

"The mind has exactly the same power as the hands;
not merely to grasp the world, but to change it."
~Colin Wilson

Each teacher's behavior is influenced by a largely unexamined set of beliefs and assumptions about how the world does and/or should work—the individual's worldview. In addition to values, this pervasive worldview is unconsciously taught in every classroom regardless of the content or instructional methods. Just what is a *worldview?*

A *worldview* is a set of fundamental assumptions about the world in general—about the basic nature of reality and how we come to understand it. A worldview is the internal geography through which the human mind organizes its myriad categories of people, places, objects, information, and experiences. It is how people maintain their world as a consistent whole. It allows them to sense the world as a predictable place and to gain a certain measure of security. People frequently couch their worldview as a story or metaphor: The world is like....

When people use phrases such as "it went like clockwork" or "I need some downtime," they are, in effect, saying *the world is like a machine.* They are using a machine metaphor to organize experience. As a part of a machine, each person must function properly if the machine is to work. This worldview is somewhat like the Mouse Trap game where the action of part A causes an action in part B, which in turn causes part C to move and trap the mouse.

Shifting the worldview metaphor from a machine to an interactive system (such as weather or an ecosystem) encourages people to consider the relationships among the various parts of the system in addition to the parts themselves. Rather than sequential cause-and-effect relationships of the machine metaphor, they view events as a web of interactions. None of these interactions, in isolation, is solely the cause or effect of another. For example, humans have learned through experience that messing with one part of an ecosystem produces a ripple effect that may adversely affect the entire system. Those effects are not apparent when one looks at the parts of the system separately because they depend on the synergistic interactions occurring in the system. Science has recognized the insights available in the systems perspective. What about education?

Education's Dominant Metaphor

"The dominant metaphor for today's education is the Newtonian Machine: The school is a more or less well-oiled machine that processes (educates?) children. In this sense, the education system (school) comes complete with production goals (desired end states); objectives (precise intermediate end states); raw material (children); a physical plant (school building); a 13-stage assembly line (grades K–12); directives for each stage (curriculum guides); processes for each stage (instruction): managers for each stage (teachers); plant supervisors (principals)…uniform criteria for all (standardized testing interpreted on the normal curve); and basic product available in several lines of trim (academic, vocational, business, general)."[11]

Any worldview necessarily brings some aspects of the world into the foreground and focuses less attention on others. A worldview that perceives reality as a machine focuses on *parts*. The underlying belief is that if you understand those parts, you will then understand the whole. Reform efforts arising from this metaphor focus on "fixing" parts— effective teaching, cooperative learning, motivation, discipline, thinking skills, standards, facilities, evaluation, the role of the teacher, without consideration for the relationships among those parts. Thus, simplistic "answers" to the pressing questions about education are never complete.

A worldview is a single perspective. Its strength lies in the insights it makes available—the understanding it fosters. The weakness in any worldview lies in the danger of accepting it as the *only* way of understanding—of equating it with "reality." Einstein's theory of relativity and Darwin's theory of evolution, focusing on the interaction of factors within an ecosystem, both employ a Systems worldview. This is no more a "correct" metaphor of the world than is the machine. However, shifting the perspective from parts to whole necessarily shifts the focus from how each piece works to the patterns of interaction in the system. New information becomes available.

In *The Fifth Discipline*, Peter Senge says,

> "...Human endeavors are also systems. They...are bound by invisible fabrics of interrelated actions, which often take years to fully play out their effects on each other. Since we are part of that lacework ourselves, it's doubly hard to see the whole pattern of change. Instead, we tend to focus on snapshots of isolated parts of the system, and wonder why our deepest problems never seem to get solved. Systems thinking is a conceptual framework, a body of knowledge and tools that has been developed...to make the full patterns clearer, and to help us see how to change them effectively."[12]

What is a more "human endeavor" than education? Yet as more and more scientists and business organizations shift their thinking to a systems worldview, education persists in the mechanistic metaphor. Schools boast they are at the leading edge of technology, yet they steadfastly remain at the trailing edge of ideas. Even as educational theorists come to recognize the range of factors—the incredible number of variables—that impact the student's readiness, willingness and ability to learn, the Newtonian/machine worldview remains the dominant metaphor of education. What are some effects of this worldview

The Newtonian Worldview as a Source of Conflict

Nowhere are the effects of the Newtonian worldview more apparent than in reform efforts. Attempts to improve or re-form education by addressing parts without, at the same time, considering the system as a whole result in often-unrecognized conflicts.

41

Reforming Part 1—Improving the Curriculum

One part of the educational machine presently at the forefront of reform efforts is content—*what people should learn*. Reform groups insist that having rigorous standards and benchmarks—carefully spelled-out lists of information and skills every student should be expected to know and/or possess—will improve the education of our young people. Powerful prose enhances their arguments.

> "The educational foundations of our society are presently being eroded by a rising tide of mediocrity that threatens our very future as a nation and a people.... We have, in effect, been committing an act of unthinking, unilateral educational disarmament." (A Nation At Risk, National Commission on Excellence in Education, 1983, p 5).

In 1995, Diane Ravitch, author of National Standards in American Education: A Citizens Guide stated:

> "Americans...expect strict standards to govern construction of buildings, bridges, highways, and tunnels; shoddy work would put lives at risk. They expect stringent standards to protect their drinking water, the food they eat, and the air they breathe.... Standards are created because they improve the activity of life." (pp. 8–9) Ravitch asserts that just as standards improve the daily lives of Americans, so too will they improve the effectiveness of American education: "Standards can improve achievement by clearly defining what is to be taught and what kind of performance is expected" (p 25).

How could one begin to criticize such lofty goals? Is there any teacher who doesn't want students to use their minds well, to be responsible citizens, to gain productive employment? Who could possibly support the "shoddy" education Ravitch implies would exist without standards? The language is so powerful that to question the standards arising from these goals seems unthinkable.[13]

Reforming Part 2—Improving Teaching Methodology

While one set of reformers focuses on content, others are calling for more in-depth learning[14], situated learning[15], authentic learning[16], attention to multiple intelligences[17], and learning styles[18], and greater student involvement and choice in the learning process. The "part" of the machine they are focusing on is *how people learn*. What teacher has the temerity to suggest that individual students should not be the focus of a deeper educational process that more closely reflects the "real world" in which they live and encourages them to use the knowledge they acquire to solve authentic problems?

❧

These are just two of the reform approaches that aspire to improve education. Admirable rhetoric argues for each approach. Each focuses on a different "part" of the educational process—one on the curriculum and another on teaching methodology. The goals of each approach sound both reasonable and desirable. Let us, however, step back for a moment and view these two approaches in a different metaphor.

Your boss tells you that you must drive from New York to San Francisco in one week, covering a specified route and passing through dozens of specific locations. At the end of the week, a device attached to the car will verify you have covered the required ground. If you fail to cover any of that ground or fail to reach your destination in the required time, you will be penalized. You may even lose your job. Oh, and by the way, you are also required to stop at each of the locations and get to know the residents. Acquire an in-depth understanding of the history and geography of the place. Gain a real sense of the way each location fits into its geographic region in particular and the country in general.

In the "real world," there would be an immediate outcry among employees that such a task is impossible. The timeframes for each of the two parts of the task are contradictory. One can *either* cover a lot of ground in a short time or take a more leisurely trip, spending sufficient time in each location to acquire a sense of the place. *It is physically impossible to do both, unless one has tapped into time-distortion technology!*

In a 1998 study done by the Mid-Continent Regional Educational Laboratory (McREL), Robert J. Marzano and John S. Kendall compiled a list of more than two hundred national and state K–12 standards, addressing 3,093 specific topics, commonly referred to as benchmarks.[19]

Estimating the time it would take to adequately address each benchmark, Marzano and Kendall calculated that mandatory schooling would have to increase from K–12 to K–22 or –23![20] Clearly, that proposal has not accompanied the call for more and tougher standards. As benchmarks continue to proliferate, there are no provisions for an increase in available time.

Because each reform group focuses only a small *part* of the system, they simply do not consider such irrelevant things as time. They fail to perceive the ways in which their proposed change influences other parts of the educational system. This is not to suggest it is impossible to have standards and still address the individual needs of students. However, until reformers specifically address the relationship between the two, the present demands are impractical, at best.

Despite the outcry employees in the business world would make at such outlandish demands, teachers accept these mandates with little or no question. Many of them recognize the practical impossibility of accomplishing both tasks. They create compromises to bring contradictory parts of their reality into some semblance of order that is the most consistent with their values and sense of well-being, and with which they can live. They "leave out" a few of the standards and "beef up" a few more. They "touch on" deeper ideas, "mention" relevant issues, or perhaps assign more in-depth study as "extra credit." The political ideas of Hobbes, Locke, and Rousseau are "covered" in a twenty-minute "discussion." "To be or not to be" is quickly summarized as, "He couldn't decide."

The test at the end of the year, the "device" testifying to their performance of the assigned task, namely covering the standards, is the one constant. Recommendations for in-depth learning, having students apply what they have learned, exploring the foundations of knowledge, and teaching to the needs of individual students are seldom accompanied by a similar assessment. It takes little thought to realize which of the mandates will receive the most attention. The "numbers" are, after all, how one's teaching will be judged.

The failure of teachers to say, "Hey, wait a minute. This is impossible!" ultimately results in an increased sense of failure in their purpose. Michael Fullan suggests the teachers who become the most disillusioned are those who began with the highest ideals.[21] How can one realize those ideals under the burden of scattershot reform mandates that fail to recognize the interactive nature of the parts and place an impossible burden on both the teachers and the students?

Given that teachers shape their classroom environment in their own image and "adjust" requirements to suit their beliefs and values, why not do so openly? Why not act as experts and point out the flaws in the piecemeal reasoning that results in such contradictory requirements? Why are teachers so afraid of expressing aloud what experience has taught them is unreasonable or unworkable? The criticisms voiced in the safety of the teacher's lounge or cafeteria are, in many cases, valid commentaries from unrecognized educational experts!

An *expert* is defined as one who is skillful and well informed in a field. Isn't a teacher who spends his or her working life in the classroom— who has day-in and day-out experience with the complex interactions that take place between and among students, teachers, and knowledge— an expert? Doesn't the teacher who has daily verification of what works and what doesn't have some measure of expertise? *It's time to stop looking to others for your own expertise.*

As the person ultimately responsible for the implementation of the various reform programs and approaches, you are the one who experiences them as they work together in a system of individuals. Reformers who insist on the same standards for all students do not work with the student who comes to school hungry or fearful. Reformers who insist on in-depth coverage of topics may be unfamiliar with the student whose struggles with the basic skills of reading and writing permit little beyond improvement of those skills. The effective teacher sees all of them—works with all of them—and offers them what, in that teacher's best judgment, they need at that moment in time. In this situation, the individual teacher is the only expert who counts.

I don't suggest that teachers declare themselves the ultimate judges of the validity of attempts to improve education. However, when everything in your experience and that of your fellow teachers tells you something is wrong, that critical factors such as available time have been overlooked or swept away as insignificant, you'd be doing everyone, especially the students, a big favor by speaking out.

The Newtonian worldview has produced tremendous advances in science and technology. Researchers can apply scientific principles and methods to studies of educational issues. They can quantify those studies, yielding the statistics that make people more willing to believe their findings. Despite all of this, it may be time to admit that educators don't get the same results by experimentally manipulating living human beings that scientists can get by manipulating inert materials and processes. If educators limit their beliefs about students to factors for which there is "hard data"—if they continue to make decisions based on group statistics rather than individual human interactions, how many productive approaches to change will they have overlooked?

In describing how scientists are making the shift from the Newtonian worldview to a Systems approach, Fritjof Capra says:

> "Gradually, physicists began to realize that nature, at the atomic level, does not appear as a mechanical universe composed of fundamental building blocks, but rather as a network of relations, and that, ultimately, there are no parts at all in this interconnected web. Whatever we call a part is merely a pattern that has some stability and therefore captures our attention."[22]

Educational theorist Seymour Sarason acknowledges that systems thinking isn't easy, particularly in education.

> "Thinking in terms of a system, whether it is a family or school or school system, is intellectually demanding and messy. ...Is it any wonder, then, that people concentrate on what they feel secure about doing even though they know that what they will do is an exercise in futility?"[23]

Which Worldview Is "Correct"?

Which worldview—Newtonian/machine or Systems—is "correct"? Which will provide "the answer" to the problems of education? This question arises from the belief that there is "an" answer. We must realize that the system of education is not only complex but also adaptive. Like other biological systems, it changes over time in response to its environment. Therefore, even if it were possible to find "an answer" that works today, it may not work tomorrow. Change must be ongoing and equally adaptive. Even if what you did five years ago was tremendously effective, it may not work tomorrow.

Both the Newtonian and the Systems perspectives yield good information. When forced into opposition with one another, valuable information is lost. Examining parts is useful in focusing on details. Systems theory forces people to adopt a broader perspective—to speculate about "action at a distance." What else will change when we "fix" the curriculum? What else must change for the "fix" to work? And what changes will this "fix" require after the system adapts to it?

In short, there is no "correct" worldview. Insisting that one must adopt either the Newtonian worldview or the Systems worldview is counterproductive. Dichotomies force people to take sides and inhibit them from seeing other alternatives that may address everyone's concerns. Productive questions become buried under mountains of name-calling and incorrect assumptions.

The mechanistic worldview is the defining aspect of educational thought. Although we speak of the education *system*, we seldom perceive it as such. Educators rarely acknowledge the complexity of interactions and the system's adaptive nature. Theorists will continue to get the same answers—answers that have proven unworkable and ineffective—until they open themselves to multiple ways of characterizing the process of education. Isn't the future of your students worth the effort?

The first three chapters have introduced a few of the ways in which individual beliefs, values, and worldviews can influence the choices teachers make. The goal of this book goes far beyond pointing out potential problems. Identifying problems leads only to frustration unless people are empowered to act. Those actions must begin with exploring *your* beliefs, *your* values, and *your* worldview in terms of the choices you make and the effect of those choices on your students. Numerous ways to accomplish those tasks will be suggested in later chapters.

---

1 Pajares, M. F. (1992). Teachers' Beliefs and Educational Research: Cleaning Up a Messy Construct. *Review of Educational Research, Vol. 62, No. 3*, 307–332.
2 Ibid, 309.
3 Dilts, R. B. (1999). *Sleight of Mouth: The Magic of Conversational Belief Change*, Capitola, CA: Meta Publications.
4 Marchese, T. J. (1998). The New Conversations about Learning: Insights From Neuroscience and Anthropology, Cognitive Science and Work-Place Studies. New Horizons for Learning. URL: http://www.newhorizons.org.
5 Lawley, James, personal communication. With his partner, Penny Tompkins, Lawley trains therapists and works extensively with beliefs and metaphors. They

have written a book entitled *Metaphors in Mind*, available at their website URL: http://www.cleanlanguage.co.uk.

6 Palmer, P. J. (1998). *The Courage to Teach*. San Francisco: Jossey-Bass, 2.

7 Dilts, R. B. (1999). *Sleight of Mouth...*, 81.

8 Postman, N. (1995). *Redefining the Value of School*, New York: Alfred A. Knopf.

9 Introduction to the Framework, New Jersey Mathematics Curriculum Framework. (1996) Available at URL: http://www.dimacs.rutgers.edu/nj_math_coalition/framework/intro.html.

10 Peter, Laurence J. (1977). *Peter's Quotations: Ideas for Our Time*. New York: Bantam Books, 39.

11 Sawada, D. & Caley, M. T. (1985). Dissipative Structures: New Metaphors for Becoming in Education. *Educational Researcher, Vol. 14, No. 3*, 15.

12 Senge, P. (1994) *The Fifth Discipline: The Art and Practice of the Learning Organization*. New York: Doubleday, 7.

13 As powerful as these words are, they overlook one very important point. The standards to which Ravitch refers are for inanimate objects—not living, breathing, thinking organisms that resist being shaped and formed into "standard" products.

14 Curriculum and Evaluation Standards for School Mathematics (1989), National Council of Teachers of Mathematics, 12.

15 Brown, J. S., Collins, A., & Duguid, P. (1989). Situated Cognition and the Culture of Learning, *Educational Researcher, Vol. 18*, 32–42.

16 Berryman, S. E. (1995). *Designing Effective Learning Environments: Cognitive Apprenticeship Models*. Institute on Education and the Economy, Box 174, Teachers College, Columbia University New York, New York 10027; (212) 678-3091.

17 Gardner, H. (1997). *Extraordinary Minds: Portraits of Exceptional Individuals and an Examination of our Extraordinariness*. New York: Basic Books, 35-36.

18 Gordon, H. R. D. (1998). Identifying Learning Styles. (ERIC Document Reproduction Service No. ED 424 287)

19 Marzano, R. J. & Kendall, J. S. (1998). Awash in a Sea of Standards. Mid-Continent Regional Educational Laboratory. URL: http://www.mcrel.org.

20 Mid-Continent Regional Educational Laboratory (2001, April 28). URL: http://www.mcrel.org/standards-benchmarks/docs/process.asp

21 Fullan, M. (1993). *Change Forces: Probing the Depths of Education Reform*. London: The Falmer Press.

22 Capra, Fritjof. (1991). *The Tao of Physics*. Boston: Shambhala, 329.

23 Sarason, S. B. (1991). *The Predictable Failure of Education Reform: Can We Change Course Before It's Too Late?* San Francisco: Jossey-Bass, 42.

Chapter 4 ~ Metaphors Create Meaning

"In all aspects of life,...we define our reality in terms of metaphors and then proceed to act on the basis of the metaphors. We draw inferences, set goals, make commitments, and execute plans, all on the basis of how we in part structure our experience, consciously and unconsciously, by means of metaphor." ~George Lakoff and Mark Johnson

Beliefs, values, and worldviews are not the only ways in which individual teachers create and maintain their inner worlds. This chapter will explore several other mental processes that people use to shape their realities.

Teaching Is Like...

"My classroom is a zoo!"

"I try to weave all of the concepts together."

"Those kids are really blossoming."

"He's one of my top students."

"We're always falling behind."

Teachers typically use this kind of language when they talk about their work. What do the statements have in common? Each of the sentences contains a metaphor. Before I get into trouble with teachers of English or linguistics, let me clarify the way in which I will be using the word *metaphor*.

In literature classes, metaphor is often taught as a linguistic device that adds interest to the written or spoken word. A *metaphor* is defined as "a figure of speech in which one thing is spoken of as if it were another." The example used in Webster's dictionary comes from Shakespeare—"All the world's a stage..."[1] Now, we know that "the world" is not "a stage." They are two different conceptual categories. Yet, Shakespeare's metaphor encourages people to experience the world in a specific way, particularly when he continues:

"…And all the men and women merely players: They have their exits and their entrances; And one man in his time plays many parts, His acts being seven ages."

For the sake of simplicity, I will use *metaphor* to mean any circumstance where a person uses one conceptual category, experience, or "thing" to describe or define another conceptual category. It may be simple or extended, and with or without the words *like* or *as*. "The essence of metaphor is understanding and experiencing one thing in terms of another."[2]

Just a Figure of Speech?

What do figures of speech have to do with how individual teachers perceive their profession and make their choices?

Karl comes into the teacher's lounge shaking his head. "My classroom is a zoo today!" If what we learned in literature is correct, Karl is simply using a figure of speech, making his description of his classroom more interesting or unique. Other teachers recognize that Karl's classroom is probably noisy and unsettled. The "animals" may be on a rampage and difficult to control. Is it just a "figure of speech"—a linguistic device? Or does a statement such as this spring from something much deeper—from Karl's conceptual system?

Linguist George Lakoff and philosopher Mark Johnson[3] provide convincing evidence that metaphors may be people's *primary mode of mental operation*. They argue that because the mind is "embodied"—because it experiences the world through the body in which it resides—people cannot help but conceptualize the world with respect to bodily perceptions. Our concepts of *up-down, in-out, front-back, light-dark,* and *warm-cold* are all related to orientations and perceptions acquired through our bodily senses. The "teacher talk" sentences at the beginning of this chapter contain several such metaphors. A *top* student represents a vertical orientation, whereas *falling behind* suggests a horizontal orientation. (Italics will be used to draw attention to metaphors.)

Lakoff and Johnson suggest that the metaphors through which people conceptualize abstract concepts influence the way in which they understand them. In *Metaphors We Live By*, they provide a number of examples of common metaphors people use when describing the concept of *ideas*. The heading for each group is the primary metaphor—*ideas* are conceptualized as *food, plants,* and *commodities*. The rest of the sentences are common expressions that people use—idioms that arise from the metaphor.

Ideas Are Food

What he said *left a bad taste in my mouth*. All this paper has in it are *raw* facts, *half-baked* ideas, and *warmed-over* theories. There are too many facts here for me to *digest* them all. I just can't *swallow* that claim. That argument *smells fishy*. Let me *stew* over that for a while. Now there's a theory you can really *sink your teeth into*. That's *food* for thought. We don't need to *spoon-feed* our students. He *devoured* the book. Let's let that idea *simmer on the back burner* for a while. This is the *meaty* part of the paper. My ideas haven't *gelled* yet.

Ideas Are Plants

His ideas have finally *come to fruition*. That idea *died on the vine*. That's a *budding* theory. It will take years for that idea to come to *full flower*. He views chemistry as an *offshoot* of physics. Mathematics has many *branches*. The *seeds* of his great ideas were planted in his youth. She has a *fertile* imagination. He has a *barren* mind.

Ideas Are Commodities

It's important how you *package* your ideas. He won't *buy* that. That idea just won't *sell*. There is always a *market* for good ideas. That's a *worthless* idea. He's been a source of *valuable* ideas. I wouldn't *give a plugged nickel* for that idea. Your ideas don't have a chance in the intellectual *marketplace*.[4]

It should come as no surprise that humans attempt to understand vague, abstract, or complex concepts in terms of more familiar experiences. The point is that the metaphor a person selects to frame a concept/experience necessarily focuses attention on some aspects while ignoring others—much like a worldview. Thinking of ideas as *commodities* focuses our attention on how those ideas will be received *(bought)* by other people and whether they are *salable*. By contrast, ideas as food concentrates on the satisfaction (olfactory or gustatory) that one gets by *chewing on* an idea.

It's important to recognize that the two categories that are compared don't share identical characteristics. However, a well-chosen metaphor has the potential to reveal interactions and processes that may be missed when thinking of the concept or experience itself.

Metaphors provide cognitive economy. Rather than having to describe a number of particular events that occurred in his classroom, Karl got his point across by saying that it is a zoo. Because people are familiar with zoos, they "get the picture." That picture would have been quite different had Karl said, "My classroom is a beehive."

Each metaphor has certain entailments—necessary conditions contained within the metaphor. If ideas are *commodities*, then they must be *marketable*. Having an idea just for the sake of having it isn't consistent with this metaphoric structure. You want to *crank out* lots of ideas and *get them out the door.*

In the *ideas-are-plants* metaphor, it's perfectly consistent to hold an idea for quite a while without trying to sell it. After all, plants take time to *ripen* and *mature*—to *come to fruition.*

The language we use reflects our ongoing metaphors—the ways in which we unconsciously structure various parts of our world. By listening to that language, we can investigate our internal metaphoric landscape. What does this have to do with teaching?

In recent years, educational researchers have begun to study teacher metaphors.[5] They have consistently concluded that *the metaphors teachers use to describe their work significantly influence their actions.*

Are metaphors merely literary devices—figures of speech used to decorate conversations? Neil Postman joins those who think not.

> "A metaphor is not an ornament. It is an organ of perception. Through metaphors, we see the world as one thing or another. Is light a wave or a particle? Are molecules like billiard balls or force fields? Is history unfolding according to some instructions of nature or a divine plan? Are our genes like information codes? Is a literary work like an architect's blueprint or a mystery to be solved?"[6]

Discussing the influence of metaphors on behavior, Lakoff and Johnson state,

> "Metaphors may create realities for us, especially social realities. A metaphor may thus be a guide for future action.

Such actions will, of course, fit the metaphor. This will, in turn, reinforce the power of the metaphor to make experience coherent. In this sense metaphors can be self-fulfilling prophecies."[7]

Early Metaphors in Education

Postman cites early writers on the topic of education such as Plato, Comenius, Locke, and Rousseau. These people "made their metaphors explicit and in doing so revealed how their metaphors controlled their thinking."[8]

In ancient texts such as the *Mishnah*, an early part of the *Talmud* written in the second century, four kinds of students are proposed:

"…The sponge, the funnel, the strainer, and the sieve. It will surprise you to know which one is preferred. The sponge, we are told, absorbs all; the funnel receives at one end and spills out at the other, the strainer lets the wine drain through it and retains the dregs; but the sieve—that is the best, for it lets out the flour dust and retains the fine flour."[9]

These metaphors contain within them beliefs about knowledge and the expected role of the student. Each suggests that knowledge is something that is "taken in" as opposed to being generated internally. Even in the second century, students weren't expected to retain everything. The preferred role of the student was to "separate the dust from the fine flour." Would you agree?

His mind is like a sponge. Although this statement may elicit a picture of a student "soaking up" knowledge, one shouldn't simply take a metaphor at face value. Sponges are living creatures before someone cuts them from their beds and delivers them to your local store. As living creatures, they don't "absorb all." They take in nutrients from their environments, metabolizing what they can use and excreting the waste. Dead sponges may absorb everything, but they can't "use" it. Living sponges can. If you think or speak of your students as sponges, are those sponges alive or dead?

Interpreting Metaphors—An Individual Process

Let's consider a couple of common teaching metaphors. Some teachers describe themselves as *entertainers* or *performers*. Does that mean the teacher is a stand-up comic, constantly cracking one-liners for the sole purpose of keeping his kids amused? Or is she a dramatic actress, holding her audience spellbound as she draws them into a story? Does the teacher's *performance* challenge, inform, make one think, or merely entertain?

What of the *teacher-as-gardener* metaphor? Does the teacher perceive her garden as a profusion of various flowers and plants, each requiring different nutrients and special care to achieve maximum growth? Or is she tending a field of corn, giving all the plants the same amounts of water and nutrients at the same time? Whose fault is it when a particular plant fails to grow—to bear healthy fruit? Perhaps the seed was genetically weak and would not have grown under any conditions. Or was there something missing in the environment?

Does *teacher as policeman* automatically imply that students are prospective criminals? What sort of expectations does that set up? Is this policeman's approach to teaching—"Go ahead. Make my day!"—or is he more like Officer Friendly, explaining how some laws are in everyone's best interest?

Examining the subtext—the entailments of a metaphor—yields fascinating insights into the role of the teacher, the student, the curriculum, discipline, and many other aspects of the educational environment. The common language used among teachers is filled with metaphors. The concept of *standards*, for example, arises from the factory metaphor in which *students are products*.

Putting students in *tracks* carries with it the idea that, like a train, one must *stay on the track*. *Switching tracks* is a complex process that isn't easily accomplished. Then again, one can get *off the track*, in which case one won't *get anywhere*. The larger, underlying metaphor here is that *learning is a journey*. Let's see where that journey takes us.

Current Metaphors in Education

A Lesson Is a Journey

One of education's most influential metaphors is the idea of *covering* material. The primary meaning of the word *cover* in the educational use of the word is that of *covering ground*—moving across a terrain of some kind. In this metaphor, *knowledge is a landscape* traversed during the learning *journey*.

Lessons as Moving Objects

Researchers frequently quote "teacher talk" that almost exclusively uses the metaphor of lessons as moving objects. Here are some examples from an interview of a single teacher by Hugh Munby.

"I just went ahead..."

"They're always a step ahead of the other classes because everything goes so smoothly..."

"We move along faster."

"We'll probably even back up a little bit."

"These kids need a push in every direction"

"If he's lost, he's just going to get further behind..."

"They like to get off of the subject on to different topics."

"We didn't get to that."

"We didn't even get past those ten sentences today."

"I get carried away sometimes."

"If I go right back to the basics."

"I hate going over that two and three times."

"I might move on...it was time to move on very quickly."

"I'm pushing and backing up as far as I can..."

"I thought the class went fairly slow."

"He's kind of a slow starter."

"She was slowly plowing through it."

"I finally got to the point..."

"They get behind."[10]

Not only is the lesson a moving object, but the journey appears to be along a fixed two-dimensional road. This teacher defines her role in terms of covering a specific distance along that road in a specific amount of time. In this metaphoric context, some behaviors, such as discussions about topics that interest students (getting off the subject) are unlikely to occur. Notice how the metaphor puts the subject matter—the road to be covered—in the foreground and assigns value to the students with respect to how much of that road they have traversed.

Many teachers think of the concepts and principles they teach—the bits of human wisdom considered "essential knowledge"—as ends in themselves. This adds yet another layer to the *knowledge is a landscape* and *learning is a journey* across that landscape metaphor. *Concepts and principles are objects* that reside at various locations on the knowledge landscape. As students move across the knowledge landscape, they must *pick up* the concepts until they have *covered* it all and arrived at their final destination—Testland. Here, teachers make sure that students *possess* the knowledge objects acquired during the journey.

Being Educated Is Possessing Knowledge Objects

There is a rarely questioned assumption that everyone who has *covered* the knowledge landscape—the terrain of a given concept—*possesses* the *knowledge objects* of that concept. As one looks at a student's life in school, it is as if they were on a years-long *scavenger hunt*—moving quickly from place to place and collecting a pre-specified list of treasures. The greatest prizes at the end of the hunt go to those students who have managed to collect and hold onto the most treasures—those that haven't fallen under the burden, or dropped too many treasures along the way, as the load became too heavy. Scores on tests such as the ACT or SAT determine who these students are.

An even more critical assumption made by educators is that after students *possess* the essential concepts and principles, they will be able to *transfer* their knowledge from one context to another. Is that assumption justified? Students would need to transfer knowledge only if they wanted to *use* the knowledge in a different context. Where in the *coverage* metaphor is there any talk of students *using* the objects they have ac-quired? With the exception of a few examples that the teacher may mention in passing, there is little time spent on the journey actually *using* concepts in *any* context—*even the one in which it is acquired.*

Keep in mind that this is only one possible interpretation of the *learning is a journey, knowledge is a landscape,* and *concepts and principles are objects* metaphors. I once heard someone say that each class in school provides students with a piece of a puzzle. Throughout their years of schooling, they pick up more and more pieces, putting this piece in one pocket and that piece in another. Nowhere in the course of their educational experience are they encouraged, or even given the opportunity, to put the pieces together and see what the *big picture* is. Notice that both of these metaphors focus on the goal of education as *possession* of the pieces—the knowledge objects.

The thousands of bits of information listed in standards and benchmark documents are collections of "required" knowledge objects. Despite research demonstrating that *rote memorization is the least effective form of learning,* the prevailing "coverage" metaphor forces any consideration of the learner into the background, except as a repository for knowledge objects!

An Alternate Interpretation

The previous interpretation of the *covering territory* metaphor presupposes that the goal of the journey is to *pick up* knowledge along the way. The underlying belief is that the more knowledge objects students possess, the more they have learned.

If, instead, a teacher believed that learning requires students to interact with their environment, the goal of the *journey* takes on a whole different look. It becomes a *journey of discovery* instead of a flat-out *race* across the *landscape* of a discipline. In the original metaphor, one can visualize the journey as a busload full of students with the teacher driving at full speed along a predefined road to reach the destination— the test—before nightfall. Leave No Child Behind!

In a discovery-oriented interpretation of the metaphor, the teacher and students travel more or less together, along a loosely defined route toward that same destination. But they make frequent stops along the way as students notice something of interest that they wish to explore. There are occasional side trips to unexpected places. At times, groups pursue different paths and, after returning to the main road, report to the class about what they have found.

In this interpretation, learning is still a journey, but a very different type of journey. Compare the two interpretations with an around-the-world trip. The first is like a two-week flight around the world— cramming in as many sights as you can in your limited time. When you return from the trip, about all you can say about those sights is that you saw them. The second is an around-the-world cruise, stopping at interesting ports of call and returning to the ship only when you have explored to your heart's content.

Right! Like you have time to make a leisurely exploration of the subject matter! Since when can teachers choose how much or little of a subject they *cover*. They can't change the date of the test—and getting the kids ready for the test is what they've been hired to do!

I would only ask if *coverage* of the knowledge landscape, the collection of predefined knowledge objects, and verification of that collection in

Testland are the most efficient or effective metaphors in which to characterize and insure student learning.

Time Is a Resource

> "...We can make the trains run on time, but if they do not go where we want them to go, why bother?"
> ~Neil Postman[11]

This is where another metaphor comes into play—a metaphor that drives much of what teachers do (and don't do) in teaching. *Time is a resource*. Frequently, that resource is similar to money. Time is something that people can *spend* or *waste*, wisely *invest* in productive activities or *squander* in questionable pursuits. Thus, time becomes the *cost* of discovery—all this exploration on the part of the students.

Further, time is not a resource that teachers *own*. The traditional content of a given course or school year *allots* specific amounts of time to accomplish certain tasks. Time is, after all, a *scarce* resource. Teachers must *budget* that time, *spending* only within the limits of what they have been *allotted*. *Wasting* time on material that isn't part of the assigned curriculum means that they will *run out* before they have covered all the material. Heaven forbid that time *runs out* before the test and the class hasn't *covered* everything!

Think about the issue described previously, wherein teachers are mandated to cover the standards at the same time as they are told to do more in-depth, individualized, and authentic teaching. The *time-is-a-resource* metaphor is *the single most influential factor many teachers use in making decisions about content and methodology*.

In Western culture, *time is a resource* is so much a part of our shared metaphor it would never occur to us that there might be other ways to think about our lives. People in other cultures don't necessarily think of time as a resource.

> "According to anthropologist Elizabeth Brandt...the Pueblos do not even have in their languages a means of saying the equivalent of 'I didn't have enough time for that.' They can say 'My path didn't take me there' or 'I couldn't find a path to that,' but those are not instances of time being conceptualized as a resource."[12]

Lakoff and Johnson state that:

> "Cultures in which time is not conceptualized and institutionalized as a resource remind us that time in itself is not inherently resource-like. There are people in the world who live their lives without even the idea of budgeting time or worrying if they are wasting it. The existence of such cultures reveals how our own culture has reified a metaphor in cultural institutions, thereby making it possible for metaphorical expressions to be true."[13]

In Western cultures, people no longer recognize that *time is a resource* is a metaphor. They just assume that it is true and act accordingly.

Concepts Are Objects. What Kind of Objects?

What if, instead of perceiving concepts as generic *objects*, we perceived them as *tools*? People often collect *objects* just to possess them but only collectors with a specific interest simply collect *tools*. *Tools* are objects that people *use* for a specific purpose. The *tool* metaphor, interpreting knowledge as something to be *used* rather than acquired, has entailments very different from the *tools-as-collectibles* metaphor.

We may acquire a tool, such as an electric drill, to drill holes for the screws that hold up our curtain rods. By installing a screwdriver tip instead of a drill bit, we can use the drill to drive the screws themselves. Later, we use the drill to repair or make a piece of furniture, or attach a lock to the door. Over time, we find many uses for our combination drill/driver. We also find that it's not particularly useful for pounding nails, chopping wood, or tightening a nut on a bolt. When a person has explored the various uses of a tool and found it wanting in some situations, the person develops the need for other tools and is motivated to go looking for more useful tools.

The behavior of a teacher who thinks about *concepts and principles as tools to be used* is quite different from one who thinks about them as *objects to be collected* or possessed. The first teacher is more likely to spend time having students learn to use the tools once they have collected them. She might, in fact, give students a problem requiring a specific tool that they didn't already have. When students recognize that they need the tool, the motivation is in place to acquire it.

Once they possess sufficient tools, this teacher often has students confront real issues, real situations, to see how their tools can be used to operate on those issues. Students explore the range of situations in which they can use each tool and begin to recognize places where the tool's usefulness ends and what other kind of tools they might need.

Beliefs Behind the Metaphor

Depending on a teacher's beliefs, the same metaphor can create different realities. The interpretation of the tool metaphor as it is described above stems from the following beliefs.

1. Learning includes the ability to use the knowledge (tools) one has acquired;
2. students gain something worthwhile by working with knowledge to find ways in which it is and is not useful; and
3. students will be motivated to acquire other tools when they discover a need for them.

On the other hand, a teacher who *believes* every educated person must *possess* the same "body of knowledge" will employ the tool metaphor in an entirely different way. If *concepts and principles are tools*, that teacher will perceive his job as *giving* those tools to the students. He will feel he has done his job well when each student *possesses* the deluxe set of tools (the 512-piece set complete with metal boxes and compartments into which each tool fits). Even though concepts have been described as tools, this teacher's goal reverts to *possessing* those tools—the concepts and principles—rather than *using* them. Therefore, examining the beliefs behind the interpretation of the metaphor is essential.

Journeys, Tools, or Something Else?

You may be thinking, "What's this got to do with me. I don't think about learning in terms of journeys or tools. I just go in there and teach!" Although you may be unaware of them, you almost certainly represent teaching, learning, the classroom environment, and other contexts within teaching as metaphors. People have no choice about using metaphors in their language. They automatically emerge. Your metaphors and their entailments are a wonderful way to unlock some of the deeper beliefs that you may not even realize you hold. With a little practice, you can begin to recognize the metaphors that you and other teachers use, and speculate about what beliefs reside below the surface.

Remember that the mind uses metaphor to understand complex concepts and experiences. The educational process is about as complex as it gets. A single metaphor is unlikely to illuminate that process. Instead, teachers use different metaphors to make sense of different contexts within their profession, such as discipline or their relationship with students. As you've seen, even when teachers appear to use the same metaphor, they can interpret it in very different ways.

Keep in mind that there are no "correct" metaphors any more than there are "correct" beliefs everyone should use. The question is one of identifying how you and your fellow teachers individually perceive your roles and those of your students, and the effects of those perceptions on the classroom environment.

In one study of teacher metaphors, researchers conclude:

> "[It] …makes a great deal of difference to our practice…if we think of teaching as gardening, coaching, or cooking. It makes a difference if we think of children as clay to be molded or as players on a team or as travelers on a journey"[14]

Education professor Kenneth Tobin, in researching the effect of metaphors on the behavior of teachers, goes so far as to suggest that metaphors act like a "master switch" for beliefs.[15]

> "The metaphor used to make sense of a [teaching] role was a master switch for teachers' associated belief sets. If…the metaphor is changed…new beliefs are deemed relevant to the role. Reconceptualizing a role in terms of a new metaphor appeared to switch an entirely different set of beliefs into operation."[16]

Categories—The Stuff of Experience

> "…It is not just that our bodies and brains determine that we will categorize; they also determine what kinds of categories we will have and what their structure will be."
> ~Lakoff and Johnson[17]

Categorizing objects and situations in the world is an intrinsic function of living brains. From the simplest organism "deciding" that one substance is food and another is not, to the theoretical physicist proposing that the universe consists of ten-dimensional strings, living systems cannot help but seek out patterns and organize their perceptions into categories. Linguist George Lakoff and philosopher Mark Johnson[18] explain that those categories are determined by the way we perceive life from the perspective of our bodies.

1. *Human thought processes are shaped by physiology.* Reason—the ability to "think logically"—is a highly valued thought process. Lakoff and Johnson argue that reason is not a disembodied capacity separate from the mind and it is largely out of a person's control. Reason cannot be the ideal "pure" thought, unaffected by subjectivity that some would wish because it "arises from the nature of our brains, bodies, and bodily experience."[19] People are not free to think just anything. The concepts that people are capable of forming arise from the perceptions that human bodies are capable of producing.[20]

Such basic terms as *in/out, up/down, in front of/behind* are fundamental spatial references that people use and understand because they experience those orientations in their bodies. If humans existed as clouds of gas with no distinct boundary, if they existed in a gravity-free environment, or if they possessed senses capable of 360-degree perception, these concepts would not be part of human thinking processes nor of their "language."

2. *Abstract concepts are mostly metaphorical.* The human mind attempts to understand a new or a complex phenomenon in terms of prior experience. The mind identifies certain features of the new situation and unconsciously searches for similar features in categories and experiences it already has stored. This is the essence of metaphor—mapping of the features of one experience or domain, such as *life*, onto another.

Forrest Gump's mother told him, "Life is like a box of chocolates. You never know what you're going to get." Jawaharlal Nehru said, "Life is like a game of cards. The hand that is dealt you represents determinism; the way you play it is free will." Samuel Butler claimed, "Life is like playing a violin in public and learning the instrument as one goes."

Abstract concepts, such as *life* or *education*, may be defined in a literal way but are generally described and understood through metaphor. Few of the statements people make or read in print are literal. The literal statement "I achieved my purpose" sounds flat and relatively uninteresting. More commonly, a person might say "I *reached* my *goal*," categorizing the achievement as a *journey to a destination*. Similarly, "I *got* what I *wanted*" metaphorically compares the achievement to *gaining possession of a desired object.* Most of the richness in human thought and language emanates from metaphors.

"I saw him *in a new light*" (visual), "That doesn't *ring true*" (auditory), and "I *don't like the feel* of this situation" (kinesthetic) are simple examples of how the speaker's internal sensory representation—and understanding—of a situation is represented metaphorically.

The categories people unconsciously select to explain an unfamiliar concept often reflect the familiar ideas of the times. For example, theories about the brain/mind have included *a great raveled knot, a homunculus (little man), a demon, a switchboard, an underground stream,* and *hemispheres.* The brain is characterized as having *doors* of perception. *Maps* of the mind have been drawn as *cubes, fields, geometric shapes, hierarchies, arrows,* and *disjointed body parts.*[21] These to understand the brain/mind in terms of other, more familiar, ideas are metaphors.

The Strengths and Weaknesses of Metaphor

"A metaphor is a characterization of a phenomenon in familiar terms. To be effective in promoting understanding of the phenomenon in question, the familiar terms must be graphic, visible, and physical in our scale of the world. To characterize teaching as pouring knowledge into the empty vessel of a student is to describe the phenomenon in physical terms at a very 'handy' size. In our imagination, we can see ourselves physically 'doing teaching' in this way."[22]

Complex phenomena present problems for the human mind. They contain too many features to be efficiently processed simultaneously. Metaphors serve the purpose of reducing that complexity to a couple of key features. It's obvious that students are not *empty vessels* and that knowledge is not a substance that can be *poured* into students by teachers. The metaphor focuses on the idea that teachers have something to *give* students. Whether that giving is characterized by pouring a liquid or writing on the *tabula rasa*—the blank slate of the student's mind—the focus is on the process of *filling an empty space.*

Because people are familiar with pouring a liquid, the metaphor encourages further questions about the system. If *learning is like pouring a liquid into a container,* if the teacher pours faster, does learning increase? Are all containers the same size and shape? Do they all have the same size opening?

In addition to providing a place to start in understanding a complex idea, metaphors can reduce cognitive anxiety. Complexity often generates feelings of confusion or stress—there's too much information coming in. Decisions are difficult and worrisome. What does it mean to *teach*? What do I do first? *Teaching* is too big, too vague. *Pouring a liquid into a container* is something I can do; I can give students information.

The very thing that gives metaphors their power is also their greatest weakness. By focusing on a limited number of features of a complex phenomenon, other important features are ignored. These may be critical to understanding the concept. Obviously, in the *learning as filling an empty vessel* metaphor, individual variability and the role of the student in learning are ignored.

Comparing the brain to a computer places expectations and limits on that brain. The limitations of a computer are known, so the same limitations are assumed for the brain. Computers are unemotional; therefore emotions are ignored in this model. Computers do what they are instructed to do and generate correct answers. They are not asked what they would like to learn, nor are they given choices about what programs they will run. Therefore, those factors are not considered because they are not supported by the metaphor.

Neil Postman makes the point that

"...Such simple verbs as *is* or *does* are, in fact, powerful metaphors that express some of our most fundamental conceptions of the way things are. We believe there are certain things people 'have,' certain things people 'do,' even certain things people 'are.' These beliefs do not necessarily reflect the structure of reality. They simply reflect an habitual way of talking about reality."[23]

Postman cites Samuel Butler's book *Erehwon*, which portrays a society in which "...illness is something people 'do' and therefore have moral responsibility for; criminality is something you 'have' and therefore is quite beyond your control."

"In schools, for instance, we find that tests are given to determine how smart someone is or, more precisely, how much smartness someone has. If, on an IQ test, one child scores a 138 and another a 106 the first is thought to have more smartness than the other. But this seems to me a strange conception—every bit as strange as "doing" arthritis or "having" criminality. I do not know anyone who has smartness. The people I know sometimes do smart things (as far as I can judge) and sometimes do dumb things—depending on what circumstances they are in, how much they know about a situation, and how interested they are. Smartness, so it seems to me, is a specific performance, done in a particular set of circumstances. It is not something you are or have in measurable quantities. In fact, the assumption that smartness is something you have has led to such nonsensical terms as over- and underachievers. As I understand it, an overachiever is someone who doesn't have much smartness but does a lot of smart things. An underachiever is someone who has a lot of smartness but does a lot of dumb things."[24]

Whether or not you agree with Postman, it is clear that even the most common ways of categorizing the world should not be above examination. Teaching that is *like pouring liquid into a container* is very different from teaching that is *like mining for gold*.

When people become trapped in a single metaphor, they have access to only those perceptions that "fit" the metaphor. "Getting a new perspective," itself a metaphor, is used to describe the shift in perceptions that accompanies changing the metaphor used to understand a situation. Try this: Jot down a few ideas that complete the following statement: *Teaching is like coaching because....* Then shift the statement to *Teaching is like weaving because....*

Notice how each of the metaphors focuses your attention on different aspects of teaching. The first metaphor might bring to mind teamwork, execution of basic skills, and practice. The second might trigger thoughts of the various activities, skills, or ideas that a teacher must "weave together" effectively during the day. Your own interpretation of the metaphors may have been very different from these examples. Once again, it is not the words, but the meaning that each individual attaches to those words that determine a person's perception and behavior.

Neuroscientist Candace Pert[25] offers the example of two "beings" strolling across a pasture. One is a botanist and the other is a cow. Both perceive the grass—but the *meaning* of grass is different for each. The definition of "grass" as an objective substance does not provide us with the complete picture. The way the observer *categorizes* the grass—the observer's *interpretation*—is "the difference that makes the difference."[26]

Language—Externalizing Internal Processes

People have traditionally used stories—extended metaphors—to "teach" morality and "proper" behavior. Aesop's fables, fairy tales, and the parables of the Bible are obvious examples. Even when the conscious mind attends only to the literal actions of the wolf and the three little pigs, the unconscious mind quickly absorbs the "messages" about wise and clever thinking and transfers them to other relevant contexts through its natural process of categorization.

The metaphors we unconsciously use when describing our world offer remarkable insights into the way we conceptualize and understand that world. A teacher who describes his work as *combat teaching* and speaks of *hammering home ideas* conceptualizes teaching much differently than the teacher who speaks of *guiding students along the path* of learning. People have little choice about thinking in metaphor and expressing their thoughts in metaphoric language. They can, however, consciously choose another metaphor.

In *Metaphors of Thought*, Michael Reddy[27] suggests "...problem setting, not problem solving is the crucial process." People spend too much time trying to solve problems and too little defining what the problem really is. In effect, a metaphor tells a story. Problems arise when people are using different stories to describe the same situation. Because they haven't taken the time to communicate and compare their stories—the meanings and interpretations through which they understand the situation—they assume they are discussing the same situation when, in fact, they are not.

The Conduit Metaphor

Reddy lays much of the blame for the failure of people to communicate on the pervasive use of what he calls the "conduit" metaphor. In this metaphor, ideas are captured in words *(knowledge as objects)*. These knowledge objects can then be transferred to the minds of other people or stored in books or other media. "All the ideas are 'there in the library,' and anyone can go in and 'get them.'"[28]

According to this metaphor, ideas are external to the mind. Education involves transferring knowledge objects from one person to another. One need only look at the language of educational reform to recognize that concern for packaging of knowledge objects and more efficient transmittal are primary goals.

Here are a few examples of the conduit metaphor in language.

1. I'm trying to *get this idea across* to you.

2. I *got* the idea from John.

3. That idea *came across* beautifully.

4. That article *gave me* lots of good ideas.

What's wrong with the conduit metaphor? With its focus on the transfer and storage of knowledge objects, the conduit metaphor ignores the issue of how the human mind processes information and creates meaning. It ignores the capacity of the human mind to *use* ideas once they are possessed, and to generate new ideas. Educational theorist Asghar Iran-Nejad estimates that 70 percent of educators' metaphoric language regarding thought, ideas, and knowledge uses a conduit metaphor.[29] The pervasive use of this metaphor maintains the focus of education on knowledge rather than the learner.

The *conduit* metaphor is consistent with the mechanistic worldview and the concept of cause and effect. As part of the educational machine, *knowledge objects* are moved from teacher to student with assembly-line precision. One can reasonably infer from standards documents that the goal of this *assembly line* is to *turn out* productive citizens, all of whom *possess* the same *knowledge objects*.

Notice that in this set of metaphors, *teachers are parts of the machine* and *students are products*. How often, in a production line, does the machine stop to ask the raw material what it thinks? The "thoughts" of the student are addressed only during final quality control—to verify that the proper knowledge objects have been transferred and stored. In other words, the conduit and mechanistic metaphors themselves prohibit or limit behaviors that focus on the individual.

Here's a typical example of "teacher talk" using the conduit metaphor.

"Do you teach *grammar*?"

" Yes, I taught *it* last semester." (Notice that grammar—defined as a system of rules for speaking and writing a language—is referred to as a preexisting object.)

"How did you teach *it*?" (Here, to teach means to transmit.)

"I had the kids memorize all the parts of speech and diagram some sentences." (The implication is that the knowledge object *grammar* can be transferred from teacher to student as a package of definitions and sentence diagrams.)

Where, in this exchange, is there any recognition of student effort, ability, or interest? Students are either willing recipients of the knowledge objects or sometimes impediments to its efficient transmission. Regardless of the rhetoric that supposedly addresses individual differences, there will be little appreciable change in the transmission model of education unless and until the *language*—the stories we are telling ourselves about what knowledge is and how it is generated and manipulated—change.

Beliefs and Metaphors

"To the man who only has a hammer in the toolkit, every problem looks like a nail." ~ Abraham Maslow

The relationship between beliefs and metaphors is complex. There are many theories and little agreement about how one arises from the other. We've seen how changing the beliefs underlying a metaphor result in different behaviors. But how are the metaphors chosen by the unconscious mind in the first place?

As previously noted, beliefs focus people's perceptions. They determine which features of a situation will be noticed. The mind then tries to find a match for those features in prior experience. For example, a teacher who believes students are naturally unruly and undisciplined will perceive behaviors that support that belief. As the mind works to categorize these perceptions, it unconsciously seeks out similar situations of random noise and motion with the same "feeling tone" the teacher associates with "unruly" and "undisciplined." Metaphors related to *riots* or *police work* can easily arise.

A teacher who believes students learn through active interaction with their environment will perceive the same levels of noise and motion, but with a more positive interpretation and a very different "feeling." That teacher may unconsciously find a match in situations where productive activity is taking place, such as a *beehive* or a *construction site*.

To this extent, the metaphor a person uses reflects that person's beliefs. Often, however, people's beliefs arise from a larger metaphor. This occurs when the metaphor becomes the "myth" of a culture. The

Scientific Revolution shifted the study of nature from philosophy and biblical decree to personal experimentation about cause and effect. The *machine* metaphor was born. It is interesting that a movement that freed humans to learn through their own efforts has resulted in a system of education that rarely permits such behavior within its walls.

Social institutions are often grounded in the science of the day. Although the science of the 21st century has moved away from the mechanistic paradigm, education remains firmly entrenched within its confines. Church authorities strongly resisted the evidence presented by Copernicus and Galileo that the sun, not the earth, was the center of the known universe. In the same way, traditional educators now resist the evidence that people are not machines; that thought is not linear and predictable; and that learning is not simply the acquisition of information, but the active processing of experiences.

Doctors use a variety of imaging techniques, such as MRI, CT scans, or X-rays to diagnose health problems. Each type of image contains information about a specific function or structure in the body. In the same way, each teacher metaphor gives a different picture of education. No single metaphor provides the "right" picture. That is why using a variety of different metaphors is so useful. Changing a metaphor provides a new, and potentially more revealing, map to the territory.

Metaphors and Predispositions

"The process of teaching and learning is more than a process of transmitting information. Cognitive processes interact with emotions and predispositions...educators' predispositions about students shape the process of teaching and the way schools are organized. From a practical standpoint, revealing some of the basic predispositions and underlying assumptions teachers possess about students...may be an effective route to better understanding and deeper insight into some of the problems and difficulties with which school is faced. Furthermore, such understanding and insight may turn out to be an effective means of...changing teacher practice, and school organization." ~ Dan Inbar

Researcher Dan Inbar[30] suggests that one of the more interesting and effective ways to expose predispositions is through an examination of metaphorical images. He studied more than seven thousand such images gathered from hundreds of students and teachers. They were asked to complete the following statements: *The pupil is like…. The teacher is like…. The principal is like…. The school is like….* After completing the statements, participants were asked to briefly explain their statements.

Students were seen as *receptacles*—a *mind as container* metaphor—by 17.6 percent of teachers. In terms of discipline, the teacher expects the students to behave as proper receptacles—sit down, be quiet, and listen.

More than 10 percent of teachers saw students in metaphors such as *clay in the potter's hands*—*raw material* whose attitudes and values can be *molded*. With this metaphor, the student is perceived as a formless entity waiting to be property shaped by the teacher. The teacher, of course, decides the shape.

The largest group of teachers (27.2 percent) characterized students as various flora and fauna. They used terms such as *tiny seedling, little bush, delicate bud,* or *tender flower.* Although the metaphors focus on the student's helplessness and dependence, and the educator's responsibility and obligation, they at least acknowledge the inherent potential of the student for development. This metaphor encourages the teacher to focus on the environmental conditions that students need to develop these potentials. However, what many horticultural metaphors overlook is the student's role in organizing his/her learning.

Another very common metaphor explains many of the feelings students have about school."…The most striking phenomena is that 54.9 per cent of all the metaphorical images about students generated by the educators…imply authoritative control…"[31] Is it any wonder, then, that almost 45% of students perceived teachers as "jailers" or other custodial terms. About the same percent saw school as a "framed world"—a *bolted and barred fortress, a prison*, or a "square labyrinth, like a square, equilateral box, which molds a square equilateral student to an identical society."[32]

Inbar suggests the helplessness felt by students who are viewed by their teachers as *receptacles* or *formless shapes* contributes to the students' feeling of being a prisoner. This can occur when students refuse to buy into a teacher's metaphor. What is interesting is the number of teachers who share that perception.

Fortunately, metaphors and the predispositions they suggest have become an increasingly popular topic for research in schools of education.[33] There is growing recognition that "…the metaphors created by teachers to make their roles explicit also can enhance or limit student opportunities to learn."[34]

Metaphors and Teaching

"You don't see something until you have the right
metaphor to let you perceive it."
~Robert Stetson Shaw, physicist

Beginning teachers come into the classroom with an already robust image of education based on their own experiences. Some of their metaphors may arise from a vision of what education could be like *(a community of learning)* or a reaction to what it has been like *(police state, dictatorship)*. Once the new teacher is actually working with students, the reality of classroom life may alter the existing metaphor or the teacher may work to get students to conform to that metaphor. In this situation, it's easy to forget students have stories of their own that may be inconsistent with the stories teachers are telling.

In a study done in British Columbia, 151 students preparing to become teachers were asked to provide their own metaphor of the teaching/learning process. The researchers analyzed the responses in a number of different ways.[35] All quotes are from this source.

1. Image. What types of images were presented? Journeys, horticultural metaphors, and finding treasure were fairly common. A couple examples follow:

"Teaching is like raising a plant. Give it water (information) and sunlight (stimulation) and it will grow and mature."

"The teacher, like the sun, radiates her knowledge in beams onto the faces of her pupils, or plants. Some plants wither and die, others convert this energy into food which can be assimilated to enhance further life."

"Teachers are tug boats, tiny but strong, pulling the giant ships of society's youth toward knowledge and understanding that will allow them to survive in the ocean of the future."

"The teacher is a miner using the proper tools of the trade searching and bringing out precious gems or minerals that he knows are there."

If you think about the implications of each of these metaphors, the beliefs contained within them are apparent. The first is unidirectional. The plants have little or no responsibility or input. The second admits that the plant has some choice, but the focus is still on the sunlight emanating from the teacher. The third implies that society's youth must be pulled toward learning. It ignores the fact that learning is an innate process in which children naturally and eagerly engage—when it is appropriately presented. The fourth statement is the only one that acknowledges something of value already within the student.

Clearly, these are more than interesting ways of speaking about teaching. They reflect very fundamental beliefs about the role of both the teacher and student.

2. Effort. Some teachers saw teaching and learning as requiring active effort: "like climbing a hill of sand." If teachers approach every day with the unconscious belief that their work will require painful effort and will often be unrewarding, those teachers are predisposed to interpret their experiences in that way.

Others suggested that learning occurs without any effort on the part of the teacher. "Learning is like breathing—if one is alive, it is inevitable" focuses on the ease of learning. The teacher's role becomes one of creating an environment in which students can more easily learn the appropriate content.

3. Affect. Some respondents had a very positive attitude toward teaching. Others saw it as a distasteful chore. "A mother spoon feeding a young child—to have the food swallowed or spat back into her face."

4. Control. Many teachers perceive the learning process as teacher-centered with only benign cooperation required of the student. "Teaching is like throwing a snowball at a wall. Some of the snow sticks but most bounces back. It also seems that just throwing harder doesn't necessarily make more of the snowball stick."

Other teachers bring the process of *learning* more into the forefront, acknowledging greater control on the part of the student. "The teaching/learning process reminds me of crystals forming in a magma chamber. They (the students) acquire their particular habit from the physical and chemical properties of the magma (teacher) to form their own unique shape, growing ever larger." In this case, the teacher is the resource—the substrate upon which the student grows in its unique way.

5. Themes. The researchers grouped the responses according to four themes of delivery, change, enlightenment, and human development.

a. Delivery. Unidirectional transmission of knowledge from teacher to learner. Knowledge itself remains largely unchanged. Teaching is like *a messenger, like pouring water on a sponge, like marketing—packaging knowledge so that the student wants it*, or like *filtering sand*—separating out the important information from "undesirable chunks of useless or unnecessary material."[36] These teachers believe they have the responsibility to decide what information is "useless or unnecessary" for all students. *Delivery* metaphors are a form of the *conduit* metaphor.

b. Change. Change metaphors center on what happens to learners as a result of learning. Horticultural metaphors with the student as a *growing plant* and the teacher *providing the nutrients* are common versions of these metaphors. The general idea is that growth is dependent on the learning environment. These metaphors have a consistently positive affective tone in student-centered versions. More teacher-centered versions imply the change is not always positive.[37] "Teaching is like cooking; you need the correct ingredients and supplies and do it in the proper order. Hopefully you can stomach the results."

c. Enlightenment. These metaphors tend to use images of *journeys, discovery, vision, exploration,* and *treasure hunting.* The underlying idea is that there is some pre-existing quality—valuable knowledge or some hidden potential within the learner—that is discovered during learning. "You see *Star Trek?* Well...the teacher leads others boldly (one hopes) into new worlds and facilitates their discovery of things they have never known before" or "...Like the role of an optometrist: you take a piece of raw glass and slowly alter its optical properties so that the wearer of the glasses sees the world more clearly."[38]

d. Humanistic. Metaphors placed in this category focus on teaching and learning as human activities and stress the importance of the interaction and cooperation between the teacher and learners. "...A tennis match. There is a continual interchange between teacher and student." Not all interactions are positive. One teacher evoked the common metaphor, "You can lead a horse to water, but you can't make it drink."

In the self-inventory, how did you complete the sentence, *Teaching is like...?* As you analyze your response using the categories listed above, is your image teacher- or student-centered? Does it carry a positive or negative affect? What roles are implied for both the teacher and student?

A Case in Point—The Gardening Metaphor

Horticultural metaphors are common among teachers, particularly those of elementary grades. The image of *teacher as gardener*, nurturing her students, sounds benign and helpful, but all gardens are not created equal. The general metaphor is less important than the subtext—the entailments that go along with the story as a result of the particular *meaning* assigned by the individual. Here are a couple of examples.

1. Gardener number one first plows the land to remove all the weeds. The ground is then laid out in neat plots and the same type of seed is planted in each plot. The gardener regularly waters the seeds and gives them doses of fertilizer. What the gardener expects from those efforts is a field of healthy plants that will yield a productive harvest. They are, of course, all the same plants. Failure to grow and produce is seen as the fault of weak and stunted plants—the bad seeds. The gardener is judged by the yield of his fields (test scores).

2. Gardener number two creates unique and beautiful bonsai trees. Working with what is already there, the gardener judiciously snips and prunes, feeding each tree with just the nutrients it needs to become a one-of-a-kind specimen—to bring out the innate beauty of each tree.

3. Gardener number three tends a large botanical garden. Different plants occupy each area of the garden. Some require more or less water, more or less fertilizer, more or less sunlight. The gardener recognizes the unique requirements of each type of plant and provides the environment most conducive to growth and development. The gardener's reward is in helping each plant produce the healthiest flowers and fruits that are within its nature.

There are, of course, many variations on these themes. Even the most benign gardening metaphor casts the students as plants or seeds. They are essentially dependent on the gardener for their environment and nourishment. They are also fixed in position. If a teacher uses a *gardening* metaphor, what insights does the metaphor give that teacher when a student is unruly and wants to *expand outside his plot*? Must he be *pruned or staked down* to keep him within his part of the garden? Does the plant have any choice as to the *nutrients* it receives?

What happens when teacher/gardeners two and three are confronted with standards and standardized testing? Aren't standards much more consistent with the metaphor of gardener number one?

Other Common Educational Metaphors

Metaphors for the processes of teaching and learning and the role of the teacher are not the only ones that influence education. Many other metaphors are used to characterize the school, the curriculum, and other factors in the educational process. Here are just a few examples.

Schools

Schools have been characterized as shopping malls, zoos, and war zones. The latter is exemplified by phrases such as *in the trenches, frontline experience, combat teaching,* and *putting up a united front.* The *factory/workplace* metaphor is extremely common and has been previously discussed.

Educators who focus more on individuals often use *hospital/medical metaphors* in describing schools.[39] They give *batteries of tests* to *diagnose* student difficulties. *Treatments are prescribed* based on individual needs. Sounds good, but in discussing traditional teaching, professor Michael Battista asks, "How would you react if your doctor treated...your children with methods that were ten to fifteen years out-of-date, ignored current scientific findings about diseases and medical treatments, and contradicted all professional recommendations for practice?"[40]

Parker Palmer describes a faculty meeting where the teachers complained about getting too many low-quality students. Palmer told them they sounded like "doctors in a hospital saying 'Don't send us any more sick people—we don't know what to do with them. Send us healthy patients so we can look like good doctors.'"[41]

Palmer goes on to say that when the medical metaphor is used,

"The dominant diagnosis...is that our 'patients' are brain-dead. Small wonder, then, that the dominant treatment is to drip data bits into our students' veins, wheeling their comatose forms from one information source to the next until the prescribed course of treatment is complete, hoping they will absorb enough intellectual nutrients to maintain their vital signs until they have graduated...our assumption that students are brain-dead leads to pedagogies that deaden their brains."[42]

The Curriculum

The curriculum is often perceived as a race or journey over a prescribed course. Educators use many orientational metaphors referring to that *course,* such as *going over, covering,* and *going back.* Some students *fall behind* and must *get caught up*. *Getting off the track* often means the class will have to *really move* during the next part of the course.

Another common way of speaking about curriculum arises from the conduit metaphor. Curriculum content (information) is perceived as objects to be *broken down into simpler parts, given, tossed around, thrown in,* or *touched on.* These objects must be *gotten out or given* to the kids who may *catch them, miss them,* or *pick them apart.*

Content can also have a vertical orientation. Some information is *fundamental* (lower as in a foundation) while other ideas are *above or over their heads*. Teachers get *down* to basics and work *up* to more advanced topics. This metaphor includes *top* students and *lower-ability* groups. Because people share the primary metaphor that *more is up and less is down, top* grades and *low* scores are consistent with the vertical curriculum.

Intelligence

The subject of intelligence itself is not free from metaphoric interpretation. In his book, *Metaphors of Mind*, Robert Sternberg discusses the different metaphors or models of intelligence that have influenced education. These include the use of cognitive maps, computer-like programs and information processing, structural metaphors such as Piaget's schema and Guilford's "structure of intellect," and systems made up of parts, such as Gardner's Multiple Intelligences and Sternberg's own Triarchic model.[43]

The idea that intelligence can be quantified is in itself a metaphor, categorizing intelligence as an observable and measurable entity separate from the total functioning of an individual's mental operations. Contrast this with a metaphor that conceptualizes *mental operations as a river*. The river is a collection of drops, one of which is intelligence. Categorizing intelligence as a separate entity is an artificial categorization. Drops don't exist separately unless removed from the river. The behavior of a drop does not provide much insight into the behavior of the river.

How Institutional Metaphors Influence Education

"Metaphors have a way of creating realities. And since different metaphors create different realities, truth is always relative and related to its generative metaphor."
~ Thomas J. Sergiovanni[44]

Lakoff and Johnson[45] explain that truth is both subjective and objective. While ideas may have consistency—truth—within a given conceptual system, the truths change from one system to the other.

For example, educational theorist Thomas Sergiovanni[46] says that schools are commonly perceived as *organizations*. Organizational theory is useful in understanding how large corporations run and how their operation can be improved. Is it equally useful for schools? Sergiovanni compares the entailments of *schools as organization* vs. *schools as communities*. Here are a few of the "truths" that arise with each metaphor—truths that define and limit the behavior of people living within that metaphor.

Organizations	Communities
To *organize* means to put in order— to arrange the "parts"—subject areas, grade levels, etc.—logically. Each part has a predefined role within the organization.	Communities arise among people with common goals. Subgroups arise internally in response to a need rather than as an external framework.
Those "higher" in the hierarchy of responsibility are assumed to have more expertise. They have more authority and less supervision.	Members of a community share common interests, goals, and beliefs. Roles are assumed in support of those concepts.
Self-interest is the primary motivational factor. Rewards and punishments are traded for rule compliance.	Communities are held together by commitments rather than contracts. Rather than rules, there are shared values and beliefs.

Schools run as *business organizations* have a very different look and feel from schools run as *learning communities*. Further, both of these metaphors fail to account for many aspects of what schools are about.

When new ideas or reform efforts are introduced, they are judged by their consistency with the prevailing metaphor. This contributes to the failure of many well-intentioned reform efforts. Teachers in an *organizational metaphor* do not see the logic of relinquishing control to students—it is inconsistent with the hierarchical structure of the organization. On the other hand, members of a *learning community* resist the imposition of standards and external assessments when they don't arise from the needs of the community.

Regardless of how much effort schools expend trying to become like enlightened corporations,

> "We are still using economic principles and vocabulary to express educational ideas. We are still allowing economy and production to shape and determine our understanding of education. We are still seeing students as raw materials to be processed in the most efficient way."[47]

Sergiovanni suggests that it is time for educational administrators to stop borrowing their metaphors—the way they conceptualize schools—from other disciplines and segments of society such as business.

> "A major problem facing educational administration today is that as a field of inquiry and practice it is essentially characterless. It has been too receptive to influences from too many other areas of knowledge and too many other disciplines. As a result educational administration has little or no identity of its own...little or no sense of what it is, what it means, where it is going, or even why it exists. And I believe that educational administration will remain characterless as long as it keeps importing its mindscapes and models, concepts and definitions rather than inventing them...You can't borrow character, you have to create it."[48]

Clearly, the unconscious metaphors used in education have a tremendous influence on both individual and collective behavior. Recent articles in leading educational publications are filled with terms such as *high-stakes testing* (gambling), *taking the helm of a district* (nautical), *deeply rooted problems* (horticultural), *a sea of contradictions* (nautical), *arena of controversy* (sports or war), *team effort* (sports), *gearing up for change* (factory), *blueprint* for schools (architecture), and programs *targeted* at specific students (military). Each of these metaphors operates from a different set of "truths." Is it any wonder there is so little consensus about what works and how to improve education?

One example of how a single theorist's metaphor can profoundly shape educational thought is seen in the work of influential educational theorist Madeline Hunter.[49] Hunter's *Effective Teaching Model* was based on solid research—in behaviorist psychology. Behaviorists accept the presuppositions inherent in the conduit metaphor—knowledge exists as *objects* that can be *transferred* from one person to another. Therefore, any technique that increases the efficiency of those transmissions is seen as positive. Hunter's "eight steps" were designed for just that purpose.

In 1985 Ron Brandt, executive editor for the Association for Supervision and Curriculum Development, said Hunter has had "more influence on U.S. teachers in the last ten years than any other person." Is it any wonder that the transmission metaphor is so difficult to dislodge from the thinking of educators when it is at the heart of many popular (and often required) professional development programs?

Mapping the World of Education

The first step in understanding the complex system that is Earth is a set of accurate maps. A good world atlas contains maps of population density, topography, the layers within Earth, natural resources, and political boundaries. Each map is drawn in answer to a particular question about Earth. Each map enriches people's understanding, but no map is the territory that it represents. In the same way, no metaphor is the complex phenomenon that it represents.

Alternative metaphors are ways to create the richest possible maps that respect the systemic nature and ecology of social systems such as education. If the goal is to create the deepest and broadest understanding of teaching and learning, the information gained from multiple maps moves educators closer to that goal. The first step is for you and your fellow teachers to identify the map(s) you already use.

1 Shakespeare, W. *As You Like It*. Act II, Scene VII.
2 Lakoff, G. & Johnson, M. (1980). *Metaphors We Live By*. Chicago: University of Chicago Press, 5.
3 Lakoff, G. & Johnson, M. *Metaphors...*, 56–60. See also Lakoff, G. & Johnson, M. (1999). *Philosophy in the Flesh: The Embodied Mind and its Challenge to Western Thought*. New York: Basic Books. Johnson, M. (1987) *The Body in the Mind: The Bodily Basis of Meaning, Imagination, and Reason*. Chicago: University of Chicago Press.
4 Lakoff and Johnson. *Metaphors...*, 46–47.
5 See for example Tobin, K. (1990). Changing Metaphors and Beliefs: a Master Switch for Teaching? *Theory Into Practice, Vol. 29, No. 2*, 122–127. Bullough, R. V., Jr., & Stokes, D. K. (1994). Analyzing Personal Teaching Metaphors in Preservice Teacher Education as a Means for Encouraging Professional Development. *American Educational Research Journal, Vol. 31*, 197–224. Taylor, W. (Ed.). (1984). *Metaphors of Education*. London: Heinemann Educational Books.
6 Postman, Neil. (1995). *The End of Education: Redefining the Value of School*. New York: Alfred A. Knopf, 174.
7 Lakoff and Johnson. *Metaphors...*, 156.
8 Postman, *The End of Education*, 174–175.
9 Ibid., 175.
10 Munby, H. (1986). Metaphor in the Thinking of Teachers: An Exploratory Study. *The Journal of Curriculum Studies, Vol. 18*, 197–209.
11 Ibid., 61.
12 Lakoff, G. & Johnson, M. (1999). *Philosophy in the Flesh...*, 164.
13 Ibid., 165.
14 Connelly, F. M. and Clandinin, D. J. (1988). *Teachers as Curriculum Planners: Narratives of Experience*. New York: Teachers College Press, 71.
15 Tobin, K. (1990). Changing Metaphors and Beliefs: a Master Switch for Teaching? *Theory Into Practice, Vol. 29, No. 2*, 122–127.
16 Ibid., 126.
17 Lakoff, G. & Johnson, M. (1999). *Philosophy in the Flesh: The Embodied Mind and Its Challenge to Western Thought*. New York: Basic Books, 18.
18 Ibid.
19 Ibid., 4.
20 Ibid., 37.
21 Hampden-Turner, C. (1981). *Maps of the Mind*. New York: Collier Books, MacMillan Publishing.
22 Dickmeyer, N. (1989). Metaphor, Model, and Theory in Education Research. *Teachers College Record, Vol. 91, No. 2*, 151–159.

23 Postman, N. (1995). *The End of Education: Redefining the Value of School.* New York: Alfred A. Knopf, 180.

24 Ibid.

25 Pert, C. (1997). *Molecules of Emotion: Why You Feel the Way You Feel.* New York: Scribner, 257.

26 This phrase was first used by Gregory Bateson.

27 Reddy, Michael J. (1993) The Conduit Metaphor. In A. Ortony (Ed.). *Metaphors of Thought*, 2nd ed. (p. 188). New York: Cambridge University Press.

28 Ibid.

29 Iran-Nejad, A. (1990). Active and Dynamic Self-regulation of Learning Processes. *Review of Educational Research, Vol. 60, No. 4*, 573–602.

30 Inbar, D. E. (1996) The Free Educational Prison: Metaphors and Images. *Educational Research, Vol. 38, No. 1*, 77–92.

31 Ibid., 85.

32 Ibid., 88.

33 See, for example, Bullough, R. & Stokes, D. (1994). Analyzing Personal Teaching Metaphors in Preservice Teacher Education as a Means for Encouraging Professional Development. *American Educational Research Journal, Vol. 31, No. 1*, 197–224; Munby, H. (1990). Metaphorical Expressions of Teachers' Practical Curriculum Knowledge. *Journal of Curriculum and Supervision, Vol. 6, No. 1*, 18–30; and Tobin, K. (1990). Changing Metaphors and Beliefs: a Master Switch for Teaching? *Theory Into Practice, Vol. 29, No. 2*, 122–127.

34 Strickland, C. R. and Iran-Nejad, A. (1994) The Metaphoric Nature of Teaching and Learning and the Role of Personal Teaching Metaphors. A paper presented at the Annual Meeting of Mid-South Education Research Association, Nashville, (ERIC Document Reproduction Service No. ED 399 208)

35 Gurney, B. F. (1990, April). Tugboats and Tennis Games: Preconceptions of Teaching and Learning Through Metaphors. A paper presented at the annual meeting of the National Association of Research in Science Teaching, (ERIC Document Reproduction Service No. ED 326 382)

36 Ibid., 6.

37 Ibid., 7.

38 Ibid., 17.

39 Schlechty, P. C. & *Joslin, A. W.* (1984). Images of Schools. *Teachers College Record, Vol. 86, No. 1*, 156–170.

40 Battista, M. T. (1999, February) The Mathematical Miseducation of America's Youth. *Kappan*, February 1999. URL: www.pdkintl.org/kappan/kbat9902.htm.

41 Palmer, P. J. (1998). *The Courage to Teach: Exploring the Inner Landscape of a Teacher's Life.* San Francisco: Jossey-Bass, 41.

42 Ibid., 41–42.

43 Sternberg, R. (1990). *Metaphors of Mind: Conceptions of the Nature of Intelligence.* New York: Cambridge University Press, 5.

44 Sergiovanni, T. J. (1993). Organizations or Communities? Changing the Metaphor Changes the Theory. Invited address, American Educational Research Association. (ERIC Document Reproduction Service No. ED 376 008)

45 Lakoff, G. and Johnson, M. (1980) *Metaphors We Live By*. Chicago: University of Chicago Press, Chapter 23 156–158.

46 Sergiovanni, 2–7.

47 Sztajn, P. (1992). A Matter of Metaphors: Education as a Handmade Process. *Educational Leadership*, November 1992, pp. 35–37.

48 Sergiovanni, 1

49 Steiner, J. N. (1993). A Comparative Study of the Educational Stances of Madeline Hunter and James Britton, NCTE Concept Paper No. 6, Urbana, IL: National Council of Teachers of English.

Chapter 5 ~ Teaching Is Like...
A Teacher Is Like...

"It may be hard for an egg to turn into a bird: it
would be a jolly sight harder for it to learn to fly
while remaining an egg. We are like eggs at present.
And you cannot go on indefinitely being
just an ordinary, decent egg.
We must be hatched or go bad."
~C. S. Lewis

Chapter 4 examined different metaphors through which educators characterize teaching, learning, school, the curriculum, and intelligence. Now, let's turn our attention to ways in which you can interpret your own metaphors and how to use metaphors in a generative way to create your ideal classroom.

Entailments—Strings Attached to Metaphors

If I am a *shepherd* when I am teaching, are my students *sheep*? If I am a *master* of my subject, does that make my students *disciples*? If I am a *gardener*, are my students *helpless buds* who must depend on me for sustenance?

Educational researcher Robert V. Bullough states, "Metaphors that define the self automatically define the Other."[1] Problems arise when the "Other" rejects the role in which he or she is cast. When nearly half of students polled perceived teachers as *jailers* and themselves as *captive or programmed*,[2] perhaps it's time to modify the metaphors that cast them in these roles.

Teachers who are aware of their metaphors can safeguard their students from inappropriate roles imposed on them by those metaphors. But teachers themselves are the "Other" when the policymakers in a school possess a pervasive metaphor of their own, such as a *factory* or *organization*. Because the language used in everyday communication reflects and sustains that metaphor, there is a passive acceptance of its "truths." "Institutionalized discourses press conformity, and discourage alternative metaphors: They anonymously co-author our stories."[3]

Teachers' values are influenced by their perceptions of what administrators, other teachers, parents, students, and the community expect of them. Because the *conduit* metaphor is so prevalent in the language of schools, teachers unconsciously accept the "truths" inherent in that metaphor. Those truths include the idea that *transmission* is the most efficient way to *cover* the material required by the curriculum. But according to many research studies, this is anything but true!

Metaphors also define the nature of the classroom, the curriculum, modes of instruction, assessment, and perhaps of greatest importance, the interactions among students and between teacher and student. For example, if a teacher sees the *classroom as a workplace*, such as a *factory* or *business*, it follows that students must *work*. The role of the teacher is to *supervise* that work. If a student is "off task," the *workplace* metaphor dictates that additional rewards or punishments are in order. This is part of the behaviorist theory inherent in the *organizational* metaphor. The teacher offers additional rewards (or a threat of punishment) and the student briefly returns to the task, but the improvement is short-term. Of greater importance, the assumption that *working*—staying on task— results in more *learning* remains unexamined.[4]

If, however, the classroom is characterized as a *learning place*, getting a student back "on task" may involve increasing the child's curiosity or interest in the task, or examining the task to see if it is relevant to the child's learning. Unlike the *workplace* metaphor, the *learning place* metaphor recognizes the role of the student in learning. The teacher shifts from a supervisory role to one of mentor, guide, or diagnostician.[5] Solutions to problems arise from the needs of the individual student's learning rather than through external "fixes" such as increased rewards or punishment. Rewards or punishment are still appropriate for some students in some contexts. The difference is that the individual student is the basis for the decision to use them.

If we take this one step further—to classroom as *learning "community,"* interactions among students take on even greater importance. The goal of learning is now shared among students and teacher. With this metaphor, authentic group and cooperative learning is more likely. Keeping individual students "on task" becomes a problem addressed by the entire community. Even the word *task* takes on a different meaning because *tasks* in a *learning community* are not assigned from outside but emerge from the process of learning itself.[6]

As you recall, the *entailments* of a metaphor are the truths, assumptions, roles, and perceptions that arise from the nature of the metaphor itself and from the "reality" it creates. Recall the three different interpretations of *teacher as gardener* from the last chapter. Each interpretation conceptualizes the work of the gardener in a different way. Therefore, the entailments of each interpretation are different.

Variations on a Theme

Although others may recognize your general metaphor, you are the only one who can identify its entailments. Your metaphor is your own personal way of making meaning. Metaphors are rarely interpreted in the same way by different individuals.

Teacher as Sheep Dog

When he thinks about what he is like when he is teaching at his best, Parker Palmer identifies himself as a sheep dog: "...not the large, shaggy, lovable kind, but the all-business Border collies one sees working the flocks in sheep country." Palmer envisions his sheep dog as having four main functions:

1. It maintains a space where the sheep can graze and feed themselves.
2. It holds the sheep together in that space, constantly bringing back strays.
3. It protects the boundaries of the space to keep dangerous predators out.
4. When the grazing ground is depleted, it moves with the sheep to another space where they can get the food they need.[7]

When I first read this description, I was amazed. Palmer's book, *The Courage to Teach*, is an extremely personal and honest self-examination that makes clear the author's high regard for students and for the process of learning. The image of a sheep dog nipping at the heels of helpless students to keep them penned within a prescribed pasture of knowledge did not seem at all consistent with the image I had of Palmer. The problem, as it turned out, was not with Palmer's metaphor but with my interpretation of that metaphor.

What makes this metaphor work for Palmer is his belief that a teacher creates a "bounded but open" space for learning. Unlike many traditional classrooms, Palmer's teaching/learning space is not composed of some predefined set of facts that must be *digested* before students are allowed to leave the pasture. Instead, the boundaries are created by a question or a great idea around which the teacher and learners gather. The materials used to explore that question or idea "must be so clear and compelling that students will find it hard to wander from the subject...." In other words, the sheep will find the grass so appealing that they aren't tempted to wander off looking for greener pastures. Students are, however, free to wander where they will within the confines of the pasture. "If boundaries remind us that our journey has a destination, openness reminds us that there are many ways to reach that end."[8]

Palmer's *sheep dog* permits the *sheep* great freedom within the *pasture* defined by the subject of the lesson, yet *nips at their heels* when they get *too far afield*. This metaphor suggests a way to balance a student's freedom with the responsibility of the teacher to guide learning toward an appropriate end.

Palmer acknowledges that the metaphor has a "dark side" because it necessarily casts the students in the role of sheep. He admits to getting upset when students are passive, docile, or mindless. Because he is aware of this "dark side," he is able to recognize it when it influences his behavior. "If the sheepdog metaphor does nothing else but keep me alert to the appearance of my own shadow, it will have served me, and my students, well."[9]

Palmer's metaphor clearly works for him, but it would not work for me. Although I find the "bounded but open" space and the other positive aspects of the metaphor appealing, that appeal is insufficient to overcome the more compelling *meaning* that I attach to sheep. When I look at a flock of real sheep, there is little to differentiate one from another. They all *graze* in the same pasture and require essentially the same diet. They are *easily led*. The points of correspondence I first notice in the metaphor are negative for me because they are inconsistent with my beliefs about students. Therefore, I would not be comfortable with a *shepherd* or *sheep dog* metaphor and would be unlikely to choose one, consciously or unconsciously.

No metaphor is, in itself, good or bad. Palmer makes effective use of the *sheep dog* metaphor because his focus is on the *pasture*. It doesn't serve me because my focus is on the *sheep*. A metaphor is appropriate to the extent that it is useful in creating the environment you want. It is useful in focusing you on the perceptions you need to work effectively in that environment. It is inappropriate when it places limitations on you or your students or contains "truths" that are not consistent with your beliefs or supported by research.

Here is another example demonstrating that it is not the metaphor but the interpretation of that metaphor that makes it more or less useful.

Teacher as Cook

Basic Premise

If lessons are conceptualized as *mental meals*, it is the responsibility of the teacher to prepare those meals—meals intended to *nourish* the mind.[10]

Some insights available from this metaphor:

- The more appetizing a meal, the more likely a person is to eat it.

- In many cases, people prefer fresh foods to those that are dried or canned.

- With the exception of infants, people prefer to chew their own food rather than having it mashed or pureed by the cook. In the process of chewing, the person adds enzymes that aid digestion. It takes some people longer to digest certain foods.

- Diners have different appetites—some are hungrier than others.

- Diners have different food preferences and some are even allergic to certain foods.

Sample Interpretations

Cook number 1: Cook number 1 focuses on efficiency, preparing the same basic meal for every diner (the facts). He ensures that everyone gets a balanced diet by filling each plate before it is delivered to the diner. The diners must clean their plates or no dessert!

Cook number 2: Cook number 2 focuses on variety and choice, providing a banquet table filled with nourishing foods (ideas) from which the diners may select. To ensure a balanced diet, this cook requires that diners take something from each food group and finish everything they take.

As you think about these two different "takes" on the *teacher as cook* metaphor, you can undoubtedly think of other entailments—both appropriate and inappropriate in terms of learning and students. Both interpretations have limitations. Some teachers would be appalled at the thought of having to prepare a buffet-style meal for every lesson—it takes too much time to create all those different dishes. Other teachers would be bored with the thought of preparing the same menu every day. One potential "dark side" to the *teacher as cook* metaphor is that it casts the students in the role of *diner*—dependent on the teacher for sustenance. A potentially more useful variation on the metaphor might cast the teacher as the head of a cooking school—teaching the students to cook their own meals.

Think of several different ways that you could interpret *teacher as sculptor, teacher as orchestra leader, teacher as coach*, or *teacher as ship's captain*. Taking a few minutes to think about alternative interpretations will make it easier to interpret your own metaphor.

It's often helpful to have someone else point out the metaphors that you typically use. However, it is imperative that each teacher determines the *meaning* inherent in his or her metaphor. Just because you share one of the general metaphors mentioned in this book doesn't mean that you will share the same perceptions or that the metaphor will serve you in the same way. What is important is the internal state that the metaphor creates in you as an individual, the environment that it produces, and the behaviors that it generates.

Identifying Your Metaphors

"As good teachers weave the fabric that joins them
with students and subjects, the heart is the loom on
which the threads are tied, the tension is held, the
shuttle flies, and the fabric is stretched tight.
Small wonder then, that teaching tugs at the heart,
opens the heart, even breaks the heart—
and the more one loves teaching,
the more heartbreaking it can be."
~Parker Palmer in *The Courage to Teach*

As you've read about various metaphors teachers use to describe their work, you may have already recognized some of the language you use when you speak about teaching, students, and education in general. What is important is that you identify the metaphors you *actually* use rather than those you think you *should* use. There are a number of approaches for doing this. Use any or all of them that you feel are appropriate. Remember that your unconscious use of language is a rich source of information about your internal map of reality.

1. Go back to the Self-Inventory and notice how you completed the statements, such as *Teaching is like...*, *Learning is like...*, and *Students are like...*. If you didn't spend much time on the original statements, you may wish to complete them again.

Your metaphors for these complex concepts may be related, but don't be surprised if they're not. They are often part of a larger story or may reflect the kind of day you were having when you filled out the Self-Inventory. It's not enough to simply identify a metaphor. You want the one that really drives your behavior in a given context. You'll know it when you find it!

2. One of the richest sources of information about your metaphors is the language you use when speaking casually to other teachers. Begin by simply listening to the conversations at lunch or in the teachers' workroom or office. Pay particular attention to the metaphoric language other teachers use. This will help you recognize your own. As you get better at it, remember that even simple (and common) words like *cover, higher/lower,* and *give* are metaphors.

If you're comfortable with doing so, share these ideas about metaphors with a couple of other teachers and ask them to listen for your commonly used metaphors. Another option is to tape record the conversations for later analysis. Of course, you will want to tell the other teachers why you are doing this. They might be interested to discover their own metaphors.

In this exercise, remember to withhold judgment about your own or anyone else's metaphors. You can't make any valid assumptions about their beliefs or behaviors without knowing much more about how they *interpret* or make meaning with that metaphor. Teachers will occasionally use language that sounds very out of character to describe a particularly stressful or unusual experience. They may simply be having a bad day!

3. Another approach is to identify the story—the broader metaphor—that characterizes what goes on in your classroom. Is there a movie, book, or television show that reminds you of what it's like to teach or of the atmosphere in your classroom? What character do you represent in that story? What roles do your students play?

4. If a general story isn't easily forthcoming, try talking about specific instances or contexts. Complete the statement, "When I am teaching at

my best, I am like a…." Repeat this for a situation that didn't go as you would have liked—perhaps the class was unruly or you just couldn't find a way to help a student understand a difficult concept.

5. If all else fails, go off somewhere with a tape recorder and talk to the walls about teaching. Imagine you're making a speech to a group of fellow teachers or to parents. What would you say as you accept the Teacher of the Year award? Talk about your successes, your failures, your joys and frustrations, your hopes and dreams, and what you want for your students. What would it be like to teach in your ideal classroom? What is it like to teach in your present classroom?

As you do this, don't monitor your language. The more natural language you can access, the greater the opportunity to identify your story—your metaphors. Don't be surprised if you use several different metaphors. Some teachers adopt a role for its presupposed efficiency in covering large amounts of material. They slip into that role only occasionally when they are feeling pressured from outside or inside to catch up with some mythical or imposed schedule.

One or Many?

"The tales persons spin about themselves provide the substance of their concept of self." ~ J. W. Murphy

As you explore your metaphorical language, do you tend to use similar metaphors for different aspects of your teaching, or does your metaphor change from context to context? For example, Carol speaks of *keeping the kids in line, deciding who was guilty* of cheating, and *cracking the whip*. The roles of *military officer, judge*, and *animal trainer* come to mind. On the surface, these seem unrelated. If, however, we move to a larger context, all three of these roles represent authority figures with control over others.[11]

Similarly, the underlying (or overarching) metaphor for a teacher who talks about *bridging the gap* between content and student understanding, providing a *good foundation* of the basics, and *building* understanding is *construction/engineering*.

Some teachers are fairly consistent—using the same or related metaphors for most situations. One individual can, for example, be a spouse, a parent, a friend, an employee, a boss, a cook, a golfer, a health nut, and a dog lover. As the context changes, the metaphor that the person uses to conceptualize his role in that context may also change—sometimes radically. As a parent, he *keeps a tight rein* on his children but lets his dogs *run wild* (related, but opposite metaphor). A person in middle management might be a *mousy* employee, but a *tyrant* as a boss (different metaphors).

A teacher might use a *gardening metaphor* when describing interactions with students, a *weaving* metaphor when describing lesson planning, and a *mediator* metaphor when talking about discipline. This teacher is comfortable switching roles. As long as the teacher's behavior is consistent *within* each of the roles, the students adjust to the changes. They know what to expect in various situations and behave accordingly.

For one person, the consistency of a single set of metaphors offers stability and predictability—characteristics the person values. Another person values flexibility and open-mindedness, so shifting from one metaphor to another in different contexts feels appropriate. Despite apparent differences, their multiple metaphors may still be part of a larger story, such as *teacher as guide*, or *teacher as explorer*.

You can become more aware of how a metaphor influences your perception by stepping into the role suggested by a metaphor. Notice what perceptions follow. How do your perceptions change when you think about teaching a lesson as a *gardener* or as a *police officer*?

Analyzing Your Metaphors

Assuming you've identified at least one of the metaphors you use to conceptualize your teaching roles, it's time to decide if that metaphor is serving you. Is it providing you with the perceptions and conceptual tools you need to do your job in the way you would like?

Here are a few important questions to ask as you analyze your metaphor:

- How does the metaphor conceptualize *educational processes* such as teaching and learning?

- How does the metaphor conceptualize the *relevant actors*—you, your students, other teachers, parents, administrators, educational policymakers, curriculum directors, the community, and so forth?

- How does the metaphor conceptualize *educational artifacts*, such as the physical facilities, materials used in the classroom, the curriculum, class schedules, rules of the school, and so forth?

• How does the metaphor conceptualize *social relationships*—placement, grouping, interactions between teacher and student and among students, classroom governance—the social context in which all come together to bring about teaching and learning?

Although we've already examined many metaphoric entailments, let's pick apart one more metaphor as an example of how these questions can be answered. Remember that there are many interpretations of the same metaphor. This example contains only a few possible "meanings."

Teacher as Caregiver

Teachers who talk about *helping students develop sound minds and bodies*, of *diagnosing* problems, or of *providing tough love* may be employing some form of the *caregiver* metaphor.

Conceptualization of educational processes:

Teaching—Caring for the physical and/or mental health of the learner.

Learning—The metaphor focuses on the *teacher as caregiver*, so learning is only indirectly addressed. One might infer that learning is allowing oneself to be taken care of, following directions, taking the treatment that is prescribed, or doing as one is told. Alternatively, a caregiver may help people become better informed as a way of improving their health and well-being. The meaning of learning will depend on how the individual interprets the role of caregiver.

Conceptualization of relevant actors:

Keep in mind that defining self also defines others. Caregiver roles for self/other include the following:

If the caregiver/teacher is like a parent or guardian, the student is cast as a child or dependent.

If the caregiver is like a doctor, the student is a patient.

If the caregiver is like a psychologist/counselor, the student is a client with a problem.

Notice some of the beliefs and presuppositions built into these roles. The primary belief is that students must be *cared for* and responsibility for that care lies mainly with the teacher. This may arise from the teacher's kindness or concern for others. However, with this metaphor, students are often assumed to have less expertise, ability, and experience. Less may be expected of them. Some roles even presuppose the student has a problem of some kind. Although some caregivers take the opinions or thoughts of their charges into account, this metaphor has the potential for being teacher-centered.

Conceptualization of educational artifacts:

Classroom—Depending on the role chosen by the teacher/caregiver, the classroom can become the *family home, a hospital or place of diagnosis and treatment, holy ground,* or a *mental institution.*

Curriculum materials—The curriculum may be characterized as *chores* by a parent, *treatments* by medical professionals, *sermons* by the clergy, or *therapy* by mental health professionals. Again, the decision lies with the caregiver rather than the client.

Schedules/class size—How much time does the parent have to spend with each child? How long is the doctor or psychologist's appointment? For how many patients does the nurse or attendant care?

Conceptualization of social relationships:

Caregiver roles suggest a number of very different relationships between teacher and student. A *parental* relationship may be warm and caring, strict (tough love), or minimal if there are many children in the family demanding the attention of the parent. A *physician* may be an old-fashioned GP who takes the time to sit down and chat or an impersonal doctor who has to consult the chart to remember the patient's name.

As for student-student relationships, some *parents* expect siblings in the family to help one another. The *psychologist* may insist that people need to stand on their own feet or engage in group therapy. The social climate in the classroom—the tone that is set for behavior—will, of course, depend on what type of caregiver the teacher conceptualizes.

Working with Your Metaphor

Apply the following ideas to your own metaphor:

- According to your metaphor, what is your role? Just as an actor may write a "biography" for his or her character, jot down a few ideas to "flesh out" your role. What other metaphors emerge? Is your metaphor teacher-centered or student-centered?

- According to your metaphor, what role is implied for the students? What insights does this give you about learning? What limitations, if any, does it place on students?

- What does your metaphor suggest about artifacts of teaching, such as the classroom, curriculum content, grades, or testing?

- How does the metaphor define social relationships among you and your students; among; between you and your administrator? How does your metaphor affect your response to disciplinary issues?

- What are the strengths and weaknesses of your metaphor? On what factors does it focus most heavily? What factors does it ignore? Does it serve you in most or all situations in the classroom—from lesson planning to personal interactions to disciplines problems?

One of the easiest ways to determine whether your metaphor is serving you is to think about your level of satisfaction in your classroom. If you are generally dissatisfied with your students or your teaching, try to figure out what it is about your metaphor that might be leading you to that dissatisfaction. Keep in mind that metaphors direct both what you perceive and how you interpret those perceptions.

If you are generally pleased with the environment and productivity of your classroom—if what you see, hear, and feel is mostly positive—it is often useful to focus on the metaphor(s) you may use in less satisfying situations. These may include unusual disciplinary problems or pressure from others to teach in ways that are inconsistent with your beliefs.

People sometimes unconsciously shift metaphors when they feel threatened. A person who generally uses a metaphor that embodies a sense of confidence or effectiveness may suddenly switch to a passive or aggressive stance. This new metaphor produces different nonverbal signals, so people with whom that person is interacting shift their own stances in response. Those shifts may actually make the problem worse.

Digging Deeper

There is no simple way to analyze your own personal metaphors. Only you fully understand the meanings and implications built into a "throwaway" comment about *nurturing* students or *weaving* a lesson. I can only suggest that the more you think about the entailments of the metaphor, the more productive will be your efforts. Do these exercises alone or with others, remembering that the purpose here is not to lay blame or find fault. It is merely to learn more about yourself.

1. Follow your verbal metaphor into the realms of visual, auditory, and kinesthetic experience. As a requirement of your metaphor, what do you focus on visually? What do you *see* as you look around your classroom? What are you constrained from seeing? A *police officer* "looks for trouble" and "barely notices" people who are doing positive things. A *beekeeper* "looks for signs of productive activity" and expects the bees to be active.

What kinds of things do you *hear*? Teachers who adopt a *conduit/transmission* metaphor generally expect silence so there is no interference with the ideas you are trying to *get across*. This may cause the teacher to negatively interpret any "noise" in the classroom. A *learning community* metaphor, on the other hand, attunes you to thoughts, comments, reactions, and ideas of others.

How do you *feel* during the various parts of your teaching day? Is there a warm feeling that comes with a student's success? Do you get butterflies in your stomach when confronting a troublesome student or presenting an unfamiliar topic? How does your metaphor determine or influence those feelings?

2. Compare the metaphor you've identified with your actual behavior. In one study, a prospective teacher described himself as a *husbandman*. He gave an eloquent description of the role he expected to play:

> "As husbandman to a group of growing human beings, I see my role as teacher being most importantly one of providing the very best climate in the classroom for the maximum growth and development of each student…. My experience as teacher will be one of ongoing discovery…that will help me understand not only who needs more or less light, more or less water, or who needs to have the weeds pulled up from around them, but also what methods for administering this care will

contribute the most to healthy growth.... As husbandman I
will cultivate an appreciation of the intrinsic dignity and beauty
of the living beings I will be entrusted to care for."[12]

Later in his student teaching, this teacher was required to videotape
himself in action. He was deeply disturbed to discover "the teacher he
heard talking to the students...was not the nurturing and responsive
teacher he imagined himself to be.... [Instead,] the classes were
dominated by monologue; he was imposing his will on the students."[13]

Because he continued to believe in the validity of the *husbandman*
metaphor, this teacher was determined to discover why his actions did
not reflect his beliefs. He found that he was so strongly influenced by
the dominant metaphors of the American culture—productivity and
efficiency—that he automatically chose what that culture believes is the
most productive and efficient method of teaching—the *conduit*
metaphor. This teacher's experience demonstrates that a belief in what
should be done does not necessarily agree with deeper, but hidden, beliefs
that drive how it actually is done. This is a fascinating example of the
power of the traditional metaphors that hold teachers in their grasp.

Assuming your metaphor contains all of the highest ideals you
believe you hold, what evidence do you have that you actually live that
metaphor? Videotaping your own classes can be extremely revealing.
Does the teacher you see on tape match your self-image? It might also
be revealing to ask your students to describe your teaching as a
metaphor. How close is it to the way you perceive yourself?

3. A simple test of the focus of your metaphor is noticing how often
you use the words *I, my, them, their, us,* and *our.* Do your pronouns tend
to focus on you, your students, or a combination of the two? Do they
represent a split in your perception—a *me* versus *them* mentality, or a
sense of cooperation and co-participation?

4. If you could eliminate one aspect of teaching—one duty or
responsibility, one educational role—what would it be? What do you
really dread? What metaphor do you use to characterize that role?

Shifting this metaphor can create a rapid and pervasive change in
both your own perceptions and those of others. A different metaphor
cannot help but change your non-verbal behaviors, causing others to
respond to you in remarkably different ways.

Evaluating Your Metaphors

Once you've picked apart your metaphors and their entailments, it's time to decide if the metaphor is serving you as effectively as you'd like. Imagine what your ideal classroom might be like. Pay particular attention to what the students are doing. What *roles* come to mind? Don't hesitate to say to yourself, *"The students are like...."* That will automatically send your mind in search of a metaphor. In many cases, your internal dialogue about the scene suggests a metaphor: "They're busy as bees."

Once you identify a metaphor, what is your role? For example, if your students are bees:

- Are you the *queen (or king)*? Does that mean the other bees are there to serve you? This is an unlikely scenario for an ideal classroom, but there are other interpretations for being the "queen bee."

- Perhaps you *tend the garden* in which the beehive sits. In that case, your role is to provide a variety of food sources.

- Are you the *beekeeper*? If so, what are your duties?

- Perhaps you are simply an *older and wiser bee* who leads the swarm to the choicest flowers.

How does the metaphor of your ideal classroom compare to the metaphor(s) you are now using? Would the "ideal" metaphor serve your needs more effectively? What is it about your present metaphor that limits you from behaving in ways that you admire in other teachers? Perhaps you like the way a certain teacher interacts in a friendly or collegial way with his students, but your metaphor demands that you retain control and authority. Can you think of an effective authority figure who retains control while being friendly and collegial? People sometimes assume that one quality precludes the other. It doesn't! A simple change of authority figures may be all that's needed to remove limits on your behavior.

Trying on alternative metaphors need not be threatening. In fact, it can be liberating. It's like trying on a new piece of clothing. If you like it and it fits, you buy it. If not, you return it to the rack and keep looking. There's no need to give up that comfortable old pair of jeans, but you may enjoy occasionally dressing up (or down). Isn't it interesting to notice how people respond to you differently depending on your attire?

Getting What You Want

Think about what you want your metaphor to accomplish. On what aspects of teaching/learning do you *want* to focus? How do you *want* to behave? How do you *want* your students to behave? What will you see, hear, or feel that lets you know learning is taking place? Here's an example of the answers a teacher might give:

- I want a balanced focus on learning and teaching.

- I want to be able to behave flexibly rather than having the same rules for everyone.

- I want students to assume more responsibility for their own behavior.

- I want to see and hear students actively involved in their own learning.

This is a beginning, but the statements are too general. They resemble the high-sounding statements that appear in educational journals but rarely translate to actual classroom experience. It's helpful to ask, "How, *specifically*, will I know that this is occurring?"

What, *specifically*, will you see, hear, or feel if students are "taking responsibility for their own behavior"? What will the classroom look and sound like if students are "actively involved in learning"? How, *specifically*, will you know that you have achieved a "balance between learning and teaching" or that you are "behaving flexibly"?

If the metaphor you presently use does not help you achieve these goals, look around at other contexts in life. In what role, what profession, what field of endeavor is there a "balanced focus" on participants who have different responsibilities?

In basketball, for example, the players must do their part, but good coaching can improve their play. In construction, plumbers, electricians, and carpenters must each perform their tasks well, but the general contractor schedules them appropriately and oversees their work. The *meaning* you assign to teaching will, of course, influence the metaphors you select. They will depend heavily on whether you lean more toward an *organizational* model with hierarchical structure or a *community* model with a more democratic approach—or something entirely different!

After comparing potential new metaphors with your goals, notice which one "feels" more appropriate. With a good metaphor, people often get an "aha." The mind runs with it, ticking off multiple insights the person hadn't previously noticed—different perceptions that shed new light on teaching and learning.

Acquiring a New Metaphor

Once you've identified a new metaphor that shows promise, making the switch is often simply a matter of saying, "Okay. Now I want to pay attention to ways in which my classroom is a *community* rather than an *organization*—how I can be more like a *mentor* rather than a *general.*" It's a bit like breaking an old habit and acquiring a new one. Write down a few words associated with your new metaphor. Start introducing them into your language. Rerun the tape of your day, noticing events/interactions that were successful. What role did you play in producing that success? Were you *nurturing*? Did you *weave a particularly beautiful pattern* of knowledge? Did you *motivate your team* to success?

Then identify events/interactions in which you could have been more effective. How did these events relate to your metaphor? Did you inadvertently shift to another metaphor? Does your new metaphor fail to include a mechanism to deal with such a circumstance?

The new metaphor may feel something like a new pair of shoes. They feel a bit unfamiliar until you get used to them, but unfamiliar is different from uncomfortable. You may also find that your new metaphor suddenly clashes with something in the old metaphors. That's great! It gives you the opportunity to explore even more beliefs of which you've been unaware. The conflict brings those beliefs into your awareness so that you can examine them and decide if they serve you.

Don't forget that you are human. It's okay to have a bad day when some internal state totally unrelated to teaching overrides your altruistic metaphors. It's also common for some personal value to take the forefront. The built-in human mechanisms of downshifting into survival mode for self-protection are there for good reason.

Often, it takes only a few days of success with a new metaphor to make it "stick." Develop a sense of curiosity about your own metaphors and that of others. If you consciously attend to metaphoric language, your unconscious mind will pick up on the fact that you want to focus on that and take over the job.

When Metaphors Collide

The more you become aware of and play with metaphors, the more insights you'll get into the complex phenomenon that is education. Other insights can arise from noticing the subtle metaphors that permeate your school and how they support or contradict your own.

Principals characterize their roles in a variety of ways:

- *Moral* leaders often see themselves as *pastors* or *missionaries*. Their task is to spread the "truth" to the congregation—the pagans. *Commandments* of good behavior are posted on the school walls. The curriculum guide becomes *holy scripture*. One problem with moral leadership is the assumption that all teachers and students share the same *religion*—values.

- Leaders who perceive themselves as *servants* work for the teachers and students in whatever capacity they require. The strength of this form of leadership is that it empowers others. The "dark side" is that the leader isn't really leading. She's allowing teachers and students to make decisions about what does or doesn't get done. They may not agree or may not be aware of what is possible, so nothing gets done.

- The *stewardship* metaphor puts leadership in the role of conferring values on various aspects of the school environment. As *steward of the earth*, man has assumed the power to decide what "lives or dies" and what resources are or are not used. Assigning values to different programs and the allocation of resources to those programs puts that same power in a principal employing the stewardship metaphor.

- A *transformational* leader shares his or her vision and leads, at times, by charisma or sheer will. This leader stays somewhat apart from the group as the "holder of the vision". The "dark side" is that this puts teachers and students in the role of carrying out the vision. Some are simply not interested. In this case, the vision often disappears if the leader is replaced.[14]

What metaphors are apparent in your supervisor, other teachers, the school board, or the community? Viewing disagreements from the perspective of metaphors can increase your understanding of why you feel fulfilled or frustrated in your job.

Tapping Into the Metaphors of Others

Once you get accustomed to identifying metaphors in everyday language, you may begin picking up on metaphors used by your students. The ability to step into a student's metaphor—to use language from that metaphor when working with that student—is a powerful tool. It provides access to the student's unconscious mind and gives the student the sense that you understand him or her. If, for example, the student constantly uses *sports* metaphors, you'll get a lot further saying "You need to be more of a *team player*" than you will with "You need to *get in tune* with your group."

Think about the way people describe adversarial encounters with another person. "We didn't *see things in the same light.*" "I didn't *like the sound of his ideas.*" "He was *playing by a different set of rules.*" Each of these expressions suggests the parties were conceptualizing the issue, not only in different metaphors, but in different sensory systems! The first is visual, the second, auditory, and the third, kinesthetic!

An analysis of metaphors can provide fascinating insights into parenting, marital or partner relationships, working relationships, and many other facets of life. What metaphor might you use to describe your relationship with your spouse, children, or friends? What role do you play in the story of your life?

The wider the range of metaphors you use, the more insights you will gain. Educators owe it to students whose lives they influence to investigate these powerful tools that, up to now, have been unconscious.

---

1 Bullough, R. V., Jr., with Stokes, D. K. (1994). Analyzing Personal Teaching Metaphors in Preservice Teacher Education as a Means for Encouraging Professional Development. *American Educational Research Journal*, Vol. 31, No. 1, 201.

2 Inbar, D. E. (1996). The Free Educational Prison: Metaphor and Images. *Educational Research*, Vol. 38, No. 1, 77–92.

3 Bullough, R. V. Jr., 201

4 Marshall, H. H. (1988). Metaphor As An Instructional Tool in Encouraging Student Teacher Reflection. *Theory Into Practice*, Vol. 29, No. 2, 128–132.

5 Ibid., 129.

6 For a valuable view of school as community—a community of truth—see Palmer, Parker J. (1999) *The Courage to Teach.* San Francisco: Jossey-Bass.

7 Ibid., 148.

8 Ibid., 74–75.

9 Ibid., 149.

10 Ormell, C. (1996). The Eight Metaphors of Education. *Educational Research*, Vol. 38, No. 1, 67-75.

11 If you resist the idea that teacher as authority figure is a metaphor, consider that this role is so much a part of the school as organization metaphor it goes unquestioned. Authority figures arise from the context of that metaphor. While authority may temporarily be given to individuals within a community, the role of authority figure is not part of a community's internal structure as it is in an organization.

12 Bullough, R. V, Jr. (1991). Exploring Personal Teaching Metaphors in Preservice Teacher Education. *Journal of Teacher Education*, Vol. 42, No. 1, 43–51.

13 Ibid., 47.

14 Aviolo, B. J. (1994) The Alliance of Total Quality and the Full Range of Leadership. In B. M. Bass & B. J. Aviolo (Eds.). *Improving Organizational Effectiveness Through Transformational Leadership* (121-145). Thousand Oaks, CA: Sage.

Chapter 6 ~ Beliefs—Lenses of Perception

"It is hard to let old beliefs go. They are familiar. We are comfortable with them and have spent years building systems and developing habits that depend on them. Like a man who has worn eyeglasses so long that he forgets he has them on, we forget that the world looks to us the way it does because we have become used to seeing it that way through a particular set of lenses. Today, however, we need new lenses. And we need to throw the old ones away."
~Kenichi Ohmae

For many years, educators have run from one theoretical optometrist to another, seeking the lenses that will ultimately give them the clearest vision of teaching and learning. As each new prescription fails to meet that expectation, it is tossed out, despite the fact that each of those lenses may work beautifully *in some contexts.*

Try this simple experiment. Think of an unpleasant situation you've experienced with a student. Spend a moment playing through that situation in your mind. Notice the dialogue that went on during the situation, as well as how you describe the situation in your thoughts— your internal dialogue. What do you see and hear? What feelings or emotions do you experience in the situation?

Now, mentally step out of yourself and into the body of the student, physically "stepping across" into the student. *Take on as much of the actual posture of the student as possible.* Once you feel you have fully engaged the student's point of view, replay the situation. See, hear, and feel the situation once again—this time from the student's perspective.

Step out of the student and into a third position—a neutral observer who watches the interaction between you and the student. What insights does this neutral observer have that neither you nor the student had?

Just as in the movie *Rashomon*, the *story* changes as the perspectives change. The *meanings* of the actions change. Harvard psychology professor Ellen Langer suggests that a mark of intelligence is the ability to generate options rather than an immediate leap to quick answers.[1] One way to do this is to withhold interpretation of a situation until you've examined it from several different perspectives. What are some alternative beliefs that teachers might hold? How might each belief influence teacher behavior?

In the following chapters, we'll be exploring a variety of alternate beliefs—many of which may seem like heresy in the light of conventional wisdom. If it appears that I'm criticizing one of the "sacred cows" of education, remember that I'm merely suggesting another way to graze the educational pasture—offering another perspective. I'm not arguing that the "cow" should be ground into hamburger! I promised earlier I'm not going to tell you what to believe. That doesn't mean I'm not going to try to shake up what you presently believe!

Beliefs and Behavior

"At some point early in our lives, we decide just how conscious we wish to be. We establish a threshold of awareness. We choose how stark a truth we are willing to admit into consciousness, how readily we will examine contradictions in our lives and beliefs, how deeply we wish to penetrate. Our brains can censor what we see and hear; we can filter reality to suit our level of courage. At every crossroads we make the choice again for greater or lesser awareness." ~ Marilyn Ferguson[2]

The quotation reminds us that teachers must possess a certain level of courage to question directives from on high. They must possess strong convictions to teach in ways that run counter to traditional wisdom. Teachers must balance courage against their individual "survival instincts." Thus, it is a very personal choice. It is for you to decide how much risk is appropriate for you, but remember that the development of your students is a factor that can't be ignored.

Research indicates that teachers "…generate belief systems because they need to explain their efforts in ways that give them a sense of accomplishment…. These belief systems may help educators feel more successful, but may also prevent them from imagining what could be."[3]

Parts of Beliefs

Beliefs can be described as having three parts or components—cognitive, affective, and behavioral. Here is one possible scenario surrounding a belief.

1. A teacher says with conviction that *It's important for students to get good grades.* That teacher can typically provide several *cognitive* arguments in support of the belief, such as the heavy emphasis that college admission policies place on grades.

2. When a student's grades drop, the teacher *feels* an urgency to do something about it. Notice the difference between this feeling and the more intellectual exercise of explaining to the student why it's important to work harder. Triggers for this *affective* component come from the goal, need, or value the belief supports. One teacher might interpret the lower grades in terms of self—he isn't doing his job. Another teacher might worry about the student. Either motivation triggers an emotional or affective response.

3. What does it *mean* when a student gets poor grades? What *reasons* might you assign to that behavior on the part of the student? A teacher's response—*behavior*—will depend on the answers to those questions. The table shows some of the possible meanings a teacher might assign to poor grades and how the teacher might respond to those meanings.

Meaning (reasons)	Teacher behavior
The student is lazy	Attempt to motivate the student
The student is troubled about something	Ask the student if he needs help
The student is incapable of getting better grades	Do nothing
The student is overly tired from work outside of school	Discuss situation with parents and student
I didn't do a good job of teaching (threat to self-concept)	Reduce threat to self, often by blaming student
I didn't do a good job of teaching (concern for student)	Find a different way to present material to that student

While the last two *meanings* are the same, they generate different *behaviors* depending on whether the teacher is focused on self or student. Notice that *meanings* and *reasons* are also beliefs. The original belief that *it's important for students to get good grades* is generic—a generalization apart from any particular student. A belief about why a *particular student* gets poor grades is colored by one's beliefs about that particular student. Notice how important the expectations of the teacher are in terms of the choice of behavior. Those expectations are very different from any externally imposed standards.

Where Do Beliefs Come From?

Experience early in a person's life has a tremendous influence on the development of that person's beliefs. At that time, people are building their mental map of the world. Once a feature is in place on that map, it's difficult to admit it doesn't exist.

Some beliefs originate in the preverbal world of the infant. Studies have shown that babies recognize different emotions in the facial expressions of adults and alter their behavior accordingly. If a strange dog approaches a baby, the mother's facial expression may project fear. The child's brain makes a connection, associating the dog with the emotion of fear. Later, when the child becomes verbal and is asked why he is afraid of dogs, he "explains" this belief in words that make sense in his inner reality—dogs are *scary* or *mean looking*. He honestly doesn't know why he believes that, but his future encounters with dogs will likely give him more evidence it is true. He *expects* it to be true and notices information supporting that expectation, ignoring evidence to the contrary. So much for the logical basis of beliefs.

It's less important *why* we have certain beliefs than *how* those beliefs affect us. Beliefs often form as the result of experiences that are not only limited but fail to represent the most common examples of a given situation. This is particularly true if there is a strong emotion associated with the experience, such as being betrayed by a friend or being injured in an accident. Subsequently, the belief acts as a lens, allowing in only supporting evidence.

If you want proof of how a belief influences you, try this. The next time you're in a group of people, look around with the conscious thought, "Everyone is out to get me." For a few moments, "take on" that belief just to see what happens. Notice how the belief influences not only what you perceive but also the way you interpret the facial expressions or actions of other people. Take note of your own posture and the tension of your facial muscles.

Now, change the belief to, "Everyone wants to help me succeed." Once again, notice what expressions and actions you perceive and how you interpret those perceptions. How is your facial expression and body posture different while holding this belief?

Many people notice a significant difference in their experience when they "take on" these two beliefs. Here are a couple of reasons why.

1. First, beliefs focus perception itself. The senses gather all of the information that's out there, but people pay attention to a very small portion of that information. With the "everyone is out to get me" belief, you may have been aware of more frowns or of body language that you might interpret as hostile. With the "everyone wants to help me..." belief, smiles and "friendly" body language pop into focus.

2. Second, beliefs influence the *meanings* that you give those perceptions—your interpretations or secondary beliefs. You will interpret *the same* facial expression as hostile with the more negative belief and friendly or neutral with the positive belief.

3. Third, because beliefs can change your own nonverbal communication (facial expression, voice tone, or body language), people respond differently to you. If you frown and look at someone suspiciously, a person is less likely to smile in response.

You may wish to "play with your beliefs" in your classroom. Look around with the belief that *students are naturally disruptive*, and then with the belief that *students are full of energy that can be directed to a worthwhile task*.

The important thing to remember is *you are already doing this all the time*. At the unconscious level, you host beliefs that determine *what* you perceive and *how* you interpret those perceptions. The items with which you strongly agreed or disagreed in part A of the Self-Inventory are just a few of the beliefs that filter your personal perceptions.

To this extent, each person lives in a world of his or her own making. Through their beliefs, people choose the feedback—the things they notice—about their world. Few people, unfortunately, are consciously aware of those beliefs. The good news is that if you're not happy with the feedback you're getting from the world, you can figure out what belief is forcing you to perceive and interpret the world in that way and change it!

Perhaps you're thinking, "You can't just go around changing the way things are." That's the whole point! The way things "are" is the way you interpret them to be because of your beliefs. Cynthia, who believes students can't be trusted, sees a student smile at her and thinks, "He must be trying to hide something." George, who believes students are trustworthy, sees *the same smile* and thinks, "That student is so friendly." Which world would you rather live in?

It is through beliefs that people create and maintain their inner map of the world. A person's behaviors are based on what is present in the map. You're not likely to allow students much freedom of choice if you believe that they are naturally undisciplined. You're not likely to encourage in-depth exploration of ideas if you believe that everything in the curriculum must be "covered" before the test.

When Charlie says, "That's impossible," he is actually saying the behavior is simply not available in his map. It may be because the behavior doesn't match Charlie's values, because he doesn't *believe* the behavior is possible, or he doesn't *believe* himself capable of performing the action. The behavior is outside of Charlie's repertoire of behaviors.

Regrettably, educational research has contributed to some of the most disempowering and destructive beliefs. For example, many teachers have little realistic hope that they can effectively teach some students because researchers consistently provide data that correlates achievement with poverty and race. Rather than seeing this as motivation to seek out and find more effective methods for these students, teachers see the research conclusions as proof that there is little, if anything, they can do.

Fortunately, some refuse to be convinced...and the results of their work demonstrates that research only shows "what is," not what has to be. For example, several years ago, George Hall Elementary school was one of the worst performing schools in Mobile, Alabama. With a student population almost entirely low-income and black, and located in an area notorious for high crime rates, the school also suffered from huge disciplinary problems. You might be thinking, "Well, that's no surprise...what would you expect."

New principal Agnes "Terri" Tomlinson answered that question. "I knew achievement wouldn't be a problem." For her and the team of teachers who shared her vision, it wasn't. By now, you may recognize that when Principal Tomlinson said, "I knew..." she was really saying "I believe..." The force of her belief was such that, within a few years, students' achievement rose to a level at or above what research predicts for white, middle-class students. The teachers accomplished this by 1.) beginning with the belief that all students can learn; 2.) assessing what students already know and are able to do, regardless of grade level "expectations"; and 3.) recognizing that, because these students were lacking in the experiences, vocabulary, and background knowledge that we take for granted in so-called "middle class" students, they had to start at the beginning when teaching any concept.[4]

This is the power of belief. The belief that all students can learn allowed these teachers, and others who truly share the belief, to re-examine what they have been doing. If, indeed, all students can learn, why aren't they doing so? It shifts the focus from "In what ways are these students unteachable," to "How can we teach these students?"

Once you recognize some of the fundamental beliefs that shape your map, you can play with those and other beliefs to see how the map changes and what other behaviors become possible. Similar to switching metaphors, it's a bit like acting—taking on a different persona for a period of time. Do people respond to your new persona differently from the way they responded to the old one? What do you notice that you didn't notice before? What can you ignore that you might have obsessed about with another belief? Unlike acting, if you like the "feel" and the feedback you get from a role, you can choose to make it part of your personality—or not.

> "Until you've tried it, you have no idea how pervasive a change can be wrought by merely changing a belief—changing what you expect to happen—changing what you look for. The world we see that seems so insane is the result of a belief system that is not working. To perceive the world differently, we must be willing to change our belief system, let the past slip away, expand our sense of now, and dissolve the fear in our minds." ~Gerald G. Jampolsky

The Robustness of Beliefs

"For those who believe, no proof is necessary.
For those who don't believe, no proof is possible."[5]

Don't confuse me with the facts—my mind is made up! Once a belief has formed, it is often highly resistant to any evidence to the contrary. If you don't believe this, try visiting the website of the Flat Earth Society.[6] The Society's website includes numerous "scientific proofs" of its claim. Those "proofs" demonstrate the lengths to which people will go to maintain their reality.

One "scientific proofs" copied verbatim from the site:

> "Picture in your mind a round world. Now imagine that
> there are two people on this world, one at each pole. For the
> person at the top of the world, (the North Pole), gravity is
> pulling him down, towards the South Pole. But for the person
> at the South Pole, shouldn't gravity pull him down as well?
> What keeps our person at the South Pole from falling
> completely off the face of the 'globe'"?

The writer's belief is so strong that it ignores the scientific explanation of gravity as an attraction between objects with mass. Many educators are as rigid in their beliefs about knowledge and the role of the teacher in "imparting" that knowledge as are the Flat Earth people. What is "irrefutable evidence" to the people who conduct educational studies is irrelevant to educators holding tightly to traditional beliefs.

One of the factors that make teacher beliefs so resistant to change is the many years teachers spent as students in traditional classrooms. Because they don't enter the profession with a "beginner's mind," as might a lawyer, engineer, or doctor, it isn't easy for them to conceive of the classroom in a way that contradicts their earlier experience.

Thought Viruses

"What you hear repeatedly you will eventually
believe." ~Mike Murdock

The statements in section A of the Self-Inventory are beliefs. Said with conviction, they take on the authority of the speaker. The mind accepts them as truth—the "correct" map of the world. Such statements are what theorist Robert Dilts calls "thought viruses."[7] A *thought virus* is a limiting belief—a generalization or a distortion once drawn from experience, but now separated from its context. The danger in thought viruses is that, because they contain *some* truth, because they are *partly true in some context*s, people are less likely to question their validity.

Statements such as *students are motivated by grades* and *students must learn the basics before they can tackle more complex problems* sound like fact. However, they are not always true. In fact, almost everyone can recall situations where the opposite is true. These are not exceptions to a fact. They are clues that the statement is a belief rather than a fact.

Simple factual statements that are part of consensus reality are often context-free. Statements such as *snow is white, the formula for water is H_2O,* and *Seattle is north of Los Angeles* are true in most of the contexts people encounter in daily life. However, the more complex a statement gets and the less defined are the terms used in the statement, the less likely the statement is to get general agreement. In order to reach agreement, people must specify the context and negotiate the definitions of the terms to be sure everyone means the same thing. Unfortunately, when people can think of a couple of instances where a statement is true, they frequently accept it as truth without further negotiation. *Thought viruses are often true in some contexts but not in others.*

Let's examine a couple of examples from the list of statements in the Self-Inventory. It doesn't matter whether you agreed or disagreed with each of these statements. The important thing is to identify on what *basis* you agreed or disagreed.

1. Students must learn the basics before they can tackle more complex problems. Have you ever learned something where you began with the basics and then worked your way up to more complex concepts? Have you ever learned something where you jumped in at a fairly complex level and eventually worked your way down to the basics?

Most people answer "yes" to both questions, so the original statement is only *partly* true. Better stated, it is true in some contexts but not in others. As such, *it is inappropriate to use the statement as a fixed truth or rule for the purposes of making decisions about how to organize academic content.*

2. It's important to keep students from failing at a given task. This statement presupposes that failure is not a good thing—that "failure" serves no useful purpose and may, in fact, negatively influence a person's self-esteem. Are there occasions where this is true? Certainly. Are there instances where failing at a task results in learning, in greater motivation, or in other positive responses? Once again, the answer is "yes." Michael Jordan "failed" at his first attempt to make his high school basketball team, yet self-esteem doesn't appear to be a problem for him. The original statement *sounds* like a statement of fact—of wisdom—of truth, yet once again it is true *in only some contexts*. It is a thought virus.

Decisions based on context-free generalizations rather than on what is actually happening in a specific context are poorly informed. For example, habitually shushing students based on the thought virus that *a quiet classroom is conducive to learning* may inhibit learning as often as it supports it.

If, in making your selections on the Self-Inventory, you were frequently aware that different contexts would change the truth of the statement, you're well on the way to recognizing the inherent danger in such limiting beliefs. If you strongly agreed or strongly disagreed with any of the statements in the inventory, ask yourself, "Is there any situation in which this *is* or *is not* true?"

Teachers use a set of basic assumptions about learning, knowledge, teaching, and the nature of students on which to base their decisions. Mindful teaching requires identifying whether those assumptions are actually thought viruses. The important thing is whether the assumption is true in the *present* context. It's undoubtedly easier to apply the same rules to every person and every situation than to have to constantly evaluate a situation and decide on the appropriate action. The cost of that "ease" is mindlessness. To the argument that there isn't time to evaluate each situation, I concur with Norman Cousins: "It is nonsense to say that there is not enough time to be fully informed.... Time given to thought is the greatest timesaver of all."[8]

Transforming Thought Viruses

If the statement *a quiet classroom is conducive to learning* is true in all contexts, the teacher doesn't have to think or make decisions. The statement juxtaposes quiet and learning. A teacher who values learning must, therefore, automatically value quiet. The instinctive response is to reprimand anyone who is talking.

What happens when the teacher acknowledges that the belief is only *partly true*—that it is context-dependent? What happens when the teacher transforms the sentence to reflect that partial truth? The sound level in a classroom *may* influence learning. Introducing the word *may* opens the door to a number of possibilities.

First, it requires further assessment of the situation. It encourages a teacher to ask, "Are there any valid reasons why students might be talking? Are those reasons related to learning?" Rather than a knee-jerk reprimand, a behavior that holds little opportunity for teaching, the teacher makes a mindful attempt to find out whether student behavior is contributing to learning.

"But you have to have rules," you may say. "Students can't be allowed to do what they want just because they think they have a good reason." How can students learn to decide on the appropriateness of an action if they are never given the opportunity to make choices for themselves? Yes, teachers can apply a rigid set of rules to everyone based on the beliefs that *people need to learn self-control* and that *a well-disciplined classroom is a productive one*. What happens when those students are on their own—when they are not bound by the teacher's set of rules? How will they know which behaviors are appropriate and which are not if they've never been given the opportunity to experience the natural outcomes of their own decisions? On what basis will they practice *self*-control if all of their control has been from outside?

If a teacher takes the time to assess the effects of student behavior on learning and the reason for talking is *not* valid, the teacher still has the option of reprimanding the student. If this is a pattern of behavior for that student, the teacher can also choose to break the cycle of misbehavior and reprimand. Remember "if you always do what you've always done, you'll always get what you've always gotten!" You bring about change in others by first changing yourself.

The willingness of a teacher to respond flexibly is, of course, based on the belief that *students are more important than information*. Does it take time? Yes. Is it time well spent? That depends on the benefits to both the student and teacher. It depends on the relative value the teacher places on a fixed set of rules or the importance of silence. It depends on the context at that moment in time. Are there times when an immediate reprimand will still be the best choice? Of course, but at least the teacher will have explored the available options.

Here are a couple of other examples from the items in section A of the Self-Inventory.

1. *Students are motivated by grades and/or other external rewards.* Whether you agree or disagree, you could broaden your choices by changing the statement to students are *sometimes* motivated by grades and/or other external rewards. Are you always motivated by external rewards? Are there times when you are motivated by interest or simply by a sense of accomplishment? Adding the word *sometimes* offers a more open-ended statement that encourages the teacher to decide what type of motivation might best be used on a case-by-case basis. Yes, that requires knowing enough about an individual student to decide what is likely to motivate him or her. Keep in mind that there is no one correct motivational tool for every student in every circumstance.

2. *Students who do poorly in school just need to try harder.* This is a complex belief that makes a number of assumptions and fails to define terms.

- One assumption is that the student is not trying as hard as he can. What, specifically, does it mean to *try*?

- What does *poorly* mean? Poor grades? Other than lack of effort, are there other reasons why a student might be getting poor grades?

- The word *just* in the original statement makes it deadly. It implies there is only one reason for the student doing poorly. If the student "fixes" that reason, he will automatically succeed. A comforting belief, but hardly accurate. Have you ever put forth a lot of effort and still not achieved your goal? Have you ever achieved a goal with very little effort? Try changing the word *just* to *may*.

Accepting generalizations that are true in only some contexts limits a teacher's choices of behavior. One of the reasons for including so many of them in the Self-Inventory is to remind you of how many beliefs take this limited view. The question you must answer for yourself is, "Do you value having more choices in what you are presently doing?"

Schools are rich incubators of thought viruses. You've taken the first step in inoculating yourself against them by becoming aware of their existence. Boost your immunity by questioning the generalizations of conventional wisdom. Remember that generalizations are often thought viruses. At the very least, ask, "Is this true in all contexts?" If it isn't, shift your perspective so that you can perceive the alternatives.

Presuppositions

"Getting rid of a delusion makes us wiser than getting hold of a truth." ~ Ludwig Borne

Recall that thought viruses are generalizations that were originally connected to some experience but are now isolated statements that *sound* like truths or facts. Because they aren't associated with any particular context, it is difficult to update or correct them by supplying new data.[9]

The statement *students must learn the basics before they can learn more complex concepts* is a thought virus. Originally, the statement may have been made in reference to some context such as recognizing letters of the alphabet before one could learn words, or recognizing numbers before one could add them together. To this extent, there is truth in the statement. But the generalization does not provide a context. It implies it is *always* true in *all* contexts. Once this statement takes up residence as a thought virus, teachers rarely take the time to decide how to present a concept—they always start with the basics and "work up" to more complex concepts.

Even more insidious is that many of these thought viruses contain hidden presuppositions not stated in the belief itself. The word *presuppose* comes from Latin words meaning "to put under." *Presuppositions* are unconscious assumptions that are must be true for a statement to make sense—the unexamined foundation "under" the belief statement.

Let's say I make the simple statement *John is a good father*. Some of the presuppositions underlying this statement include:

- There is a person named John.

- The person named John is male.

- The person named John has an offspring.

- The person named John engages in some behavior with regard to that offspring.

- I have observed that behavior.

- I am able to judge that behavior against some external standard of "good" or "bad."

If all of those statements are true, then the listener can accept the original statement as true. In reality, when such a statement is made, the listener unconsciously accepts all of those statements as true. In this way, our language communicates much more than the words themselves. This natural mental process makes conversation much simpler and produces a high degree of cognitive economy.

Unexamined presuppositions can lead to errors in judgment. Clearly, it would be inefficient to examine the presuppositions of every statement. The key is to be selective—to look for the presuppositions of those statements with the greatest potential to affect our behavior. Here's one case where it might be useful.

Presuppositions of "Back to Basics"

It's not uncommon in education to hear the cry "back to basics." This isn't even a full statement but a "catch phrase" that educators interpret to mean something like "teachers should go back to teaching the basics the way they used to be taught." Consider just a few of the presuppositions hidden within that statement.

- There are certain forms of knowledge that can be identified as "basic"—that is, as fundamental to any further learning.

- These "basic" forms of knowledge are, in some ways, more desirable or valuable than other forms of knowledge.

- Dissemination of these "basic" forms of knowledge is more desirable than what we are doing now.

- Those "basics" have, at an earlier time, been identified.

- Those "basics" have, at an earlier time, been "taught" in an appropriate and effective way.

- The student recipients of the "basics" in earlier times were in some manner "better educated" than today's students.

For "back to basics" to be a valid battle cry, *all* of these statements should be true. Yet each of the statements contains presuppositions of its own that further confuse the meaning of the original call for "back to basics." Many of the words in these presuppositions, such as the word "basic" itself, are so fuzzy and have so many possible interpretations that getting consensus on their truth would be all but impossible.

Let's assume that by "basics" we mean reading, writing, and arithmetic. Does "back to basics" mean returning to the old Dick and

Jane books—or perhaps even further back to when the Bible or other religious text was the primary focus of reading? In writing, do we return to the Palmer method? Is arithmetic new or old math? Does it mean doing one's sums, learning the multiplication tables, kitchen math, consumer math, or construction math? How "basic" are algebra, trigonometry, or computer literacy?

Aside from the letter and number systems that are the foundation of reading, writing, and arithmetic within a culture, on what other "basics" would all educators agree? If there are "basics" that were once taught and that proved innately better than what we are doing today, why did schools ever change?

Is there any evidence that some concepts can be learned without first learning these "basics"? One need only look at the social development of children before they learn their ABCs and 123s to recognize that many complex social skills—including language—are learned through immersion rather than painstakingly building from simple to complex.

If "back to basics" means that learning to read, write, and perform mathematical operations is fundamental to continued learning, it would be difficult to argue with that belief. At issue is how those skills are taught. "Back to basics" implies the way they were taught earlier in the history of education was more effective than what is happening today. Is this true?

"Back to basics" sounds good, but it is extremely simplistic. How many other tenets of conventional educational wisdom are based on such weak presuppositions? Aren't they worth the time to investigate?

The Upside of Presuppositions

People can select desired behaviors by actively choosing the presuppositions—the beliefs—under whose influence they operate. These presuppositions are not necessarily any truer than ones previously held, but they may be more useful. I admit to being pragmatic. If a presupposition serves me—if it gives me the feedback I want from the world and allows me to behave in ways that support my values—I will use it. I don't need proof that it is true in any absolute sense. Indeed, for how many of our beliefs do proofs actually exist? Notice the potential effect of each of these presuppositions on a teacher's behavior.

Presupposition 1—The meaning of any communication is the response it gets. In other words, regardless of what I "think" I said, what is important is how the mind of the listener interprets it. If I consciously accept this presupposition and it is important to me that the person "understands" what I said, then I accept the responsibility to express myself clearly enough that the listener can accurately reproduce what I've said. This doesn't mean the listener must agree with me.

How does this affect behavior? When a person adopts this presupposition, she no longer says, "You didn't understand me." Instead, she says, "I didn't explain myself clearly." Her focus is on how she can improve her own communication—something that is within her power to control. Saying "you didn't understand me" focuses on what's going on in the mind of the student—something a teacher has no way of knowing or controlling. In effect, it blames the listener.

It's common for teachers to unconsciously shift the responsibility for understanding to the student, rather than questioning their own communication skills. This is one of those puzzling inconsistencies in the human mind. We expect a doctor to treat a patient in a way that will bring about improvement in the patient's condition. The responsibility for that treatment is the doctor's. Lawsuits questioning the competency of doctors are fairly common when patients don't improve or become even more ill. Can you imagine a doctor saying, "You didn't understand my treatment, so it's your fault you didn't get better"? Yet, in the context of school, teachers commonly take responsibility (credit) for their teaching when the "patient" does well, but disavow any responsibility when the "patient" fails to improve.

The responsibility for *learning* does belong to the student, but only if that student is free to learn in ways that are appropriate. When teachers impose a treatment in the name of learning and students do not respond to that treatment, they are no more responsible than the patient who does not respond to the doctor's treatment.

Presupposition 2—Failure is feedback. This presupposition encourages a shift of perspective from a negative focus on failing (not succeeding) to a positive focus on learning something from every behavior, regardless of its outcome. (One can also say that *success* is feedback.[10])

Does nine-month-old Taneesha "fail" when she first pulls herself into a standing position and immediately plops back down on the floor? Not with this presupposition. Taneesha may be temporarily upset, but before long she once again tries to stand—this time staying up a bit longer. Each time she fails to remain upright, she learns something about gravity and the position of her body—feedback that she uses in her next attempt.

What would happen if teachers removed the stigma of failure from their classrooms? Unfortunately, this requires much more than simply changing one presupposition. It taps into our cultural obsession with "success." In education, it involves a whole system of beliefs about the nature of learning and the value of "wrong" answers. Why would a student risk offering what may be a wrong answer if the teacher simply ignores it and moves on until some student provides the "right" answer? Useful feedback comes in using the student's "wrong" ideas to facilitate learning. If the only feedback the student receives is a verbal or nonverbal reminder of stupidity, the result will be a student who never volunteers an answer again.

૭~૨

Presuppositions are another form of belief. By actively choosing their presuppositions, people select the perspective demanded by that belief. They choose the point of view they want and thus, the information that

Presuppositions are another form of belief. By actively choosing their presuppositions, people select the perspective demanded by that belief. They choose the point of view they want and thus, the information that becomes available to them. Fundamental presuppositions influence much of what people do in life, not just in teaching. Whether they are objectively "true" or not, presuppositions are useful to the extent they allow people to make positive changes in their lives, to better understand their behavior, to live more in keeping with their values, and to move closer to their goals.

An Unspoken Presupposition that Drives Education

Although it is rarely overtly stated, one of the most pervasive and firmly entrenched presuppositions of traditional education is that *preparing students to get good grades on a test is the purpose of education*. This is particularly true in the age of standards. The statement carries the following presuppositions:

- Learning outside of what the test assesses is of insufficient value to "waste" time on.

- The test is the most important indicator that learning has occurred.
- The concepts on the test have been agreed upon as not only the most important, but the only concepts worthy of teaching.
- The test is an accurate and sufficient assessment of learning.

Are any or all of those statements true in *all* contexts? A critical component of this presupposition is the meaning of the word *learning*. Many studies have shown that the type of "surface" learning that occurs in most classrooms does not result in a student's ability to either *use* information or *transfer* it to other contexts. Even students who achieve the highest grades can produce right answers on tests but fail to understand the meaning of those answers.[11]

If people look at the actual behaviors of many teachers and administrators, rather than listening to their words, it seems apparent *the present purpose of education focuses on information rather than students* and *possession of information is the primary goal.* Why is there so much "surface" learning and so little "depth" learning? Because teachers consciously or unconsciously believe this is the only way to cover the ever-increasing number of concepts on the mandated tests.[12]

Notice the cause-and-effect nature of this issue. The very tests that are supposed to assess the effectiveness of teaching and learning make it impossible for teachers to teach effectively and for students to learn much of lasting value. Even Paul Barton, former president of the Educational Testing Service, suggests "...testing is turning into a means of reform, rather than just a way of finding out whether reforms have been effective."[13]

Education professor Thomas Sergiovanni argues that tests are used by many states to determine which schools are

> "...most successful, regardless of the content of standards and the substance of teaching and learning...What if the standards that are used do not fit all students? What if the standards are the wrong ones? *What if the assessments become the curriculum?* What if students learn a lot about what is tested but little else?"[14] [author's emphasis]

In fact, in the U.S., the assessments *have* become the curriculum in many schools, particularly since the testing frenzy mandated by the *No*

Child Left Behind Education Act. Dozens of educational theorists have pointed out the flaws in this system. Dozens of scientific studies have demonstrated that traditional teaching is, at best, only marginally effective. At worst, it is damaging to students. Yet we see little movement within education as a whole toward anything different. Why? Because change can only occur when the beliefs and metaphors that form the underpinnings of that system are examined and updated.

What goes on in classrooms is unlikely to change until teachers choose to change it. Many of the reforms forced on teachers do not reflect mindful practices or systems thinking. Reformers ignore research about learning in favor of statistics about test scores. Yes, it requires more courage to openly question such practices instead of muttering about them in the teacher's lunchroom, but when it comes to the future of students, what is more important? In the words of Cicero, "If we are not ashamed to think it, we should not be ashamed to say it."

In the time that passive resistance takes to sink ineffective practices, how many students will have lost out on opportunities to develop their unique abilities? Passive resistance will, of course, continue to undermine reforms, but it does little to prevent the next ill-considered reform effort from taking its place. Teachers must insist that reformers confront and spell out the presuppositions of their reforms. They must question the validity of any presuppositions not supported by research or experience. In doing so, teachers can help to stem the flow of mandated reforms that reduce their effectiveness. They can take the first steps to create a more mindful teaching practice and to eliminate the thought viruses that have so weakened educational decision making.

---

1 Langer, E. (1997). *The Power of Mindful Learning*. Reading, MA: Addison-Wesley.
2 Ferguson, M. (1980). *The Aquarian Conspiracy*. Los Angeles: J. P. Tarcher, 112.
3 Fine, M. (1991) Framing Dropouts: Notes on the Politics of an Urban Public High School. Albany, NY: State University of New York Press. Quoted in *The School Culture*, published by Southwest Educational Development Laboratory, URL: http://www.sedl.org/change/school/culture.html
4Chenoweth, Karin. "It can be done, it's being done, and here's how: all schools could learn something from the qualities shared by schools that have been successful in educating poor and minority students to high levels." *Phi Delta Kappan* 91.1 (2009): 38+. *General OneFile*. Web. 19 Aug. 2010.
5 John and Lyn St Clair Thomas, in *Eyes of the Beholder*

6 See URL: http://theflatearthsociety.org/cms/

7 Dilts, R. (1999). *Sleight of Mouth: The Magic of Conversational Belief Change.* Capitola, CA: Meta Publications, 117.

8 Peter, L. J. (1977). *Peter's Quotations: Ideas for Our Time.* New York: Bantam Books, 494.

9 Dilts, R. B. (1999). *Sleight of Mouth...*

10 Success and failure are categories some humans have assigned to certain events. Our culture has deified success and demonized failure. There are cultures in which those categories are meaningless. People simply experience the outcomes of behavior without assigning value. You may find it interesting to reconceptualize outcomes strictly in terms of feedback to one's efforts to progress or grow in knowledge rather than as success or failure.

11 Marchese, T. J. (1998) Quoting Ellen Langer in *The New Conversations About Learning Insights From Neuroscience and Anthropology, Cognitive Science and Work-Place Studies.* Published on the web by New Horizons for Learning, www.newhorizons.org.

12 This issue is compounded by the content of textbooks. Textbook publishers focus on making sure that all standards and benchmarks from major states are "covered" in their books. Because there are so many of these benchmarks and standards, there is little or no room in the books for examples of how content can be applied. Because many teachers assume that textbooks contain the essential information, they believe that they have adequately "covered" the information when students complete the book.

13 Sergiovanni, T. J. (2000, February 16) Changing Educational Change: Substance—Not Process—Is What Matters. *Education Week*, 27.

14 Ibid.

Chapter 7 ~ Beliefs and Habits of Mind

*"It requires a very unusual mind to make
an analysis of the obvious."
~Alfred North Whitehead*

Educators have barely scratched the surface in understanding teaching, learning, and the nature of students. There are so many interactions among so many different factors that *knowing* with certainty what to do in any given circumstance may ultimately be impossible. "If precise sciences such as mathematics cannot know for certain, how can people in social sciences know for certain when working with minds, which are infinitely more complex"?[1] Therefore, teachers are forced to choose from among the available options.

The range of those options increases enormously when teachers examine their underlying beliefs. They are often surprised at what they've taken for granted—how habitual their thinking has become. This chapter examines several habitual thinking processes that limit teacher perception and therefore, those available options. These processes arise from the way the human mind works, but that doesn't mean that we can't interrupt the process and question some of the results.

Beliefs about Cause and Effect

People often agree that A is the cause of B if A takes place immediately before B. Clouds cause rain. Pressing down on the accelerator causes an increase in a car's speed. In truth, the clouds did not directly *cause* the rain nor did pressing the accelerator directly *cause* an increase in speed. In thinking, the mind often simplifies a cause-and-effect sequence by omitting steps and by ignoring other factors that play a causal role in the process. Eventually, people may forget that those other steps—other factors—exist.

Attribution of cause and effect sometimes goes astray. Our early ancestors believed that a heavenly event such as an eclipse caused earthly events such as earthquakes or crop failures. People today call such beliefs *superstition*, yet they make similarly unfounded assumptions

123

themselves. For example, I've heard a teacher say, "He misbehaved to make me look bad." The teacher is assigning a cause-and-effect relationship to two events that may have little or nothing to do with one another. If the teacher feels she looks bad, those feelings may arise from a sense of inadequacy or inability to deal with the student effectively. The student's misbehavior, on the other hand, may arise from peer pressure, a confrontation at home, or many other reasons unrelated to the teacher.

Who's in Control?

When teachers utter a statement such as, "He *made* me mad," "She *gave me no choice*," or "My principal *won't let me*," they are saying that someone else caused (or inhibited) their behavior. At times, that's an unconscious way of transferring responsibility for their action (or lack thereof) to another person—to a student, an administrator, or a parent.

An insidious result of such statements is that they prevent people from acting on the choices they actually have. In effect, they are *transferring control of their lives to someone else*. Personally, I would rather retain the choices for myself. I can choose to get angry—or not. I can choose to do what the other person wants—or not.

Blaming administrators for one's own lack of action is a common practice among teachers. At least one research study showed that, when a principal was questioned about what teachers said he "wouldn't let them do," he responded he would have been happy to support the action if they had only asked him.

You may find it helpful to "watch your language" to determine if you're turning over control of your choices to others—and if you are, why.

Beliefs and Categories

People generally process and represent basic categories, such as *chair, banana, daisy, man,* or *bicycle,* in roughly the same way. When they hear the term, they see an image of the object in their mind's eye. Once we move away from basic categories, the representation of a term in two different minds is seldom the same. What do you "see" when you think of *furniture, fruit, flower, person,* or *vehicle*—categories one step up from the basic categories listed above? People are much less likely to form the same internal pictures in response to those words because there is no generalized image that represents the word. *Furniture* may be anything from a chair to a china cabinet. *Vehicles* can range from rickshaws to the Space Shuttle.[2]

What does this have to do with education? If we take this process up a few more steps—away from concrete objects and into the realm of abstract concepts—the variations in people's realities increase enormously. Words such as *success, learn, teach, respect, study,* or *know* evoke very different internal representations in individuals.

The "mind's-eye view" is much more complex than most people realize. People hold information in their minds as a set of internal sensory representations (ISRs). Depending on the cognitive preferences of the person, not only the content, but also the senses used in the ISR differ. For example, if asked to think about the word *success,* Jack *sees* a picture of a well-dressed man climbing into an expensive car. Rosa *hears* herself addressing the board of her own Fortune 500 company. Jason *feels* the wrench in his hand as he repairs an engine at his auto repair business. Phyllis represents success as cooking an excellent meal for her family—she *smells* and *tastes* the food and *sees* people enjoying the meal.

Most of these ISRs exist outside of conscious perception. They are *sensory metaphors* that represent the *meaning* of the word in our inner realities. What do you "see" in your mind's eye when you think about the word *success?* Do you hear, feel, smell, or taste anything? (In addition to external sounds, some people hear internal dialogue, such as "Wow" or "This is great.") After you've checked your own ISR, ask a couple of friends how they represent *success.*

The Assumption of Agreement

In education, and in many other realms of human endeavor, people assume everyone uses words in the same way. Yet that assumption is accurate only when the words represent the most basic categories. The abstract "buzzwords" in education are far from basic!

Statements of conventional wisdom about education are filled with undefined terms—*effective teaching, student involvement, motivation, assessment of learning*—for that matter, *learning* itself. Just as there is no definition of *education* that is part of consensus reality, educators rarely agree on what, specifically, it means to *learn.* How did you complete the sentence *learning means…*in the Self-Inventory? How does your meaning of *learn* differ from that of other teachers, administrators, students, or parents? Keep in mind that the meaning we give to a word is a belief.

Many statements in the Self-Inventory contain undefined words that teachers interpret in a variety of ways. For example, if you agree with the statement, *I ask questions to assess student understanding,* what, specifically, do you mean by *understanding?* Are you referring to the *possession* of a piece of knowledge or the ability to *use* it? Does a student *understand* if he is able to give you a definition or formula? Or does *understanding* involve a more pervasive change in the way a student thinks about a topic?

Some may say, "Oh, come on. Everyone knows what it means to *understand.* At least, we're all in the same ballpark." Try the same exercise with *understanding* that you did with the word *success.* A person's ISR, their internal sensory metaphor for the meaning of a word, influences the verbal definition they give. Ask several of your fellow teachers, some of whom share your educational views and some who do not, to jot down what it means for a student to *understand.* You do the same. Compare their answers with your own. The results will depend on the teachers chosen, but such definitions are often very enlightening in terms of the fundamental differences that can exist in such a basic educational term.

What difference does it make how a teacher defines the word? A huge difference! If Jerry asks questions to *assess understanding,* his definition of the term *understanding* determines the type and level of question he asks. If Jerry believes *understanding* means *possession of knowledge,* he will ask questions such as, "What is an insect?" or "When did the Civil War begin?" If he believes understanding requires a higher level of thinking, Jerry asks questions such as, "What are the advantages of an insect having six legs?" or "What role did the discovery of gold in California play in the Civil War?"

A person's primary beliefs and values heavily influence the secondary beliefs (meanings) assigned to words. The meaning of the word, in turn, influences the person's behaviors. Teachers are often surprised to discover their behaviors aren't consistent with what they *think* they believe. Trish says she teaches for in-depth learning, yet the questions she asks all begin with the words *define, state,* or *describe*—the lowest level of cognitive processing, according to Bloom's taxonomy. Paul says he believes in using student interest to shape his content, yet everyone in the class covers the same material in the same way. In these cases, other beliefs and values are at work and would benefit from examination.

Foreground/Background Reversal

"Anyone who has begun to think
places some portion of the world in jeopardy."
~John Dewey

The habits of mind present in a teacher's environment also limit teacher perception. These beliefs and metaphors determine which aspects of a situation are in the foreground and which are relegated to the background.

1. Groups/Individuals

When teachers begin to question thought viruses and make decisions based on context rather than on fixed rules, they come to realize the individual student is generally the most important part of that context. The more they know about individual students, the easier and more effective their decisions become. Yet despite the rhetoric, studies, and workshops on individual differences, studies have shown many teachers pay little attention to those differences as they teach.[3]Why?

I once projected images designed to demonstrate how mindset influences perception. One of the most remarkable was a beautiful color photograph of a chef's salad. Julienned slices of ham, chicken, and various cheeses lay, like spokes of a wheel, atop shredded lettuce and other colorful vegetables. Invariably, viewers would stare at the picture for fifteen seconds or more before anyone reacted—with disgust! Alongside the slices of meat, *in plain view*, lay a severed human finger!

People's tendency to categorize—to "name"—is at the heart of this experience. Once they had "named" the chef's salad in their minds, they saw what they *expected* to see—the typical collection of ingredients found in such a salad. Their mindset actually blocked the perception of something that was blatantly obvious once they'd become aware of it.

Individual students are the hidden ingredients in the educational picture. One major cause for this is the overriding emphasis on *groups* throughout the history of American education. Students are perceived as sixth graders, "A" students, "average" students, honor roll students, career track students, LD, ADD, or BD students—*groups*. The language of group-think predominates in education.

With groups so firmly in the foreground, individual students are relegated to the background. When teachers attend to groups, they cannot *at the same time* attend to individuals within the group. The powerful influence this mindset has on the ability to actually *perceive* individuals is particularly apparent in a most unlikely place—the study of individual differences.

Researchers studying individual differences often begin by citing mountains of data demonstrating that some students process information in a linear fashion and others more holistically; some prefer quiet when they study, while others benefit from listening to music. Some students prefer to synthesize information, others are more inclined to analyze.

Teachers learn that students have multiple intelligences—strengths and weaknesses in different modes of processing that should be recognized and respected. Students are tested to determine personality characteristics. With few exceptions, most of these studies, tests, and theories have one thing in common. *In the end, the researchers divide their findings into a fixed number of groups*—sixteen different personality types, four different thinking types, thirty-two different learning styles, eight ways of presenting information to different types of thinkers. Every one of these approaches finds ways to *group* the very students they claim are different. What's wrong with this picture?

Group-think is so pervasive that researchers fail to recognize what they're doing. Rather than use the findings to emphasize the uniqueness of every individual, and the need to focus on differences rather than similarities, they use the data to put students back into groups! In their defense, theorists may be unconsciously preparing for the outcry from teachers. How can teachers possibly create twenty or thirty different lesson plans every day? How can they possibly *cover* all the information in the curriculum guide if they have to teach differently to each student? Teachers locked into their own habitual "style" of learning may not even recognize ways to teach children who learn in very different ways.

Teachers appear no more willing to use four, eight, or sixteen different styles than they are to work with individual students. Why? Because teaching in the *traditional* way, driven by *traditional* beliefs, is incompatible with teaching to individual needs. How can a shift from groups to individuals occur when a teacher believes the following statements to be true?

- The teacher is responsible for every child's learning.

- The teacher must always have the answers to student questions.

- The teacher must control what happens in the classroom.

- All students must be responsible for the same body of knowledge.

As we've seen, traditional education emerges from the conduit metaphor—*transmission* of content from teacher to student. Despite many research findings to the contrary, traditional educators still *believe* that the most time-efficient way to transmit lots of content to lots of students is through "teacher talk" to groups of students. These extremely pervasive beliefs effectively control the behavior of teachers.

As we've seen, shifting the metaphor that describes a teacher's role often acts as a master switch for shifting their beliefs. What if, for example, the teacher's role shifted from *transmitter of content* to *organizer of content* so that students could learn it on their own? Here's one way that role might be played out.

- The teacher designs the overall lesson plan—the scope and general sequence of learning.

- He defines an essential core of content that is required of all students.

- He suggests related subject matter from which students may choose, depending on their interests.

- He sets a time frame, provides materials and resources, and recommends ways for students to learn both the required information and optional material of their choice. Students are, however, free to venture beyond what the teacher has planned, using individually chosen learning methods.

- The teacher creates an assessment tool for the required information. Students demonstrate their knowledge of the optional material by presenting it to the rest of the class in whatever way each student considers appropriate.

Does this mean the teacher never spends time talking to the whole class—engaging in discussions of mutual interest or benefit? Of course not! People who feel threatened by such a major shift in the structure of the classroom often make this and similar extreme accusations. Make the new idea look ridiculous enough and no one will take it seriously!

Benefits of Shifting the Metaphor

Changing the metaphor from *teacher as transmitter* to *teacher as facilitator* or *organizer* is certainly not the only way to shift attention from groups to individuals. However, here are a few of the benefits that accrue from such as shift.

· One teacher can work with twenty to thirty individuals with different learning styles, preferences, and interests.

· Teachers must decide what is truly important for students to learn.

· When not bound into a "lecture" mode, teachers have more time to assist and interact with individual students.

· The responsibility for learning—making decisions and carrying them out—returns to the student.

· Through student presentation of optional learning, the content base is broadened for all students without any additional work on the part of the teacher.

Teacher as organizer rather than *teacher as transmitter* contains many other entailments, many other implications in terms of what and how the classroom functions. For some teachers, breaking free of the belief they must be the experts—that they are responsible for *transmitting* information to their students—is a formidable task. Implications for classroom control are further impediments to those who hold more traditional beliefs about their role in the classroom. By at least recognizing the tenacity with which they hold onto their beliefs, teachers can become aware of why their behavior is inconsistent with what they *say* they believe.

2. Labeling the Foreground

> "A weed is just a plant whose virtues
> have not yet been discovered."
> ~Ralph Waldo Emerson

Before discussing the use of labels in education, it's important to recognize that categorization is a fundamental thinking process. Labeling is a form of categorizing. Animals categorize objects in their world as *edible* and *inedible*, *safe* or *unsafe*. Humans carry this significantly farther when they categorize another person as *good* or *bad*, *friendly* or *unfriendly*. Such labels help people make rapid decisions about their future behavior with respect to the person. If I categorize a person as *threatening*, I quickly remove myself from potential danger. I may be wrong—but better safe than sorry. This type of labeling is adaptive; it has clear survival implications.

Despite the fact that the human mind automatically labels, humans have evolved to the stage where they have choices about that behavior. The modern human has the same "biological imperatives" of their ancient ancestors, but they now choose when and where they respond to those urges. People can make those same choices in higher cognitive functions. Because humans are capable of engaging in *metacognition*, they can choose *how*, *why*, or even *if* they will use labels.

Assigning labels to people is another habit of mind that limits teacher perception. In education, labels frequently refer to something negative— learning disabled, remedial, ADD. There are those who argue that labels are simply ways to facilitate communication. When a counselor describes a student as ADD, he doesn't have to run down a whole bunch of symptoms. Everyone knew what to expect. That's the problem!

Labels are useful to the extent that they promote positive action, such as removing yourself from a threatening situation. In education, once students are labeled, they are typically plopped into a group of similarly labeled students, all of whom are "treated" in much the same way.

The inherent danger in labels is that they reduce an individual object or person to a generic class. Labels act as a spotlight for specific characteristics, bringing those into the foreground while forcing others into the background. When labels focus on negative characteristics, people no longer perceive the positives. Worse, the label sets up expectations that the student will behave in certain ways and not in others. Not surprisingly, teachers get what they expect.

A student labeled *learning disabled* or *remedial* may have tremendous gifts in areas outside of those seen as desirable in traditional schools. Where are those gifts acknowledged or nurtured once the student's day is spent trying to "fix" what the label has identified as "broken"? For that matter, the label may be incorrect to begin with—"blaming" the student for failure to respond to inappropriate teaching practices.

Thom Hartmann, a best-selling author and the father of a student labeled with ADD, has written several books in which he transforms that label. In *Attention Deficit Disorder: A Different Perspective*, Hartmann argues that the "symptoms" of attention deficit disorder are inherited adaptive behaviors. In man's early history, such individuals acted as *lookouts or hunters* for their community. Behaviors we presently perceive as *normal* are those exhibited by the *farmers* in the society—the ability to remain at a task for a long period of time and to repeat the same repetitive task day after day. Where would the farmers have been if the lookouts hadn't constantly watched for marauders or dangerous animals? Without the hunters or lookouts, the farmers would have perished or the crops would have been destroyed or pillaged. The community would not have survived.

Hartmann states,

> "...ADD is neither a deficit nor a disorder. It is, instead, an inherited set of skills, abilities, and personality tendencies which would enable a Hunter or warrior or lookout to be eminently successful—and would condemn a Farmer or an accountant to certain disaster."[4]

How did this powerful set of hunter skills come to be labeled as a disorder? Schools in this country evolved in a largely agricultural setting, so the norms for the schools were the behaviors of farmers—a more focused and concentrated way of dealing with one's environment. Despite the fact that society has shifted far from that agricultural context, the same *farmer* qualities are still prized in students. When students with hunter genes fail to achieve in these *farmer* schools, the *fault* is assigned to the students. Clearly the school could not be at fault because other students are graduating with honors and going on to great things. According to farmer standards, these hunter students must be "broken"[5] and in need of "fixing." Talk about labels!

Hartmann doesn't deny that *hunter* or *lookout* students have a short attention span or are easily distracted. He does, however, point out that these same students have a high degree of curiosity and a wide range of interests—abilities often overlooked as schools attempt to "fix" the ADD symptoms. I recommend Hartmann's book to anyone who would like a new perspective on ADD.

Positive labels can be as injurious as negative ones. Many *honors* or *gifted* students resent those labels. They no longer feel free to make mistakes—to "not know." Many of them rarely volunteer an answer they are not certain is "correct" and feel tremendous pressure to maintain their image—an image often sought more by parents than students themselves.

To what extent do labels determine your perception? Which labels prevent you from perceiving the wide range of resources in any given student? In one way or another, all students are "gifted."

3. The Experts We Rarely Consult

A teacher says, "I've tried everything. I just don't know what else to do for Juan." In many cases, there's one thing the teacher hasn't tried. With the belief that teachers are the transmitters of knowledge and that students cannot learn without a teacher's expertise, teachers rarely think to ask the students themselves how they think they could learn something. Who would know better?

Casey, a fourth grader, had great difficulty learning to spell his weekly word list correctly. Al had "tried everything" in his teaching bag of tricks to help Casey. I suggested he simply ask the boy how he thought he could learn the words. When asked, Casey replied that he'd turn them into cheers. Given the *right* to learn in his own way, Casey made up a cheer, complete with arm and leg movements, for each word. Did Casey have to perform his cheers during class? No. On his tests, Casey merely wrote the word as he imagined himself doing the cheer.

Rosa read fluently but had the habit of rocking back and forth as she read. When asked to read aloud at school, her rocking annoyed the teacher and she was told to stop. As a result, she read in a halting (and personally embarrassing) manner. Had Rosa's teacher asked, Rosa would have told her that rocking made it easier for her to read.[6]

Such insights rarely occur when teachers' beliefs about teaching and learning place all responsibility on the teacher. By bringing the students into the foreground—acknowledging their knowledge of themselves—teachers increase their repertoire of teaching behaviors.

This is a simple concept that requires little effort. If you have a student who is having great difficulty learning something, and you've "tried everything" you can think of to help, ask the expert—the student. For that matter, ask your students before you start teaching!

4. Accentuate the Positive

To a large degree, educators focus on what is *wrong* rather than what is *right*. Although some schools have begun to recognize students for effort or accomplishments, there is still an overwhelming tendency to seek out what's wrong and try to correct it. When working with students, many teachers unconsciously ask the question, "What is this student doing that needs fixing?" rather than, "What is this student doing that is exciting/remarkable/creative?" The question acts as a filter for perception. It also forces teachers to interpret what they see or hear in terms of what's "broken" rather than what's working well.

Even a student who is the most *remedial*, the most *learning disabled*, the worst *discipline problem* has positive characteristics worthy of honest recognition. (Yes, that's a belief!) What would happen if teachers focused their efforts on developing student strengths at least as often as they try to "fix" perceived weaknesses?

Many students with test anxiety experience similar unconscious images—a test paper covered with red marks. Students *see* that image *before* they take the test; it lurks in their unconscious mind as a warning of what will happen, setting them up for failure. It was bad enough when teachers used red pencils or ballpoint pens to mark wrong answers. Now that broad-tipped markers are available, student papers often look as if the teacher suffered a nosebleed while grading!

What if teachers used a green or purple pen to mark the *right* answers rather than a red one to mark what's wrong? What a simple change, but what profound implications it holds for students. Look at it this way. How do you feel when someone constantly points out what you've done wrong and rarely, if ever, mentions anything you've done right? What would happen if we made a habit of focusing on what's positive instead of what's negative?

A keynote speaker at a teacher institute began his talk with the statement, "One of us is the dumbest person in this room." Those words set me thinking about implications for the classroom. I'm not interested in ranking people from smart to dumb, but each of us has strengths and weaknesses. I decided to enter my classroom each year with the idea (belief/presupposition) that every student in that room could do something better than I could. This helped me to focus on student strengths rather than constantly searching out weakness.

I'm not suggesting teachers ignore flaws in student thinking or inappropriate behavior. In fact, teachers can often use those occasions as wonderful teaching/learning opportunities. This too requires a foreground/background shift in thinking. Rather than perceiving students as broken and in need of fixing, what if teachers perceived those "flaws" as opportunities to improve something that is already working well? How might that change teacher behavior?

Changing the complex thinking that underlies an educator's focus on groups may be difficult, but as you've seen, there are many "little" ways for teachers to begin.

The Danger of Dichotomous Thinking

"...We distort things...because we are trained neither to voice both sides of an issue nor to listen with both ears.... It is rooted in the fact that we look at the world through analytical lenses. We see everything as this or that, plus or minus, on or off, black or white; and we fragment reality into an endless series of either-ors. In a phrase, we think the world apart." ~Parker Palmer

The human cognitive process of categorization includes generating opposites. Someone says *black* and we think *white*. Someone says *hot* and we think *cold*. Binary thinking begins as the infant explores her world, playing with her fingers and toes and batting at brightly colored toys attached above her crib. She begins to recognize what is "me" and what is "not me." In short, she begins to categorize.

As adults, people classify *ideas* in terms of whether they are "me" or "not me." "Me" is anything that fits within my inner map of reality. "Not me" is anything that is not part of my belief system (and is, therefore, obviously wrong or illogical). Whatever adaptive benefits it has, binary or dichotomous thinking causes problems when done unconsciously and without regard for its potential hazards.

The first step in creating a dichotomy is simplification. Educational theorist Joseph Schwab suggests that people distill ideas into "epitomes."[7] As they explain a complex idea to others, they pick out what they believe to be the most important points. Each time the idea is explained, it is further distorted as more and more of the specifics are deleted. What happens to a Degas painting of ballerinas if it is *simplified* to stick figures, or to a Bach fugue if it is *simplified* to a melody line? Nothing remains of what made the original unique or interesting. Nothing remains of the relationships so critical to the whole. The same is true of ideas.

In education, new and promising theories undergo three destructive processes.

1. A theory is epitomized by the very people who support it. They do this to "simplify" and make the idea palatable to those they are trying to convince. However, this contributes to the theory's demise by distorting and weakening the total package.

2. Supporters of the theory do not recognize the beliefs and value system upon which the theory rests. Failing to comprehend that one must hold similar beliefs and values to effectively apply the theory, they rush to get teachers to implement the epitomized program.

3. Teachers who are motivated by a wide variety of beliefs and values use the new procedures, often failing to get the results that the originators promised. The natural reaction is to condemn the original theory—a theory that teachers have never encountered in its entirety and therefore, never fully understood

Schwab describes how this reductive way of thinking proved to be the undoing of John Dewey's progressive theory of education.

> "In Dewey's original description of his theory, (sets) of
> terms were placed in new and fruitful relations to one another:
> time, fact-idea, change, freedom, organism-environment,
> experience, individual and society. In each epitome, on the
> other hand, only one or two of these terms appear, and
> conclusions about the character of education are drawn from
> them alone. Thus each epitome inflates what was a part of the
> original into an alleged whole."[8]

Today, many people picture Dewey's progressive schools as places where students "do their own thing" with little control or planning. They think *permissive* rather than *progressive*. Nothing could have been further from Dewey's philosophy of education. Dewey's ideas were radically different from the prevailing views of the time, so people didn't recognize they were attempting to understand the new from the point of view of the old. They simply could not accurately reconstruct Dewey's ideal classroom while still holding the values and beliefs of traditional education. As a result, they condemned Dewey's theory as flawed.

Two-Dimensional Thinking

> "Mankind likes to think in terms of extreme opposites. It is given to formulating its beliefs in terms of Either-Ors, between which it recognizes no intermediate possibilities. When forced to recognize that the extremes cannot be acted upon, it is still inclined to hold that they are all right in theory but that when it comes to practical matters circumstances compel us to compromise. Educational philosophy is no exception. The history of educational theory is marked by opposition between the idea that education is development from within and that it is formation from without; that it is based upon natural endowments and that education is a process of overcoming natural inclination and substituting in its place habits acquired under external pressure." ~John Dewey[9]

Once people have simplified—epitomized—a theory, it frequently becomes one end of an imaginary line. At the other end lies its "opposite" theory. When I say something positive about the theory at one pole, I am accused of being *against* whatever is at the opposite pole. If I argue for a more humanistic approach to teaching, I am declared anti-intellectual. If I am in favor of more in-depth learning, I must be anti-standards. If I promote practical courses, I must be anti-academic.

Consider the metaphors inherent in such polar thinking. Education is a *battle zone* of dichotomies—*armed camps* prepared to *launch a barrage* of evidence for their views. Researchers and experts are the *generals*. Each *camp* has expert opinion and research data used as *ammunition* in this battle of ideas. "For every Ph.D., there's an equal and opposite Ph.D."[10]

One of the most pervasive and influential dichotomies in education is between *objectivism* and *constructivism*. Educational objectivists state that there is a reality "out there," separate from the mind. It is the duty of education to impart the truth about that reality to students. *Constructivist* theory says that learners are involved in the active process of creating knowledge—they must interact with the world as they construct their own map of reality.

There are literally hundreds of articles in educational literature in which constructivists *shoot down* objectivist ideas and vice versa. Are these two ideas polar opposites? Does the truth of one prove the other is necessarily false?

In his book *Metaphors of Mind*, Yale psychologist Robert Sternberg suggests not. Although his book is about different theories of intelligence, Sternberg's words seem applicable to the broader context of educational theories.

> "...In the study of human intelligence ..., we pay too much
> attention to answers at the expense of paying enough attention
> to questions. As a result, we often see theories as competing,
> when in fact they are not: They are different answers to
> different questions, not different answers to the same question.
> Even when we recognize that two theories address different
> questions, we may still try to compare them on some illusory
> basis that prejudices the outcome of our comparison in favor
> of one theory or the other."[11]

With apologies for my own "epitomizing," the *objectivist* view answers the question, "Is there an objective reality of which all humans should be aware?" The *constructivist* view answers the question, "How do humans internalize information?" One camp is arguing for the existence of information external to the mind and the other is arguing for how people learn. Is it logical to place these ideas in opposition to one another? Why have to choose when this is not an either/or issue?

Jean Piaget and Lev Vygotsky both believed in the importance of the interaction between learners and the environment. Piaget believed intelligence matured internally and expressed itself externally. Vygotsky believed intelligence begins in the social environment and directs itself inward. Aren't these simply two halves of the cycle of development?

Similar arguments have long existed between the nature and nurture "camps." Newer theories in the neurosciences suggest people are born with certain internal processes that may be "turned on" by the appropriate environment. Those processes are then used to create new connections and generate new results that influence what we say or do in the external world.[12] It isn't one or the other—it's both. A child is born with latent language processes that are "turned on" when the child hears the speech of his parents. His own language matures and expresses itself externally. The development of language is only one example of the critical importance of both internal and external processes. As the old song suggests, "…you can't have one without the other."

The word *opposing*, as well as our use of *armed camps*, a *barrage* of data, and *defending our position* by *shooting down our opponent's arguments* are all part of a *military* metaphor. Is it any wonder that there is so much animosity, so much name-calling among different theorists? This is, after all, *war*! The metaphor forces educators to envision ideas as opposing *armies* on a two-dimensional *battlefield*. We have Descartes' rational mind on one side and subjectivism on the other. Externally generated standards battle curricula based on student interest. Each camp is *lobbing* data and research studies at the other from their respective *positions*. When the data doesn't overwhelm the enemy, when theoretical attempts to prove the superiority of one camp over another fail to force the enemy to surrender, the battle often disintegrates into insulting the intelligence of combatants in the opposing camp. When all else fails, call them idiots!

The combatants, entrenched in their own belief systems, can see only their immediate position (the truth) and, at a great distance, the position of their opponent. "You couldn't be further from the truth."

Teachers stand by and let the experts fight it out. Is there is a right way to teach, a right philosophy of education? If so, then why, in the history of education, has one side not been able to convince the other? Whose intellects are flawed? The fundamental belief that one or the other idea must be correct blinds even the experts to the recognition that almost every idea provides useful insight into some aspect of the problems. None contains all of the answers. Lee Shulman points out that denying the value of any approach to teaching is counter-productive. There is value to be found in almost every model, every methodology, *in the appropriate context*.[13]

This war metaphor leaves observers with the impression they must take sides. It intimidates some teachers into believing they must choose A or B rather than AB or aB or Ab—even if some combination of the theories is the most logical choice for a given situation. In the words of an educational proverb, "Successful teachers are effective *in spite of* the psychological theories they suffer under." These teachers don't allow rigid rules to dictate their behaviors.

Teachers who have no great attachment to either position—who don't insist on *taking a stand*—can rise above the battlefield to view the various theories from a new and much more comprehensive perspective. Those teachers perceive *theories as resources*—ideas from which to choose depending on the current situation. Disciplinary situations require a different resource than nurturing situations. Teaching "the basics" requires a different resource than fostering creativity. Teachers who perceive the entire plane of ideas can "zoom in" to the resource that most closely fits their needs at any moment.

Let's begin by tossing out the war metaphor. Many other metaphors could provide a much more productive background for discussion. For example, what if we think of educational theories as flowers in a huge garden? People don't think to ask which is better—a rose or a daisy, an orchid or a violet. Each flower has something unique to offer. The landscape is a result of the judicious combination of color, shape, and size. The bee gets to fly from flower to flower, collecting the sweetest nectar and returning to the hive to produce the finest honey. Just imagine what teachers might produce if they were free to draw from the rich repertoire of possibilities in the garden of educational theories.

Neils Bohr once said, "The opposite of a true statement is a false statement. But the opposite of a profound truth may be another profound truth."[14] Educational theories are different points of view rather than either/or positions to be defended. Each point of view contains valuable insights. The idea that one must adopt one end of a spectrum and stay there, "defending" it against all evidence to the contrary, is as limiting as eating only one type of food or always wearing the clothing for every occasion.

Dichotomous thinking is an adaptive behavior that is part of human nature. The wonder of the human mind is that we can change it. We don't have to behave habitually. We can actively choose to think in a different way. Human minds are enormously adaptable. Establishing different patterns of thought will take some effort, but once established, those new patterns will become as natural as the old way of thinking.

> "Our mind is capable of passing beyond
> the dividing line we have drawn for it.
> Beyond the pairs of opposites of which the world
> consists, other, new insights begin." ~Herman Hesse

Only you can determine to what extent you have fallen victim to these habits of mind. You may wish to go back through your answers to the items in sections A and D of the Self-Inventory and examine them for thought viruses and evidence of limiting beliefs. Shift your focus to generating options that broaden and deepen your behavioral repertoire.

1 Glickman, C. D. (1988). Knowledge and Certainty in the Supervision of Instruction. In P. P. Grimmett & G. L. Erickson (Eds.). *Education in Reflection in Teacher Education* (p. 59) New York: Teachers College Press.

2 Lakoff, G. & Johnson, M. (1999). *Philosophy in the Flesh: The Embodied Mind and its Challenge to Western Thought.* New York: Basic Books, 26–28.

3 Prawat, R. S. (1990, April). Changing Schools by Changing Teachers' Beliefs about Teaching and Learning, Elementary Subjects Series No. 19. (ERIC Document Reproduction Service No. ED 322 144) p. 15.

4 Hartmann, T. (1993). *Attention Deficit Disorder: A Different Perception.* Grass Valley: Underwood Books, 25.

5 Some educators actually use the term "broken." See for example Flaro, L. (1989). *Mending Broken Children.* Edmonton, Alberta: Learning Strategies Group.

6 This technique has been validated through experimentation. Rocking front to back or sometimes side to side appears to influence the brains of some people in some positive way, permitting fluency in reading.

7 Schwab, J. J. (1978). *Science, Curriculum and Liberal Education: Selected Essays* I. Westbury & N. J. Wilkof (Eds.) Chicago and London: University of Chicago Press.

8 Ibid., 167.

9 Dewey, J. (1939). *Experience and Education: Traditional vs. Progressive Education.* New York: Macmillan.

10 Ohanion, S. (1999). *One Size Fits Few: The Folly of Educational Standards.* Portsmouth, NH: Heinemann, 23.

11 Sternberg, R. (1990). *Metaphors of Mind: Conceptions of the Nature of Intelligence.* Cambridge: Cambridge University Press, 284.

12 Edelman, G. M. (1992). *Bright Air, Brilliant Fire: On the Matter of Mind.* New York: Basic Books.

13 Shulman, L. S. (1988). The Dangers of Dichotomous Thinking in Education. In P. P. Grimmett & G. L. Erickson (Eds.). *Reflection in Teacher Education* (pp. 31–38) New York: Teachers College Press.

14 Palmer, P. (1998). *The Courage to Teach: Exploring the Inner Landscape of a Teacher's Life.* San Francisco: Jossey-Bass, 62.

Chapter 8 ~
Changing the Educational Mind

"We can easily forgive a child who is afraid of the dark; the real tragedy of life is when men are afraid of the light."~ Plato

Before proceeding, an explanation is in order. In Chapter 7, we spoke about accentuating the virtues of students rather than their flaws. Yet, it may seem that I'm focusing on education's flaws rather than its virtues. My intent is not to condemn education or teaching in general. I recognize there are many things the educational system does well. That doesn't mean it can't be much better. My goal is simply to awaken teachers to other possibilities. What if educators took the time to analyze what they do really well and then built on that excellence rather than constantly responding to criticisms of what's broken with piecemeal "fixes"?

Some people express irritation when education is criticized. They cite statistics about the many college-bound students who enter productive professions or about the number of students in advanced placement and honors classes. They point with pride to the winners of state or national spelling, math, or science competitions. What can be so wrong if so many students succeed in school?

As food for thought, here are some possible answers to that question.

- For some students, the present school environment is not counterproductive to their learning. Their "learning styles" are compatible with gaining knowledge through reading, listening to a lecture, or other relatively passive experiences. Although many studies have found that those are not universally effective ways to teach, some students can supplement those activities from a rich experiential base of their own. They make connections that lead to learning even when the environment doesn't facilitate those connections.

- Some students get good grades because they know how to memorize and have learned to play the school game. They recognize that grades are used to judge their "worth," so they do what is necessary to get good grades. What they learn in this way does little to inspire them, interest them, or make them want to know more about a subject, but in the statistics, they appear "successful."

- Some students succeed because of an innate drive to know, rather than because of stimulating classes. If, as scientists suggest, cognitive processes are already present at birth and are "turned on" by the environment, their hunger for learning may have been turned on by parents or other experiences long before they ever entered school. These students insist on knowing "why", often to the point of irritation. Even when teachers put off their questions as being "off the subject," the students will seek out answers on their own until they are satisfied. They are learning *in spite of schooling* rather than because of it.

- Man is extremely adaptable. Humans have learned to survive in many climates, many environments that are not natural. Although humans can fly to the moon and beyond or travel thousands of feet beneath the ocean's surface, their natural abilities are severely constrained by the devices they must use to survive. Anna Freud once said, "Creative minds have always been known to survive any kind of bad training." I would simply ask how much more even the most successful student might become if the educational environment focused on, and became compatible with, natural learning rather than on transmitting a body of knowledge external to the student.

- As educators point with pride to the students who have "succeeded" in the school environment, what of the others? What about the 30 percent or more of students who, in many schools, are labeled *remedial* or *below average*. A friend once pointed out "there will always be a third who are below average. That's the nature of statistics." That statement is something of a thought virus in itself. Averages only exist in terms of group measurements and bell-curves. They are another artifact of group-think. What might happen if we were able to forget about group statistics for just a moment and think about ways every student might get the most out of his or her years of schooling? How the strengths of each student might be developed to its fullest?

Educators often argue they can do a great job with "motivated" students but can't be expected to "waste time" with unmotivated ones. They are eager to take credit for student success but unwilling to accept responsibility for the fate of students whose needs go unmet in the traditional classroom. Instead of questioning their own methods, it's much easier to perceive students as flawed entities.

There are many extremely effective teachers in our schools. There are students who leave school brimming with promise and eager to continue learning because of what they have experienced. But until the numbers of both teachers and students in those categories represent a significant majority of those in our schools, how can educators be satisfied?

In a 1999 poll of teachers and parents done by *Phi Delta Kappa* and the Gallup Organization, respondents were asked, "How would you describe the impact school has had or is having on your oldest child's attitude toward learning?" Some of the parents who responded to the survey were also teachers in public schools.

About 50 percent of both teachers and parents said that school had caused the child to become "eager learners." However, *more than a third* said school had "caused [the] child to *tolerate learning* as [a] necessary chore." Another 5 percent of teachers and fully 15 percent of parents said schools had caused the child to be *turned off to learning*.[1]

"Tolerate learning as a necessary chore"? Learning is something every healthy infant begins in the womb and pops into the world eager to continue! How can anyone be content with a system that either turns that learning into a "necessary chore" or snuffs out the eagerness altogether *in nearly 50 percent of children*? Further, there's no proof the schools actually "caused the child to become an eager learner." In some cases, school may simply have been unable to destroy that eagerness!

Although more recent PDK polls have not repeated this question, the results of the 2009 poll still had around 50% of those polled saying that children today get a worse education than they did as children.[2]

More and more doctors now focus on wellness rather than illness. This doesn't mean they ignore health issues of concern. Society expects the medical profession to continue improving so they can lengthen life expectancy and increase the number of people who remain in good health throughout their lives. If we are not content with accepting that a third of our population will remain "below average" in terms of health, why should we be satisfied with it in our schools?

How Beliefs Affect Teaching

"A great many people think they are thinking when
they are merely rearranging their prejudices."
~William James

Why is it important for teachers to re-examine their beliefs about the purpose of education— about knowledge, teaching, learning, and students? Here is just one example of how traditional beliefs about the nature of teaching and learning relentlessly drive the choices teachers make. In this case, one example seems more than enough.

In a study by Randy Yerrick and his associates[3], teachers believed they were attending a workshop designed to improve the way they presented scientific knowledge and the manner in which they assessed student learning. In reality, the researchers were studying the way in which teachers responded to such workshops. This workshop focused on the value of a deeper understanding of science concepts as they are found in the real world. Participants dutifully listened to the ideas presented and did the activities. At the conclusion of the workshop, teacher participants were asked how likely they were to use current headlines related to science to shape their lessons—one of the techniques the workshop leaders had recommended. Here are some quotes from participants. Incidentally, these quotes are verbatim. Keep in mind that one of the standards for *Kindergarten* students is to "speak in coherent, complete sentences." Hmm.

When asked about using the state's coastal erosion problems as a focus for teaching, Ben said:

> "Well…I teach weathering…also we talk about the
> formation of rocks and see after I teach the formation of rocks
> we go into weathering and erosion so I could tie it in to then
> about the type of weathering it would be and why it could
> cause things like that…we do touch on it in the curriculum…I
> would talk about it when we talk about…"[4]

Chris responded:

> "Naturally I'd have to go by the state curriculum guide. That
> would be the first priority. I always teach that first…this much

145

needs to be taught within the first 9 weeks so that means that
the time frame if I have time for other things that's when I
bring in these that are not in the curriculum…" and "…its
most important to teach the curriculum…'cuz that's what I'm
held responsible for and I'm responsible for their learning in
certain areas and the curriculum identifies what I'm responsible
for teaching. *At least exposing them to it even if they don't learn it.* I
have to expose them to it and try to give them the concepts
and try to give them some understanding in that area."[5]
(author's emphasis)

Clearly, for Chris, education is about *what the teacher does* rather than
about *what the student learns.* As long as Chris had "exposed" students to
what was in the curriculum, he had done his job "even if they don't learn
it"! He does recognize that people don't always "catch" what they are
"exposed" to.

Molly was even more direct about her reasons for not teaching
current events.

"Well the primary reason I teach anything in my classroom
nowadays is because the end of course testing in the state
curriculum…First of all, none of these (events) much go into
my state curriculum…"[6]

Molly went on to suggest she might *touch on* those topics in the first
ten minutes of class "or something."

Analyzing the data from their research, investigators concluded that:

1. All teachers in the study *believe* science is a long list of scientifically
verified concepts, linked in some rational order and confirmed by some
external source. Teachers would justify including current issues only if
they were in some way related to these concepts. Even when they would
include current issues, they wouldn't spend much time on them because
it would take too much time from their *coverage* of the pre-specified
curriculum concepts that represented *what was already known* rather than
questions arising from contemporary scientific problems.

2. Teachers used this list of concepts almost exclusively in their
decision-making. They "interpreted their jobs as distributors of this
list…reflected upon their teaching experiences using this list, evaluated

scientific questions as worthy of study through this list, and defended reasonable choices and timeframes of completion"[7] based on the list.

3. There was an overwhelming belief in education as *transmission* of a body of facts (the conduit metaphor). Teachers used the phrase, "We talk about..." repeatedly, followed by long lists of "table of contents entries and a linear, rational, and chronological progress through these concepts." In practice, "we talk about" really means "I talk about."

These findings might not constitute a problem if (a) *the list* actually constituted the most important content in science, and (b) *transmission* was the most effective way for students to learn that content. Research has repeatedly called both of these presuppositions into question.

4. Teachers presupposed that scientific facts were linked in some rational order to be presented at a specific point during schooling as reflected in the following statements. When asked whether he would discuss the collision of the Shoemaker-Levy comet with Jupiter—an event that was scheduled to happen within several days—Ben replied,

> "Well...I don't know...see they teach the solar system in the sixth grade and...and I'm in the seventh grade...so I would have to look into it...I would have to refresh my own knowledge of it first."

When pressed, Ben explained that he probably wouldn't include it "because they taught it already...it's not part of the curriculum for the seventh grade...and um it's generally knowledge they should already have...and partly I'm not as familiar with the comet so I couldn't teach it because I would have to learn it myself first."[8]

How could students "already have" knowledge of something that had not yet occurred? Ben's statement clearly demonstrates his belief that knowledge is something to "have" rather than to "use." His concern about his own lack of knowledge demonstrates how a teacher's personal knowledge base influences his choice of content. It makes one wonder what Ben does when he isn't familiar with something that is part of his assigned curriculum.

5. Participants viewed students as recipients of knowledge having little influence over teacher decisions of what and how to teach. Molly: "It was more or less you told students information, you lectured them, and they were empty vessels and you put it in."[9]

In explaining what he looked for in evaluating student answers to specific questions about content, Guy explained:

> "I just have a list of some of the types of things I'm looking for and when I read their question I look for specifically if they've listed say three of the things that we've talked about. They might have information in there that was unnecessary...sometimes even some information that wasn't correct, but if they came up with at least three of the say five things we had discussed then they get credit for that question..."[10]

It's easy to understand how a teacher with this criterion for learning could use a computerized scoring system—even for essay questions. An individual student's thought processes are irrelevant—even if it "wasn't correct." Only items from "the list" count.

When asked what he would do if two students got into a debate about some scientific issue—if he would use this as a launch pad for inquiry-based teaching—Guy replied he would consider this as an interruption to other science topics that were intended to be taught.

> "My instruction would continue. That wouldn't interrupt my instruction." He would tell a student, "You can do it Friday afternoon, but you can't interrupt what we're doing today. You know that doesn't pertain to what we're doing today..."[11]

As Yerrick and his fellow investigators put it, "It is difficult to imagine how students' input would influence such a predetermined patter about scientific concepts." This type of response was typical of teachers in the study. Expressions of individual interest were suitable only for "extra credit" assignments done outside of class. Even when students chose to do such work, they were expected to generate lists of facts about the topic. Teachers also expected student motivation to align to "appropriate concepts from the accepted curriculum."

Teachers in this study *cognitively accepted* the value of using current topics as part of their teaching, but were unwilling or unable to change their behaviors or to replace anything they were already doing. Instead, they repeatedly spoke of "bringing that in." Current topics were viewed only as a way to lead them back to their list of curriculum topics. While some teachers saw the value of dialoguing with students to determine understanding, "it seems what is taught is non-negotiable."[12]

The researchers in this study did not confront the teachers about their beliefs. They were simply studying how those beliefs influenced the effectiveness of reform efforts. It's disconcerting to see such limiting beliefs about teaching and learning expressed so blatantly. The validity of these beliefs is highly questionable, yet that doesn't seem to be a factor. Some may secretly feel that the teachers in this study are only expressing the realities of teaching. In an increasing number of schools, standards and the tests designed to assess student acquisition of those standards have *become* the curriculum and teachers believe they have little or no choice about what and how they teach.

The presuppositions that those standards are appropriate and that objective testing is the way to prove to the world that schools are doing their job remains largely unquestioned by the people directed to implement those efforts. Teachers accept the party line that they are not doing their job if they don't teach that curriculum. Through methods of conscious and unconscious extortion, teachers are pressured to make choices that, left to their own devices, many of them would never make. How much longer will teachers who feel responsible for the development of their students continue to act in ways they know, from experience, are detrimental to those students? What personal values allow them to ignore those concerns?

The teachers in this study so mindlessly adhered to the party line they didn't even question their actions. As long as the focus of education is *knowledge* rather than *students*, why would we expect them to change their behavior? In 1999, a speaker at the State of the World Forum on Education described in detail how inappropriate our present system of education was and called for radical reforms. Participants agreed. A high official in the U. S. Department of Education acknowledged the speaker was "probably intellectually right [and] even morally right, but politics just won't let this happen." There is too much institutional inertia locked up in all of this.

Another attendee challenged the statement.

"That is simply not a good enough excuse any more. We no longer have any intellectual excuse for not reversing an upside-down and inside-out system of education. What is questionable however is whether we have the guts to do what now needs to be done."[13]

Loosening Up Beliefs

"To spell out the obvious is often to call it in question." ~Eric Hoffer

Loosening up an old belief is like trying to open a window that has been painted shut. We pry, poke, and prod the dried paint until the window breaks free from the frame. Then, whoosh, the window opens easily, allowing in the fresh air of new ideas. What follows are several strategies for prying, poking, and prodding your beliefs.

1. Turn the belief on yourself. Often, teachers hold beliefs about students that don't stand up to scrutiny if the same belief is applied to self. For example, Dorothy believes *a student's learning style is the same for all or most contexts.* She prides herself on determining her students' learning styles early in the school year. She assigns students to work areas designed to suit their specific learning styles. Dorothy has noticed, however, this doesn't improve student performance as much as she had hoped.

If Dorothy asks herself how she engages in learning, she will probably realize her preferences change from context to context. If she's trying to learn something fairly abstract, she may choose to sit in a straight-backed chair with little external distraction. If she's reading for enjoyment, she may kick back in a soft chair and have music playing in the background. If she's trying to learn a skill, she may want to work with someone who already knows how to do it. Why should Dorothy's students be any different?

If you apply a belief to yourself and find it does not fit, doesn't it seem likely there are also students for whom it doesn't fit? This process isn't intended to disprove the belief—only to suggest it isn't *always* true and therefore, shouldn't be mindlessly applied.

To deepen this process, imagine you are a student in your own class. Would you enjoy it? Would you be motivated to learn? Are there any instances where you would be bored or find it difficult to pay attention? Are there rules you might consider unfair? How do you feel about tests?

From the position of the student, ask yourself what you would like the teacher (you) to do that he or she doesn't now do? What would you like him or her to stop doing? In what ways would you want the teacher to treat you differently?

2. Reverse the belief. Let's say you believe *the teacher is responsible for students' learning.* Without any value judgment about the validity of that belief—arguments for or against it—turn that belief around. Ask, "In what ways might students learn even more if the teacher took *less* responsibility for their learning?" Questions automatically send the brain in search of answers. There is an assumption that an answer exists and *voila*, we find it. Asking that question encourages you to rethink your belief. The original belief is not under attack, so there's no need to defend it. You might think of answers like the following:

- Students would become more responsible and would select learning experiences that were most appropriate for them.

- The teacher would have more time to work with students who really needed help while other students would learn just as much or more by going at a faster pace.

- Students might be motivated to explore some subjects in greater depth than the curriculum permitted.

This process works best with beliefs about cause and effect. Let's try another belief: *Standardized tests assess student progress toward a common goal.*

Reversal: This statement can be reversed in a number of ways. Here are a couple of them.

1. How can student progress be assessed even more effectively without standardized tests?

2. In what ways do standardized tests fail to assess student progress?

Assuming you accept the presupposition that "common goals" are desirable (or even possible), you might answer as follows:

1a. Portfolios that contain writing samples give a more accurate picture of a student's ability to express what he knows.

1b. Students who experience stress on written tests might be tested orally or through performance tests.

2a. Standardized tests fail to assess what a student knows beyond what is on the test.

2b. Standardized tests often fail to assess higher level thinking skills.

Here are a couple more belief statements with one or more reversals. No answers are provided, but you might enjoy answering the questions yourself. Notice that there are generally several different ways that a belief can be "reversed."

Belief: To be fair, a consistent set of rules should be applied to all students.

Reversal: How could more flexible rules be even fairer to all students?

Belief: Grades motivate students to learn.

Reversal: How might students be even more motivated to learn without grades?

Reversal: How might grades reduce a student's motivation to learn?

Some beliefs don't lend themselves to this sort of reversal, but whenever you can reverse a belief, you are effectively reminding yourself that it is a belief, not a fact. By taking a different perspective, you're able to ask new questions and identify new possibilities.

3. Monitor ideas that get you "fired up." Remember that beliefs have an affective or emotional component. Events in the classroom or discussions about educational issues often press a teacher's "hot button." Why? There are things about which people feel strongly and that it is appropriate to "defend." Discovering the reasons behind those feelings often provides useful insights.

Many teachers get very upset when students misbehave. It's important for those teachers to understand *why* they get so upset because their response is often to punish the student. When a student misbehaves in Al's class, Al interprets the misbehavior to *mean* the student doesn't understand the difference between appropriate and inappropriate behavior. Because Al believes students must behave

152

appropriately to succeed in the world, his upset reflects concern for the child. He makes every effort to teach the child the difference.

Georgia attaches a different meaning to the student misbehavior. To her, it *means* she has somehow failed to interest the student. This threatens Georgia's self-concept or sense of competency. Her response—punishing the student—is unconsciously chosen to reduce that threat to self. The problem here is that the student's misbehavior may have little or nothing to do with Georgia. Only in her self-constructed world of meaning is there a cause-and-effect relationship. Because she interprets student actions in terms of self, her survival instincts, rather than a concern for the student, motivate her responses.

Some people defend beliefs because of an unconscious fear of what would happen if the belief proves false. Most teachers take pride in doing what they believe is in the best interest of students. If what they are doing is shown to be flawed, a teacher not only has to confront the task of changing the behavior but may feel guilty about failing to serve previous students. The fear of change is natural. The guilt is unnecessary. Only if one continues to do something after discovering its flaws might one feel guilty. If the teacher feels guilty now, how will he feel after ten more years of doing what he knows is inappropriate?

4. Challenge yourself. Many beliefs are so innate to people's thinking, they would never think to question them. Having someone else confront us with the obvious may be the only way to become aware of our thinking. The following methods will be more effective after you've identified and confronted a number of beliefs on your own. They are extremely helpful but require a level of trust that may not exist when you first begin to explore your own beliefs.

The first involves working with a group of peers, all of whom understand the purpose of the exercise. You can think of it as playing "devil's advocate." Within the group, agree to challenge one another on statements about students, teaching, or classroom practice, *even if you agree with that statement.* This forces you and others to really listen and analyze what's being said, often making you aware of some of your own hidden beliefs. A sample dialogue follows.

Hank: "I kept the kids so busy they didn't have time to misbehave."
Aisha: "*So do you believe* kids misbehave because they aren't busy enough?" (There are, of course, many other possible responses.)

Notice that Aisha's response is a question beginning with "so do you believe." It expresses neither agreement nor disagreement but merely invites Hank to expand on what he has said. This can open a discussion about how keeping kids busy is related to learning and discipline or about what triggers misbehavior. Both Hank's and Aisha's beliefs are brought into the open. Teachers spend much of their time together talking about students. Why not use that time to do some self-reflection?

It's critical that all of the teachers involved in this process withhold judgment about what beliefs are "right" or "wrong." Keep in mind that beliefs are not facts. They may be true in some contexts, but not in others. The purpose is simply to elaborate on those "throwaway" statements that teachers so often make—to determine what beliefs lie beneath the surface.

Some "teachers of the year"[14] describe another process that they typically use. They ask their students to challenge any of their behaviors for which the student can offer a valid alternative. The success of this technique depends, in large measure, on the age and maturity of your students and the degree of reciprocal respect and trust there is in your classroom. In using this method with high school students, I've found that they respect a teacher's attempts to improve and rarely abuse the opportunity given them. It is, however, important to explain what you are doing and set some ground rules. You may limit students to challenging classroom procedures or rules, but be prepared to think about your real reasons for those procedures and rules. If you permit students to challenge content, be prepared to spend time thinking about why you really include that content.

This is also a great opportunity to teach through role modeling. When you've given students the opportunity to question your actions, they are more open when you question their actions. However, use this method only when you are sincerely open to change and able to respond to a challenge without feeling personally threatened.[15]

I once used this process to "teach" students about the harmful effects of nonverbal behaviors. I pointed out that when a student in the class offered a "wrong" answer, some other students would laugh, make a face, or sigh—all of which implied the "stupidity" of the student giving the answer. I asked the students to recall how they felt when this happened to them. After we discussed it, I told them I wouldn't accept that kind of behavior in my class. To back up my words, I also told them if they ever caught me "putting down" a student—either verbally or nonverbally—they had my permission to "put me down" right back.

To be honest, it was a reasonably safe process for me because "putting people down" wasn't part of my teaching repertoire. However, several weeks later, my jaw dropped when a student insulted me to my face. He immediately pointed out something I had just said to another student and reminded me of my statement. I had been joking with the other student and we both knew it. However, I accepted the "rebuke" and admitted that the difference between "joking with" and "making fun of" someone may not always be obvious. We all learned a good lesson.

Because people use their beliefs to organize their world, challenging those beliefs may well cause discomfort. Once people understand the power of their beliefs in shaping their perceptions and behaviors, that discomfort is often worth the effort.

> "Beliefs themselves are not the issue. They are useful illusions, enabling us to manage experience...The problem is our relationship to them. To believe in something is to breathe life into it. If we know what we believe, we know what we empower. However, if we do not choose our beliefs—if, through our failure to question, they choose us, then we are unaware of the impact of our assumptions...If, wide awake, we choose to believe in something, we can also choose to let it go when the time comes."[16]

Start Small

No one is suggesting that a complete, overnight makeover is either possible or desirable. Start small. Here are a few suggestions.

If you repeatedly respond to students in the same way or habitually use the same methods even when they are not accomplishing your goal, *stop*! Examine the belief underlying your behavior by making a statement that provides a reason for your behavior.

For example, Sammy constantly taps on his desk with his pencil. You've lost count of the number of times you've said "Sammy, stop that tapping!" Of course, the fact that you've had to say it repeatedly suggests what you're doing does not work. *Stop! Think!* Why do you want Sammy to stop tapping? Here are a few possibilities.

- You find the sound personally distracting and believe you can't teach well if you're distracted.

- You believe other students find the noise distracting and it is your responsibility to maintain an environment conducive to learning.

- You believe Sammy is thoughtless and disrespectful of others.

- You believe when Sammy is tapping he's not paying attention and paying attention is necessary for learning.[17]

The first reason is personal. The second addresses student learning—but not Sammy's. The third and fourth arise from questionable assumptions. All four share the need to make Sammy stop tapping.

What possibilities have been overlooked? One issue is *why* Sammy is tapping. Those familiar with individual differences can quickly provide a possible answer. Sammy may be one of those kinesthetic kids who simply have to move. Forcing him to sit still stands a good chance of locking up his thinking processes, thus *reducing* his ability to learn rather than improving it. Suggesting that he tap on his leg rather than the desk allows him to keep moving while removing the annoying sound.

Another possibility is simply asking Sammy why he is tapping. Often, he's not even aware he's doing it. Giving him the opportunity to identify his reasons and to come up with another behavior that will serve his need without distracting others helps Sammy to develop responsibility.

Take a moment to look for alternatives other than the original "make him stop" strategy. A teacher becomes open to these possibilities only by breaking the action-reaction response cycle. When you stop and think, new possibilities emerge. Begin by thinking about the most troublesome "rut" in your teaching. Perhaps it's a disciplinary action, a teaching methodology, or the way you select (or deselect) content. Anything within your teaching repertoire is fair game. Switch from mindless to mindful decision making. The first couple of times, it will require a little work, but it soon becomes almost second nature. Once you stop, the rest becomes easy.

If you're pleased with the increase in choices you gain from doing this, try working on one new behavior each week. Do whatever is comfortable. Remember that any small change resulting in improved interactions among you and your students, or a more effective learning environment, is a step in the right direction. You're making a positive difference.[18]

1 Langdon, C. A. (1999). The Fifth Phi Delta Kappa Poll of Teachers' Attitudes Toward the Public Schools. *Phi Delta Kappa International*, URL: http://www.pdkintl.org/kappan/klan9904.htm.

2http://www.pdkintl.org/kappan/poll.htm. Downloaded August 12, 2010

3 Yerrick, R., Parke, H., & Nugent, J. (1997). Struggling to Promote Deeply Rooted Change: the "Filtering Effect of Teachers' Beliefs on Understanding Transformational Views of Teaching Science. *Science Education*, Vol. 81, 137–159.

4 Ibid., 142.

5 Ibid.

6 Ibid., 143.

7 Ibid., 142.

8 Ibid., 150.

9 Ibid., 148.

10 Ibid., 146.

11 Ibid., 147.

12 Ibid., 150.

13 Abbott, J. (1999). Battery Hens, or Free Range Chickens: What Kind of Education for What Kind of World, published online by the 21st Century Learning Initiative, URL: http://www.21learn.org/publ/abbott_speech.html

14 Agne, K. J., Greenwood, G. E., & Miller, L. D. (1994). Relationships Between Teacher Belief Systems and Teacher Effectiveness. *The Journal of Research and Development in Education*, Vol. 27, No. 3, 141–152.

15 For one teacher's description of how this process works, you may wish to read "Thanks, I Needed That!" by Mary Mortimore Dossin (1999). *College Teaching*. Vol. 47, No. 2, 42.

16 Zweig, C. (1984). Commentary: Trying Out Experimental Beliefs. *Brain/Mind Bulletin: Frontiers of Research, Theory and Practice*. Vol. 9, No. 10, 3.

17 There's an enlightening discussion of the way teachers habitually think about "paying attention" in Harvard psychologist Ellen Langer's 1997 book, *The Power of Mindful Learning*, Reading, MA: Addison-Wesley.

18For a revealing description of how one teacher went about transforming his practice, see Patterson, Thomas H., and Thomas P. Crumpler. "Slow transformation: teacher research and shifting teacher practices." *Teacher Education Quarterly* 36.3 (2009): 95. General OneFile. Web. 19 Aug. 2010.

Chapter 9 ~ Visions of Education

"I am entirely certain that twenty years from now we will look back at education as it is practiced in most schools today and wonder that we could have tolerated anything so primitive."
~John W. Gardner

Education Is...

"Do not follow where the path may lead. Go, instead, where there is no path and leave a trail." ~Unknown

As noted in Chapter 1, there is no universally accepted definition of education. Is it the transmission of our culture to the next generation, the transmission of a body of accepted knowledge, the total development of the child, or something else? Before exploring those beliefs, let's examine what education *would* be in the ideal world of your own making. Each person's definition of education often springs from that individual's ideal vision of education.

In *The Fifth Discipline*, Peter Senge suggests that one of the most important characteristics of a learning organization is *shared vision*. Senge defines a learning organization as one that continuously expands its capacity to create its future by "re-perceiving" the world and one's relationship to it. We might expect education to exist as a model for a learning organization. However, not only is there no shared vision that drives and motivates educators, but those involved in education can't even seem to agree on their primary purpose—why they are in business in the first place.

According to Senge,

> "A shared vision is not an idea. It is not even an important idea such as freedom. It is, rather, a force in people's hearts, a force of impressive power.... At its simplest level, a shared vision is the answer to the question, 'What do we want to create?' "[1]

In the early days of education, there may have been a shared vision, although some suggest it focused on the production of formulaic human beings whose behavior could be predicted and controlled.[2] As the enterprise of education grew and theorists began to isolate different aspects of knowledge, teaching, and learning, the vision splintered. Some continued to call for uniform standards while others argued the importance of a more student-centered approach. These need not be contradictory, but were often seen as such and battle lines were drawn.

You've probably seen what happens when people in a group or on a committee "pull in different directions." Frustration levels rise. Progress in any direction requires overcoming not only outside resistance, but pressures from within the group. The enterprise of education is now so large, with people pulling in so many different directions, that there is a real threat of disintegration from within.

We see the effects in the proliferation of charter and private schools and in the call for vouchers allowing parents to send students to schools of their own choosing. In some states, parents create their own schools, while others opt to take their children out of school and teach them at home. In 2003, over one million students in the United States were home-schooled, roughly the same as the total public school enrollment of Georgia or New Jersey. According to a study by the National Home Education Research Institute, by 2008, that number had increased to between 2-2.5 million, with an annual increase of between 5-12% a year.[3]

Is there any hope that education might return to a shared vision? Senge suggests shared visions emerge from personal visions—visions that generate enthusiasm, compel courage, foster risk taking and experimentation, and create commitment to long-term goals. Transformational leaders can often inspire others to their vision.[4] While it seems unlikely a single leader will emerge capable of uniting educators in a shared vision, some individual schools have achieved promising results by focusing on the visions of individual teachers.[5] What has been done in those schools can be done in many others. What it takes is one or more teachers coming forward with a sufficiently powerful vision.

Teachers sometimes forget they are leaders with the responsibility for guiding and inspiring their students toward some vision of possibility. It's time for teachers to renew those visions for themselves—to recapture the enthusiasm, courage, risk-taking, and commitment they once had as they first looked at the faces of their students.

"In scores of educational reform reports, there are no magnificent dreams for future schools. Instead, most reformers accept the system as it is and suggest that the egregious problems of education can be fixed by improving particular dysfunctional parts."[6]

What a Vision Might Look Like

"Make no little plans. They have no magic to stir men's blood and probably themselves will not be realized. Make big plans. Aim high in hope and work. Remembering that a noble, logical diagram once recorded will not die."
~Daniel H. Burnham

Seymour Papert, professor, mathematician, and author, suggests that at the heart of the problems of education lies "a shortage of bold, coherent, inspiring yet realistic visions of what education could be like 10 and 20 years from now."[7]

"Vision allows us to look beyond the problems that beset us today, giving direction to our passage into the future. Even more important, vision energizes that passage by inspiring and guiding us into action."[8]

Papert quotes a first grader in Mississippi: "The biggest thing about someone is imajunashun. Before you can be something, you must imajun it." He continues:

"Salk imagined a way to eliminate polio...not a treatment to relieve it. Kennedy imagined a man on the moon...not a faster jet. We imagine a school that revolutionizes learning for the next century...not one that reconditions learning as we have known it in the past. We imagine a school in which students and teachers excitedly and *joyfully* stretch themselves to their limits in pursuit of projects built on their own visions...not one that merely succeeds in making apathetic students satisfy minimal standards."[9]

Papert argues that vision is also the key to what education should be about—to inspire every student with "a proud vision of self as a powerful life-long learner, a vibrant vision of a worthwhile life ahead, an optimistic vision of a society to be proud of, and the skills and the ethic needed to follow these visions."[10]

Dee Dickinson, director of New Horizons for Learning, shares her vision in these words.

> "For a long time I have dreamed of a place to learn that has it all...a place where teachers and students learn with *joy* and success. It makes use of the best teaching and learning practices, all of which are in use somewhere, but not all in one place as far as I know. My dream goes something like this: Enter a community learning center that does not resemble the old factory-model schools with their egg-crate classrooms and 9 to 3 o'clock days, broken into bell-punctuated periods. Nor is it utilized in the same ways that traditional schools were, leaving them dark in the evenings, on weekends and holidays, and for three months during the summer."[11]

Dickinson elaborates on her vision, a place that would hardly be recognized as a school if viewed by today's standards. Yet it is an exciting place—one in which many teachers would be thrilled to work and that students would be excited to attend. If you need further ideas for your own vision, read her complete description.[12]

What I find discouraging is that in 1968, George Leonard described a similar vision in his book *Education and Ecstasy*. Leonard, author of a number of books on personal growth, argues for an education whose purpose is centered on the joyful development of children.

> "We cannot guess what the distant future will ask of its schools, but perhaps we can step far enough in the future to see what our children already need. Schools for what?
>
> • To learn the commonly-agreed-upon skills and knowledge of the ongoing culture (reading, writing, figuring, history and the like), to learn it *joyfully* and to learn that all of it, even the most sacred 'fact,' is strictly tentative.
>
> • To learn how to ring creative changes on all that is currently agreed upon.

- To learn delight, not aggression; sharing, not eager acquisition; uniqueness, not narrow competition.

- To learn heightened awareness and control of emotional, sensory and bodily states and, through this, increased empathy for other people (a new kind of citizenship education)....

- To learn how to explore and enjoy the infinite possibilities in relations between people, perhaps the most common form of ecstasy.

- To learn how to learn, for learning—one word that includes singing, dancing, interacting and much more—is already becoming the main purpose of life."[13]

Notice that all three of these visionaries use the word "joy."[14] When I think of children, I think of joy. When I think of children in school, the image changes. Educator John Goodlad speaks of "...epidemic boredom in the schools, the flat, neutral emotional ambience of ...classes...."[15]

The words used in reform rhetoric are frightening—devoid of any of the joy of learning described by Einstein as "...the holy curiosity of inquiry," by Nietzsche as "...ecstasy...," and by Archimedes in the simple cry "Eureka!" Instead educators are urged to "mandate...require... intensify efforts...stress motivation...demand higher standards...more rigorous grading...lengthen...." Where, in this rhetoric, do we find any indication the future will be different, more positive, more joyful, or more human than the past?

> "The verbs used in the Kindergarten standards are significant: Identify (6 times), know, follow, explain, recognize (3), distinguish (4), track (3), blend, produce, count, match, read, understand, describe, locate, use (2), connect, retell, ask, answer, listen (2), write. This sounds like a whole lot of workbook pages to me. Where are words like *enjoy, savor, laugh, contribute, help, try out, experiment, discover?*"[16]

Leonard and a few others may have been ahead of their time, but today more and more teachers are adding their voices to the cry for a more human and less mechanistic vision of education. Join your voice to theirs. Reclaim your own vision.

Some teachers' visions have dimmed, but they are alive and well just below the surface. I once invited small groups of teachers to design an educational system for a new colony on the moon. Money was no object and they were completely in charge so they were free to do whatever they wanted. As I walked around, I was disappointed to note that this lunar educational system looked and sounded very much like the school in which we worked. When I asked a few pointed questions about the ideas, it was as if a veil had fallen from the teachers' minds. Their eyes lit up. "You mean we can *really* do anything we want?"

Once freed from the burden of conventional wisdom—of traditional education—ideas flowed like fine wine. Gone were the boxy school buildings, graded classrooms, and droning teachers. The emerging vision of these teachers was both exciting *and educationally sound*. All they needed was permission to express it.

Practical Vision

Researcher Mary Kennedy suggests that teacher planning is heavily based, not on lesson plans developed in a logical or rational way, but scenarios teachers have consciously or unconsciously envisioned.

> "Teachers may derive their visions from their ideals, but the visions themselves are not idealistic imaginings; instead, they are detailed plays with scenes, episodes, and characters all organized to lead to a particular conclusion. The plays that teachers envision are the teachers' solution to the problem of balancing...multiple and competing educational goals. The plays form a path through the thickets of ideas and ideals that fight for their attention. These plays also help them adapt to circumstances as they arise, just as mental maps can help drivers plan a detour. If drivers know their eventual destination, and know the roads in the area, they can change their route when they encounter a roadblock and still eventually reach their destination."[17]

Teachers who are conscious of the intended outcome of their plays can alter the script as they go and still reach that goal. "Teachers with a vision may strive to be more thoughtfully adaptive because they have a driving personal commitment to impart more than just what is required. In this sense, vision may take teachers beyond knowledge, instilling in them a commitment to inspire students to be something more than just academically competent."[18]Indeed, visioning may be the "missing construct" in identifying high-quality teachers.[19]

If you are not aware of the vision that drives your planning, or your vision has dimmed, I invite you to go mining for your own treasures, chipping away at encrusted layers of conventional wisdom to expose the riches of your former idealism.

Identifying Your Vision

"What every man needs, regardless of his job or the kind of work he is doing, is a vision of what his place is and may be. He needs an objective and a purpose. He needs a feeling and a belief that he has some worthwhile thing to do. What this is no one can tell him. It must be his own creation." ~Joseph M. Dodge

The first step in identifying your own personal vision is to reclaim your beliefs about the purpose of education. How would you complete the following sentence" "The purpose of education is…"? Set aside the current state of affairs in education and go for the dream. Assume the decisions are in your hands, and then ask, "What do I want to create?"

When you have identified what you believe to be the fundamental purpose(s) of education, make your ideas concrete. Create a mental picture of your ideal classroom or teaching environment.[20] Notice what the students are doing and what you are doing. What words would you use to describe this ideal classroom? Ask yourself, "If every classroom in every school were like this, would education be fulfilling its purpose?"

If the answer is no, what else would have to happen? Continue to enhance that image until you can answer "yes." Then step fully into that scene and experience it. Listen to the sounds. Feel the emotions. Imagine what it would be like to teach in that classroom each and every day. Store that multisensory image so that you can access it at any time.

Once you have your ideal classroom firmly fixed in your mind, set it aside for a moment and make a mental picture of your present classroom. Jot down a few words to describe that classroom. Pay particular attention to the ways in which your present classroom differs from your ideal classroom. What are the students doing differently? What are you doing differently?

Your present classroom represents the *functional* rather than *idealistic* beliefs and values that drive your current decision-making process. A teacher's ideal classroom is a "big picture" driven by fundamental beliefs and values about the overall purpose of education. That same teacher's present classroom is part of the "real world" of education filled with external mandates and pressures, deadlines, curriculum standards, "unmotivated" students, and numerous other frustrations. Permitting external forces to control their choices without questioning their validity, teachers will find it difficult to move toward their ideal visions.

Those externals are unlikely to change on their own. The inertia[21] of education is too great. One way to implement change in so large and disorganized a system is to institute small changes from within—changes that will eventually stress the system to the point where it shifts to relieve the pressure.[22] Remember that the stronger and more compelling your personal vision, the more enthusiastic you will become. The vision will make you more courageous and willing to take risks, and you will become more committed to seeing that vision realized.

The time has come to behave proactively rather than reactively—to move the system toward a vision of what education can be. Rather than treading water in the river of reform, you are, like the salmon, actively swimming upstream to where your vision will be born.

Identifying the Conflicts

> **"I have always thought the actions of men**
> **the best interpreters of their thoughts."**
> **~John Locke**

The next step in moving toward your personal vision is analyzing how, specifically, your present classroom differs from your ideal classroom. Make a table like the one shown on the next page with more room to write. Row headings represent categories of experiences during a typical day—how you deal with various aspects of teaching.

For the "ideal" column, access the image of your ideal classroom and jot down some behaviors in which you might engage for each of the row headings. Remember—*don't think about the way things "really" are, but how you want them to be*. With your larger view of the purpose of education in mind, how would you deal with discipline, how would you select content, what methodologies might you use, how would you assess learning, and how would you interact with students? What is the role of the teacher in this classroom? Add any other categories that seem important. In an ideal classroom, you may find there are multiple behaviors you would use, depending on the specific situation. For now, you need list only one or two in each category.

Categories	Ideal classroom behaviors	Present classroom behaviors
Discipline/control		
Choosing curriculum		
Teaching methods		
Assessment of learning		
Interaction with students		
Role of the teacher		

For the "ideal" column, access the image of your ideal classroom and jot down some behaviors in which you might engage for each of the row headings. Remember—*don't think about the way things "really" are, but how you want them to be.* With your larger view of the purpose of education in mind, how would you deal with discipline, how would you select content, what methodologies might you use, how would you assess learning, and how would you interact with students? What is the role of the teacher in this classroom? Add any other categories that seem important. In an ideal classroom, you may find there are multiple behaviors you would use, depending on the specific situation. For now, you need list only one or two in each category.

After you've described your "ideal classroom," repeat the same process for your present classroom. It is helpful to "step into" specific situations. Pay attention to what is happening and what you are thinking.

The differences between the behaviors teachers envision themselves using in their ideal classroom and the behaviors they actually use in their present classroom represent the areas in which they may hold conflicted beliefs or values. To understand specifically how those changes happen, you must uncover the beliefs underlying those behaviors. Here's one way to do that.

Look at one of the behaviors you have listed in the *ideal* classroom column, such as *teaching methods used*. Complete the statement, *I engage in this behavior because....*

In Maria's ideal classroom, students work on the same general topic, but Maria allows them to use different approaches and begin with some aspect of the topic that interests them. Maria might say, "I engage in this behavior because *students begin with different experiences and have different styles of learning.*" This is a statement of a belief associated with Maria's ideal classroom.

Some of the presuppositions embedded in this belief include:

• Learning is facilitated by allowing students to learn in different ways.

• Learning is facilitated by allowing students to relate a topic to their own experiences or interests.

• Teaching is about facilitating learning.

Consider the last presupposition. It sounds like common sense but is far from universally accepted. Remember the teachers in the Yerrick study described in Chapter 8? Their presupposition was that teaching is about transmitting knowledge. There was only surface concern with learning, limited to students' abilities to retransmit acquired knowledge on the test.

What belief drives your present behavior? Look at the corresponding *teaching methods used* in your present classroom and once again, complete the sentence, *I engage in this behavior because....*

In Maria's present classroom, she is lecturing to the students about a concept. Maria might say, "I engage in this behavior because *I have to be sure we have covered all the concepts that will be on the test.*"

By completing the sentence in that way, Maria is identifying the beliefs or values that motivate her present behavior. Some of the more critical presuppositions in this statement include:

• The concepts that have been designated for testing are the most appropriate ones for all students in the class.

• Covering material means students have learned that material.

• Lecturing is the most effective way for students to learn the designated concepts.

• Teaching is about transmitting specific concepts to students.

For the belief to be true in all contexts, all of the presuppositions of that statement must also be true. Does Maria believe each of the presuppositions listed above is true? Her statement about her ideal classroom would suggest otherwise. So why does she continue to behave as if they are true?

Notice that Maria's reason for her behavior in the ideal classroom focuses on what is best for the *student*. Is that also true in the present classroom? If Maria truly believed "covering designated concepts so that those concepts can be tested" is in the best interest of students, then yes, she would still be focused on students. In many cases, however, teachers' reasons for their present behaviors focus on some belief or value related to self.

Teachers may have conflicted values in terms of keeping their jobs or good reputations versus doing what they believe is in the best interest of students. If Maria is truly convinced her job or reputation would be in jeopardy if her students don't perform adequately on tests, that value is likely to motivate her behavior.

Maria's concern for her own survival in the academic world is completely natural. Survival is one of the primary needs of any organism. *The sad thing about the present state of education is that teachers feel pressured to choose between their own survival and the well-being of their students.* That is unforgivable!

Many teachers reach the point where they are no longer willing to make that choice. Unfortunately, rather than speaking out, they choose to leave the field of education. If they believe that speaking out will cost them their jobs, what's the difference? They would have at least had the satisfaction of speaking out on behalf of their students before leaving. Who knows? Their actions might well give other teachers the courage to speak out as well. Teachers often feel as if they're alone in their feelings. Realizing others feel the same way may be all it takes.

Analyzing Your Own Vision

"The time to release ourselves from simplistic and ineffective prescriptions has passed; the time to dream is upon us." ~Carl Glickman[23]

The discussion in the previous section was based on one possible difference between Maria's ideal classroom and her present classroom.

Now it's your turn to discover what lies at the heart of any differences between your ideal classroom and your present one.

1. Select one behavior from the *ideal classroom* column on your table. Step into your mental representation of that classroom and complete the sentence, *I engage in this behavior because….* Whatever follows "because" will identify the belief or value itself or can be used to identify them.

2. Repeat step 1 using the corresponding behavior from the *present classroom* column. Step into your mental representation of the present classroom and complete the same sentence: *I engage in this behavior because….* You now have the beliefs/values that motivate your ideal and present behaviors. Explore them in the following ways:

- Notice if the belief or value focuses on the needs of the students or your own needs.

- List the presuppositions of each belief.

- To what extent does research or experience support these presuppositions? Remember that, for the belief to be valid in all contexts, all of the presuppositions must be true.

3. Repeat steps 1 through 3 for several other pairs of behaviors from the table. After only a couple of such comparisons, a pattern may develop. This pattern can give you a sense of the conventional wisdom driving your present behavior.

Here is another way to explore the differences in your behavior in your ideal and real classrooms.

A. Select one of the statements from your ideal classroom list

B. list three specific things you have done in the classroom that are consistent with this statement.

C. List three specific things you have done in the classroom that are inconsistent with this statement.

D. Analyze the factors that caused you to act in a manner that was inconsistent with your stated belief.

Here's an example.

A. Interaction with students: I will model kindness and respect.

B. Consistent behaviors:

- I listened carefully to Suzie when she told me about her home life.

- I answered Juan's question even when I wanted to get on with the lesson.
- I explained why I reprimanded Sarah so that she would learn from the experience.

C. Inconsistent behaviors:
- I had to yell at the kids to get their attention.
- I had to set down rules that probably didn't seem kind to the student.
- I ignored a question that seemed irrelevant.

D. Analysis: If I act like this sweet, kind teacher all the time, the kids walk all over me and don't pay attention. I have to holler at them to get them back inline. I can't teach unless I have their attention.

What presuppositions are included in these reasons?
- There are only two ways to behave—kind and unkind.
- Hollering at students is unkind.
- Hollering at students is the only way to get their attention.
- Hollering at students is not respectful.
- Students will not respond to kindness. (Note that this counters the original presupposition that modeling kindness and respect will have a positive effect on students.)

In many cases, self-reflection requires us to reexamine our beliefs and presuppositions about seemingly "common sense" factors. But only by doing so can we really understand the complex factors that drive our behavior.

One last exercise: Where, in the space around you, do you represent the future? As you think about next week, next month, next year, in which direction are your eyes looking? Wherever your future is in space, imagine there's a line running from your present location into that future. Put your vision of the ideal classroom out on that line—a year or two in the future. Now, move out along that line and into that classroom. Access all of the positive feelings associated with that scene. When you have made it as juicy and compelling as possible, turn around and look back at the present. Think about what steps—what actions—you will have to take to get from the present to this future. What, specifically, can you do to move closer to the realization of your ideal?

Return to the present, remembering that you can go back to visit that ideal classroom and renew your vision at any time. As long as that vision remains in your future, you will be drawn toward it.

What Can I Do?

"Each of us is—potentially—the difference in the world." ~Marilyn Ferguson

It requires tremendous effort to overcome the inertia of conventional wisdom. Many teachers who exerted that effort early in their teaching careers have grown tired of fighting. Having experienced that feeling, I can only suggest that, when your vision is sufficiently compelling, to do otherwise is unthinkable. I hope that as you confront the damage traditional education does to students because of the beliefs of conventional wisdom, you'll be re-energized in the name of the next generation and the future.

It's easy to explain away failure to act according to one's highest ideals by blaming it on something external. "I have to prepare my kids for the mandated tests." "My principal won't let me do that." "The kids aren't motivated." "I don't even have my own classroom." Some of those external factors will certainly make your efforts more difficult. Too often though, teachers have fallen into the habit of blaming outside influences for their inaction because they were simply too tired or not sufficiently motivated to stand up to those influences.

Educator Carl Glickman, who has lived through the painful process of school empowerment, advocates a realistic view. He points out that, in their enthusiasm, teachers often

> "…jump on the…bandwagon without assessing their own readiness to take on the pain and to confront the conflicts involved—and without realizing the extraordinary courage necessary to sustain such change."[24]

Glickman lists several factors teachers should be aware of as they undertake pervasive change. His original list applies to schools. I have extrapolated his points to what individual teacher may encounter.

- The more [a teacher] improves, the more apparent it is that there's more to be improved. In one study of effective schools, Wilbur Brookover found that teachers in a school that was moving toward greater success were *more* dissatisfied with their teaching than those in schools that were less successful.

- The more [a teacher] is recognized for [his or her] success, the more criticism that teacher receives. A successful teacher often gains attention and subsequently, comes under siege. Some other teachers feel the need to criticize because they interpret the success of another teacher as an implicit criticism of their own teaching.

- The more successful [a teacher] becomes, the less easily others can emulate that success. By now, the reason should be clear. The teacher's success is a synergistic phenomenon that depends on that teacher's personal beliefs, metaphors, and values, the teacher's students, and the school environment. Each teacher must find that unique synergy within his or her own mind and heart, working within the available environment.

There is one more situation that can arise when teachers recognize and acknowledge the transformative power they wield. The more teachers realize what they are capable of achieving, the more hesitant they may be to act.[25] People value "doing the right thing." As long as they perceive themselves as powerless—as long as they can transfer the responsibility for their behavior to "the administration" or "school policy"—they need not feel guilty about their actions or lack thereof.

This is hardly unique to teachers. In *The Devil's Dictionary*, Ambrose Bierce defines *responsibility* as follows: "Responsibility, n. A detachable burden easily shifted to the shoulders of God, Fate, Fortune, Luck, or one's neighbor. In the days of astrology it was customary to unload it upon a star."

Regardless of any outside factors that appear to control what goes on in the classroom, each individual teacher *is* responsible for the *implicit* curriculum emerging from who they are as human beings. I can think of no legitimate argument for failing to reflect on what students are learning from that hidden curriculum.

Not all educators are prepared to face the resistance of the establishment—to lead the way in the journey toward meaningful reform. Every educator can, however, embark on the journey. In fact, the most pervasive changes are likely to occur through actions of individual teachers in individual classrooms.

Keep in mind that the only way you can change what goes on outside of you is to change yourself. The courage to speak out about educational issues, to take the risk of trying something new, to make the commitment to face and conquer whatever annoyances are thrown in your way—all are the result of a sufficiently compelling vision. That vision must make it all worthwhile. If you have become even somewhat disenchanted with teaching because you have lost that vision, there's no better time to reclaim it.

---

1 Senge, P. M. (1990). *The Fifth Discipline: The Art and Practice of the Learning Organization.* New York: Doubleday, 206.

2 Gatto, J. (1990, September/October). Our Children Are Dying in our Schools. *New Age Journal*, 63.

3 http://www.homeschool-living.com/homeschooling-statistics.html. August 12, 2010

4 Aviolo, B. J. (1994). The Alliance of Total Quality and the Full Range of Leadership. In B. M. Bass, B. M. & B. J. Aviolo, (Eds.). *Improving Organizational Effectiveness Through Transformational Leadership* (pp. 121–145). Thousand Oaks, CA: Sage.

5 Glickman, C. D. (1990, September) Pushing School Reform to a New Edge: The Seven Ironies of School Empowerment. *Phi Delta Kappan*, 68–75.

6 Ponder, G.A. & Holmes, K. M. (1992). Purpose, Product, and Visions: The Creation of New Schools. *The Educational Forum, Vol. 56, No. 4*, 405–418.

7 Papert, S. (1999). From The Caperton-Papert Platform by Gaston Caperton and Seymour Papert, available at URL: http://www.papert.org/works.html

8 Ibid.

9 Ibid.

10 Ibid.

11 Dickenson, D. (2000). A New Place to Learn, URL: http://www.newhorizons.org/obsdeck_dickinson25htm.htm

12 Ibid.

13 Leonard, G. (1968, 1987) *Education and Ecstasy*, Berkeley, CA: North Atlantic Books, 132–133.

14 Please do not assume that "joy" means "fun." Joy is a much more complex state that can arise in many ways. Many people experience joy upon completing an especially difficult, but worthwhile, task or upon achieving understanding of a difficult concept.

15 Ibid., 255.

16 Ohanion, Susan. (1999). *One Size Fits Few: The Folly of Educational Standards*. Portsmouth, N. H.: Heinemann, 76.

17 Kennedy, Mary M. "Knowledge and vision in teaching." *Journal of Teacher Education* 57.3 (2006): 205+. General OneFile. Web. 19 Aug. 2010.

18Fairbanks, Colleen M., et al. "Beyond knowledge: exploring why some teachers are more thoughtfully adaptive than others." *Journal of Teacher Education* 61.1-2 (2010): 161+. *General OneFile*. Web. 9 June 2010.

19Shulman, L. (2004). Professional development: Leaning from experience. In S. Wilson (Ed.), *The wisdom of practice: Essays on teaching, learning, and learning to teach* (pp. 503-522). San Francisco: Jossey-Bass.

20 For the sake of simplicity, I will subsequently refer to this ideal teaching environment as the ideal classroom although it may take a very different form in your personal image.

21 Many people think inertia refers to an object being resistant to movement. This is true, but it also refers to the tendency of an object to remain moving in the direction in which it is already moving. That's the case with education. The larger the object (or system in this case), the greater the inertia.

22 Chemist Ilya Prigogine won a Nobel Prize for his work demonstrating that when a remarkably small percentage of a chemical system exerts a stress on that system, the system shifts to relieve the stress. In a chemical system, it may take only 5 percent to precipitate that shift. Prigogine and others have applied the same principle to social systems. Although the percentage may be somewhat higher, relatively small numbers of people can put enough pressure on large systems to precipitate just as rapid a shift—case in point, the fall of communism or the results of the New Hampshire primary on a presidential race. What would happen if only 5 to 10 percent of all teachers began teaching to their personal visions?

23 Glickman, C. D. (1990). Pushing School Reform to a New Edge: The Seven Ironies of School Empowerment, (1990, September). *Phi Delta Kappan*, 68–75.

24 Ibid., 68–76.

25 Ibid., 72.

Chapter 10 ~ Beliefs about Education, Knowledge, and Understanding

"Every man takes the limits of his own field of vision for the limits of the world." ~ Arthur Schopenhauer

The next several chapters will focus on various beliefs about education, knowledge, understanding, and teaching. Keep in mind that we are asking the question, "What are *some alternative beliefs* that teachers might hold?" rather than "What *should* teachers believe?"

To borrow a metaphor from Thom Hartmann, choosing to perceive the world from a single perspective is like watching a single TV show on a set that can be tuned to five hundred different channels. People throw away the remote, disable the tuning mechanism on the set, and then insist the program they are watching is the only one that exists!

When they discuss the show with others, arguments arise about what happened and why. People fail to realize their TVs are tuned to different channels! In life, those channels are the perspectives people have on a given issue. Regardless of how "good" that show is, why would anyone choose to limit their viewing to a single channel when so much more is available to them—simply by tuning in to a different channel?

Beliefs about...the Purpose of Education

"The central task of education is to implant a will and facility for learning; it should produce not learned but learning people. The truly human society is a learning society, where grandparents, parents, and children are students together." ~Eric Hoffer

"No one has yet realized the wealth of sympathy, the kindness and generosity hidden in the soul of a child. The effort of every true education should be to unlock that treasure." ~Emma Goldman

"The central job of schools is to maximize the capacity of each student." ~Carol Ann Tomlinson

"The only purpose of education is to teach a student how to live his life-by developing his mind and equipping him to deal with reality. The training he needs is theoretical, i.e., conceptual. He has to be taught to think, to understand, to integrate, to prove. He has to be taught the essentials of the knowledge discovered in the past-and he has to be equipped to acquire further knowledge by his own effort." ~Ayn Rand

"The aim of education should be to teach us rather how to think, than what to think—rather to improve our minds, so as to enable us to think for ourselves, than to load the memory with the thoughts of other men." ~Bill Beattie

"The one real object of education is to leave a man in the condition of continually asking questions." ~Bishop Creighton

These quotations demonstrate the diversity of beliefs about the purpose of education. In creating your ideal classroom, how did you describe the purpose of education?

Some theorists make a distinction between the *purpose* of education and the *functions* of education.[1] A *purpose* is the fundamental goal of the process—an end to be achieved. *Functions* are other outcomes that may occur as a natural result of the process—by-products or consequences of schooling. For example, some teachers believe that the transmission of knowledge is the primary *purpose* of education, while the transfer of knowledge from school to the real world happens naturally as a consequence of possessing that knowledge—a *function* of education.

Because a *purpose* is an expressed goal, more effort is put into attaining it. *Functions* are assumed to occur without directed effort. For this reason, it's valuable to figure out which outcomes you consider a fundamental *purpose of education* or simply a *function of education*.

In your opinion, is each of the following outcomes something that *must be included* in planning educational experiences (a purpose, *P*) or something that will occur without much or any effort on the teacher's part (a function, *F*)? Jot down your response next to each item. Each choice refers to an outcome for students.

Acquisition of information about the past and present: includes traditional disciplines, such as literature, history, science, etc.	Formation of healthy social and/or formal relationships among and between students, teachers, others
Capacity/ability to evaluate information and to predict future outcomes (decision-making)	Capacity/ability to seek out alternative solutions and evaluate them (problem solving)
Development of mental and physical skills: motor, thinking, communication, social, aesthetic	Knowledge of moral practices and ethical standards acceptable by society/ culture
Capacity/ability to recognize and evaluate different points of view	Respect: giving and receiving recognition as human beings
Indoctrination into the culture	Capacity/ability to think creatively
Capacity/ability to earn a living: career education	Sense of well-being: mental and physical health
Capacity/ability to be a good citizen	Capacity/ability to live a fulfilling life
Cultural appreciation: art, music, humanities	Understanding of human relations and motivations
Acquisition/clarification of values related to the physical environment	Self-realization/self-reflection: awareness of one's abilities and goals
Acquisition/clarification of personal values	Self-esteem/self-efficacy

The list is far from complete. Some categories may overlap, some may seem too specific, and some too general. You may wish to add others. Use them as an aid to help identify what *you* see as the fundamental purposes of education. Your choices reflect the value you place on each outcome and therefore, the amount of time you are likely to spend in an effort to attain it.

It's also worthwhile to prioritize the outcomes that you identified as purposes. Which outcome is, in your opinion, the *most* important? Which is *least* important? What specific behaviors do you currently use to "teach" or promote the development of each of the outcomes? Which "purposes" do you formally assess in some way?

Tom Peters quotes an old business "truism" that "What gets measured gets done." How might the failure to include some assessment of a "purpose" influence the time and effort a teacher makes on that outcome—particularly in today's atmosphere of high-stakes testing?

Teachers often identify the *capacity/ability to think creatively* as one of the most important purposes of education. To *create* is to bring about—to cause to be. Many constructivist educators suggest that *all* knowledge is created internally—that it cannot be transmitted from one person to another because experiences of the "receiver" are different from experiences of the "transmitter." How, for example, does a teacher *transmit* the effects of President Kennedy's "Ask not" speech on the public to students who didn't live at that time?

The teachers in Yerrick's study described in Chapter 8might well agree that *the capacity to think creatively* should be developed. However, if their statements reflect what actually goes on in their schools, there is little or no conscious effort made to enable or encourage such a capacity. In fact, the teachers' unwillingness to stray from the curriculum effectively prohibits creative thinking.

Educational rhetoric often focuses on "critical thinking skills" Current textbooks even label questions to indicate the "skill" that they address, such as *apply, identify, summarize, analyze.* But are teachers actively encouraging these behaviors? For example, how can students *recognize and evaluate different points of view* (typically listed as a valuable "critical thinking skill") if they are consistently presented with and tested in large measure only on "correct" answers?

If critical thinking skills are important, then *the capacity/ability to evaluate information and to predict future outcomes (decision-making)* would receive high marks as a *purpose* of education. Indeed, many teachers painstakingly "teach" the *steps* of decision-making—identifying alternatives, evaluating alternatives, and so on. Tests insure that students have memorized those steps. Yet, how often are students permitted to *make* any important decisions about their own learning?

What specific classroom experiences do you use that honestly support (or even permit) the purposes you identified? To what extent are students given the opportunity to *do* what educators claim to want them to do in anything other than contrived and prescribed settings?

How does your ideal classroom reflect the purposes you identified on this list? Would a student in that classroom achieve your selected outcomes? This is where your willingness to explore your own thinking must come into play. The goal here is to clarify your own thinking.

Historical Perspective

Disagreement about the purpose of education is not new. Similar issues were argued in the fifth century B.C. between the followers of Socrates and the Sophists. The Sophists were itinerant teachers from outside of Greece who recruited students and taught them for a fee. Their *purpose* was to provide the necessary knowledge and skills to obtain positions within the democratic city-state.[2]

Socrates saw education as a quest for wisdom. He believed that learning consists of being reminded of what is preexisting in the brain, a view supported by contemporary neuroscience.[3] The word *education* itself comes from the Latin word *educere* meaning "to lead out." This seems more consistent with Socrates' view than with today's practice of "stuffing in" as much information as possible.

In the Sophist view, the teacher is an autonomous dispenser of facts, rules, and beliefs. Instruction is highly structured and sequenced. The goal is for students to demonstrate their knowledge in some way. This type of education is

> "performance driven and teacher directed. Discussion is limited because it detracts from learning time...cognitive processes and cultural or linguistic characteristics of the individual learner [are] irrelevant. The transfer of learning to real-life situations is not a primary goal.... [This view] of education [maximizes] the infusion of the *what* into students."[4]

For Socrates, education focused on the development of the mind of the student rather than the dissemination of information. Learning begins with a student's point of reference rather than with some arbitrarily chosen body of information. The learner gathers more information through all of the senses. Some information fits within his present map of the world, while other information seems to conflict. At that point, the student must adjust his inner reality to fit the new information. This is what Piaget called "accommodation."

The teacher's role in this process is one of facilitation rather than dissemination. The teacher asks questions, encourages reflection, and points out meaningful connections. The student must actually *do* the learning, *using* higher order thinking skills. Transfer of these skills is less of an issue because they are already being used to address real problems. Teacher and student are "...engaged in an interactive dance of facilitation and negotiation of learning."[5] Rather than infusing the *what*, this form of education focuses on drawing out the *why* and *how*.

The Sophist/Socrates debate continues to the present day, centering on differing perceptions about what makes an educated person. E. D. Hirsch, Jr., has provided a long list of cultural references students must "know" to achieve cultural literacy. Neil Postman argues that, although it may not have been Hirsch's intent, these lists appeal to our "sound-bite" culture. The temptation is to make the lists themselves the curriculum.[6] Benchmarks that accompany standards often consist of similar lists—bits of meat picked from the rich stew of human thought.

Others in this dichotomous battle argue on the side of Socrates. They believe an educated person is one who knows how to learn and is eager to do so. They hold that the possession of a huge body of information is of little value unless one *uses* that information in some productive way. An educated person understands the *why* and *how* as well as the *what*. In this view, learning is a consequence of thinking, not simply of instruction.[7] It focuses on processes within the student rather than information external to the student.

Whether or not you have thought consciously about what you believe, your judgments are based on some similar underlying belief system. Would you align yourself more with the Sophists or Socrates? Are you interested in possibilities that lie between these two extremes?

Beliefs about...the Nature of Knowledge

"We live on an island surrounded by a sea of ignorance. As our island of knowledge grows, so does the shore of our ignorance."
~John Archibald Wheeler

The word *knowledge* is central to education. Although many assume its meaning is part of consensus reality, it is not. Once again we must question what curriculum designers, teachers, parents, or students really *mean* when they use the word *knowledge*. Beliefs about the nature of knowledge—about what it is, where it comes from, and how people acquire it—abound. Those beliefs are fundamental to the way education works. It is essential, therefore, to examine the alternatives.

Recent research has focused on how beliefs about the source of knowledge varied among both teachers and learners. They ranged from the belief that knowledge originates and is conveyed by authority figures, to beliefs that knowledge is actively constructed by individual learners. Similarly, beliefs about the stability and certainty of knowledge ranged from fixed and immutable to flexible and evolving. When these beliefs were correlated to behaviors, researchers found that beliefs about the complexity of knowledge were directly related to the openness of the teacher to new ideas.[8]

John Dewey[9] suggested the word *knowledge* has several meanings. First, it is the result of some individual's process of inquiry. Assuming the inquiry has been competent and sufficient, the conclusion—the knowledge—is trustworthy.

A second meaning of *knowledge*—one that typically supersedes the first—arises when a significant number of individual inquiries result in the same conclusion. This conclusion is accepted as more significant—more "true" than the inquiry of a single person. This *Knowledge* (with a capital K) takes on a life of its own outside of the individual processes of inquiry that generated it. It is a small step to perceiving this *Knowledge* as *true* in some absolute way—apart from the minds that conceived it. The cognitive processes that created the Knowledge are ignored. Rather than viewing Knowledge as the sum of inquiry plus the products of that inquiry—the products become answers devoid of questions and removed from the contexts in which they were developed. They become "objective truth."

Objectivist Beliefs about Knowledge

It is this "objective" truth that many educators believe they must *transmit* to students. As previously mentioned, *objective* literally means "apart from the human mind." Newton's Laws of Motion and other "laws" of nature, Euclidean Geometry, the rules of grammar, and other items listed in the content standards identified by many states, are *Knowledge* in this sense. They are taught with little concern for where they came from and why. What effect does this deliberate separation of product from process have on teaching?

In *The Courage to Teach*, educator Parker Palmer identifies four elements of what he calls the "objectivist myth of knowing":

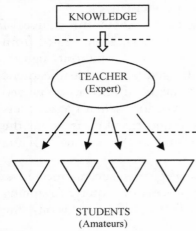

"*Objects* of knowledge...reside 'out there' somewhere, pristine in physical or conceptual space, as described by the 'facts' in a given field."

"*Experts* [teachers] are people trained to know these objects in their pristine form without allowing their own subjectivity to slop over onto the purity of the objects themselves."

Amateurs [students] are those who do not presently possess these objects. They must depend on experts for objective or pure knowledge of the pristine objects.

Baffles allow objective knowledge to flow downstream while preventing the subjectivity of the amateurs to flow back up—possibly contaminating the intellectual purity of the objects.[10]

Notice the metaphors contained within this view. Bits of *Knowledge* are categorized as *objects*. Not only are they objects, but like rare antiques, they must be protected against change of any kind lest their value diminish. These objects are *possessed* by some but not by others. In order for a person to come into possession of an object, someone (the experts) must *give* it to them. In the school context, the experts decide which of these Knowledge objects the amateurs should possess. They then dispense the chosen objects *whether or not the amateur wants them.*

The *baffles* in Palmer's model represent the efforts of objectivists to keep the knowledge free from subjectivity. Students are not allowed to probe knowledge for weaknesses lest they somehow damage it. They are rarely permitted to engage in the same process of inquiry that yielded the knowledge. When this is permitted, as for example, in a science "experiment," the expert carefully guides the amateurs so that they follow closely in the steps of the master. "Visitor must stay on the path."

Objectivist educators consciously or unconsciously accept the definition of objective as "apart from the human mind." There are those who reject the argument that the categories by which we conceptualize the world and our experience are products of the mind. For them, the categories actually exist in nature, waiting for the perfect human mind to discover them. Objectivists work toward developing the perfect mind that will abstract the true essence of nature as it exists "out there."

Many teachers have been caught up in the objectivist myth. They have for so long experienced *Knowledge* as something *given* to them by their teachers that they assume they must now *give* to their students in the same way. The adherence of those teachers to the objectivist myth is *mindless* in the sense that it is unexamined. According to Palmer,

> "In the objectivist myth, truth flows from the top down, from experts who are qualified to know truth…to amateurs who are qualified only to receive truth. In this myth, truth is a set of propositions about objects; education is a system for delivering those propositions to students; and an educated person is one who can remember and repeat the experts' propositions. The image is hierarchical, linear, and compulsive-hygienic, as if truth came down an antiseptic conveyor belt to be deposited as pure product at the end.

> "There are only two problems with this myth: it falsely portrays how we know, and it has profoundly deformed the way we educate."[11]

Palmer points out that, although many classrooms maintain this image of teacher, students, and subject as separate entities, "…I know of no field—from astronomy to literature to political science to theology—where the continuing quest to know truth even vaguely resembles this mythical objectivism."

Mind as a Container

Thinking about *knowledge as objects* is a useful metaphor. Objects take many forms and have many uses. A car is an object that carries us from one place to another. An idea can do the same thing. A screwdriver is an object that we can use as a tool. So is an algebraic equation. A map helps us find our way through unfamiliar terrain. So does an historical timeline. However, in these examples, people *use* the objects in some way, in addition to possessing them.

Problems arise when we couple the *knowledge as objects* metaphor with a *mind as container* metaphor. To "know" means the knowledge objects must be "in" that container. It is as if the mind is a filing cabinet.

Knowledge objects (facts) are documents contained in files (concepts). Addition is on one sheet of paper, subtraction on another. Both documents go into the file labeled "mathematical operations" which, in turn, is part of a larger file labeled "Mathematics."

Under the influence of these metaphors, being educated means having your file cabinet filled and well organized. Let's examine some other implications of this metaphor.

1. How does the container get filled? One teacher put into simple words what many others demonstrate by their actions in the classroom.

> "If I'm teaching facts and the things that the ITBS [Iowa
> Tests of Basic Skills] teaches, then I can open her up and pour
> it in—just open their little heads and pour it in."[12]

One of my education professors had this method down pat. He wasn't about to waste anyone's time pretending to teach us anything. He simply dictated the twenty questions that would be on the final exam along with the answers he expected to see. Our job was to memorize what he had dictated. After many hours of "study" (memorizing), the particular file he was determined to fill was stuffed to overflowing. The *test* was to successfully retrieve the proper pieces of paper when prompted by the test questions.

The label on that folder is now faded, but I can make out the words *history* and *education*. I have had no occasion to look in the folder since it was created. I have, however, managed to move that folder to a larger folder called "Ridiculous teaching practices."

2. What happens after the chosen "knowledge objects" are in the file cabinet? Of course, there is the assumption that they will be retrieved and reproduced when test day arrives. But then what? Educators are quick to point out that having those knowledge objects will allow students to access them whenever they need them. How does a student know when it's appropriate to retrieve a particular knowledge object within a file?

I once worked with a high school student who correctly solved all of her homework and class math problems but did very poorly on her tests. She couldn't understand why. Her internal representations were, in fact, similar to the documents in the file cabinet. In her "mind's eye," she actually saw separate pages lined up next to one another, representing the problems that the class did on Monday, Tuesday, Wednesday, and

Thursday. Each day's page contained a different type of problem along with its appropriate solutions. She clearly saw what was on those pages and "understood" the problems. Yet when the test came on Friday, she was totally confused!

It turned out that the tests were a mix of the different types of problems done during the week. What this student *didn't* know—what the teacher had never taken the time to explain—was *how to decide when to use each approach.* What is it about the *problem* that tells a person which solution to use? For many teachers, that is such an innate part of their personal understanding of their subject they never even think about it. They rarely think to "teach" or model it. The student *possessed* all the knowledge objects but didn't have a clue when or where to use them.

This is what happens when the ability to *use* the possessed objects is seen as a *function* rather than a *purpose* of education. "Transfer" of knowledge is something many teachers assume happens naturally. In the *mind as container* metaphor, transfer is what happens when a paper from one file is moved to another file—internal transfer from one situation to another. For instance, the paper on "electricity" in the file on "Energy" in a larger file entitled "Physics" in the subject file entitled "Science" is somehow moved to the file entitled "Lightning during a rainstorm."

Studies have repeatedly demonstrated that this type of transfer rarely occurs.[13] If the mind is like a file cabinet, apparently most of the knowledge objects students collect in school are located in a file drawer labeled "School." "Lightning during a rainstorm" is an experience-based knowledge object stored in another drawer called "Real Life." Ne'er the twain shall meet! Where is the experience that would allow a student to connect them?

In one study, students were given video cameras and asked to film things that were part of their lives. When asked why he had taken no pictures of his school or classes, one young man replied, "I thought you said you wanted this to be about my life. School isn't about my life."

"The mind-as-container metaphor is handy for talking about the acquisition of knowledge, but not for talking about what the knowledge is good for once it is in the container. A perennial concern is what Alfred North Whitehead called 'inert knowledge.' This is knowledge that just sits in the container until its name is called and does not participate actively in the

185

conduct of life. But what else could we expect of immaterial lumps of mental content?"[14]

Mind as Container plus Processor

People have many uses for the objects that surround them. With the exception of food objects, one thing that they rarely do is to put those objects inside of themselves. Yet with knowledge objects, this seems to be the primary goal. This may occur because people believe the mind—the container—also contains a machine that *processes* information. The mind processes the raw facts similarly to the way a food processor chopping or slicing carrots and onions.

Processing proceeds according to a set of rules (blades or disks). Teaching in this metaphor consists not only of giving students the raw information, but also helping students to acquire more blades or disks for the machine—more and better rules of thinking. With this model, we have explanations for reasoning, logic, drawing conclusions, higher-order thinking skills, and even behavior. However, it still doesn't help us to explain creativity, insight, or how understanding occurs. There is also a question of whether a person will use the rules that are "given." Just because someone gives you a food processor with every conceivable blade and disk, there is no guarantee you will use it in preparing meals.

Mind as Modifiable Information Processor

Is it possible for the mind to process knowledge objects in some way without storing them? This idea feels foreign because many people *feel* they have information stored inside their heads. When they explain their behaviors, their explanations are based on rules they assume are also stored within their heads—their minds. Why did I take an umbrella when I left the house this morning? Because dark clouds often produce rain. I assume that this cause-and-effect rule stored in my mind is what drives my behavior.

Computers have hard drives to store information after it is processed. In a way, we can think of this as "learning" because what is "in" the computer changes. However, a computer can also process information without storing it. It can simply output the results of its processing onto a screen or, using a printer, onto paper. Unless you "save" the work, when the computer is shut down, those results disappear. The next time the computer is turned on, it performs in exactly the same way it did originally. It doesn't "learn" in the sense of permanently changing its behavior, nor does it have access to previous output.

It's popular to think of the brain as a complex computer. We imagine that, once information has been processed, it is "stored" in memory (the container), just as it is stored in the computer's memory (hard drive). There is, however, a significant difference between computers and brains. Neurons, unlike inanimate computer chips, are living cells. As information flows between and among neurons during processing, *the neurons themselves and the connections between them are modified. The neurons change their "behavior" in response to the environment. They "learn."*

It's not necessary to have a container to store the output. Because the processor itself has changed, it will produce different output the next time it is "turned on."

> "…There is no concept, no fact in education, more directly important than this: the brain is, by nature's design, an amazingly subtle and sensitive pattern-detecting apparatus.
>
> "The brain detects, constructs, and elaborates patterns as a basic, built-in, natural function. It does not have to be taught or motivated to do so, any more than the heart needs to be instructed or coaxed to pump blood."[15]

The brains of infants perceive patterns among objects in their environment, such as faces, objects hanging above their heads in the crib, or their own fingers. Even before knowing the words with which they will later describe these categories, the child recognizes that objects with four legs are in a different category than objects with two legs. Touching four-legged objects feels different than touching Mommy or Daddy. Keep in mind these categories—patterns—are present prior to any ability to verbalize them. *There is no "rule" to which the child can refer for these categories.*

One day, Mommy points to a four-legged object and says, "Dog." A connection forms among neurons that respond to the sound of this word and other neurons that take part in the recognition of four-legged objects. Eventually, when the child encounters a four-legged object, she points and says, "Dog." Mommy shakes her head and says, "Cat."

Oops! What happens next is that the circuits associated with the perception of four-legged objects becomes tuned—changed—so that the pattern perceived by the child becomes more discriminating. The "error"—actually feedback from the child's environment—modifies the pattern recognition processes. *The brain itself changes.* It may take several trials where an adult corrects the child's pattern recognition before there are sufficient changes to assure accurate identification and naming of "dog" or "cat." The point is that *it is not necessary to store knowledge* about the difference between a dog and a cat. That difference is detected on the fly by the tuned pattern recognition circuits.

How do you tell the difference between a dog and a cat? Psychologists have a number of theories about how we recognize such categories. The *mind as food processor* metaphor would have us believe that there is a "rule" of some kind for each category—some blade or disk that allows us to process incoming perceptions and properly categorize them. Look at the following objects and tell me what *rule* allows you to categorize them.

ɑ Ａ ℛ 𝒜 ɑ Ａ ? 𝐀 ɑ Ａ ɑ 𝒜 ä Ａ ɑ 𝐀 ɑ Ａ ä ä Ａ ä Ａ ä Ａ ä

Some of these figures contain straight lines and others curved lines. All contain at least one enclosed area but so does a *d* or a *p*. Some sit on the line and some fall below it. Of course, one of the things that makes it easier to recognize these is the context in which we find the letters. How do contexts fit into rules for recognition?

Isn't it just as easy to think that the neurons in your brain have, over time, refined their pattern detection capacities so they recognize all of these variations? Doesn't that work as well as some sort of "rule" stored in your mental container? If the processor itself changes in response to the environment, the *processor* becomes the focus rather than the container. *Changing the processor* requires very different teaching techniques than *filling the container.*

The weaknesses of the container metaphor and the food processor metaphor—namely, their failure to provide much insight into the processes of understanding or creativity—can be addressed if one uses the *mind as modifiable information processor* metaphor. *Understanding* occurs when the processes become sufficiently tuned that they accurately, efficiently, and consistently recognize a pattern. I *understand* what an *A* is.

How does the metaphor help us understand other mental operations? Creativity—the intuitive leap—might occur after a number of subsystems have gradually been modified through experience. None of these individual modifications produces noticeable changes in the person's behavior until all of them have reached a particular level of change. At that point, their combined output causes the larger system to change—producing the "aha" that comes with a major insight.

Remember that there are no correct metaphors. However some metaphors are more useful than others in terms of how much insight they give us about an abstract concept. How a teacher chooses to "teach" will be radically different depending on whether that teacher conceptualizes *mind as a container* or *mind as a modifiable information processor.*

Machines that Learn

Characterizing the mind as a tunable or modifiable information processor has scientific support.[16] Researchers in the field of artificial intelligence have built machines that operate much like the child learning the difference between a dog and cat. The machine begins with no rules to guide its processing other than the simple binary operations that computers perform. Over time, the processes in the machine are modified and tuned *as a result of the feedback they get from their environment.* They don't "think" in the sense that we understand the word. They don't obey rules of logic or reasoning. They don't store any information for later use. They simply change and improve their performance in response to their environment. In a word, they "learn." Do they understand what they learn? That depends on how you define the word *understanding.*

I Understand...

"If you want to know the taste of a pear, you must change the pear by eating it yourself. ... All genuine knowledge originates in direct experience."
~Mao Zedong

You have to understand.... What don't you understand? They just don't understand. I understand...but.... Students will understand....

Understanding is one of the most often used but ill-defined words in education. Educators know they want students to do it—they just don't seem to know exactly what it is and how, specifically, people do it. As previously mentioned, people have different beliefs about what it means to understand.

Consider the following content standards from several different state and national documents:

- Students know and *understand* the symbols, icons, and traditions of the United States that provide continuity and a sense of community over time.

- Students *understand* basic economic concepts and the role of individual choice in a free-market economy.

- Students *understand* the structure, functions, and powers of the United States local, state and federal governments as described in the U.S. Constitution.

- Students *understand* how species depend on one another and on the environment for survival.

- Students *understand* the cycling of matter and flow of energy through the living environment.

- Students *understand* the basic concepts of the evolution of species.

According to these documents, these *understandings* are to be demonstrated by specific behaviors, such as "recognizes the flag of the U.S.," "describes the nitrogen cycle," or "identifies predators and prey in an ecosystem." In other words, rather than defining the meaning of the word *understand*, content writers describe the *behavior* of a person who supposedly *understands*.

In his fascinating book, *Education and Mind in the Knowledge Age*,[17] Dr. Carl Bereiter points out that the concept of *understanding* is difficult to explain using the *mind-as-container* metaphor. Some have attempted to explain how knowledge becomes understanding using hierarchies, schemas, and webs—the creation of larger knowledge objects out of smaller ones. To paraphrase Bereiter, *understanding* is then a matter of how closely one's schema or web matches the schema or web of an expert (or in many cases, the schema or web of the teacher).

If, for example, you *believe* understanding consists of the ability to recite a long list of facts about a concept, your perception of a student's "understanding" will be based on that belief. Another teacher who *believes* understanding involves the application of knowledge will assume the student who can't *apply* the information *doesn't* understand *even if that student can spout all of the related information.* How you conceptualize understanding, then, plays a huge role not only in the kind of assessments you use but also in your judgment of the abilities of individual students.

Understanding is a complex concept, such as *society* or *the economy.* Bereiter suggests that exploring the way people use the word *understanding* in everyday life may give us insight into how understanding occurs. Here are a few of the requirements leading to understanding in the commonly used sense:

- The depth of understanding that people have for a computer, for example, depends largely on how much and for what purpose they *use* a computer. A person who designs computers for a living or is a hacker has a much greater understanding than someone who uses a computer simply to send and receive email or to play games. How much do people who have merely memorized the parts of a computer *understand* about the computer?

- Understanding an object or another person depends on one's interest level. Not only does interest motivate a person to understand, but the greater the understanding the more interesting the object or person becomes to a person.

- Understanding involves comprehending relationships that objects have with one another. Observing an ant in an ant farm offers a much greater opportunity for understanding than memorizing the parts of an ant.

- Understanding is not always accompanied by the ability to explain. The understanding grows through developing the relationship, much of which a person can neither recall nor verbalize. How does a baker know when he has kneaded the bread dough long enough? How does the artist know when the painting is finished? Select one topic you "understand" and another you do not "understand." How do you know the difference? For many, there is a "felt sense" of comfort or familiarity with the understood content—a sense that cannot easily be put into words.

- Having a deep understanding requires a highly developed interaction. The more complex and frequent your interaction with the object, the deeper will be your understanding.[18]

If these are characteristics of understanding as it develops in the "real world," isn't it reasonable to assume that it is how students might come to understand information that they encounter in school?

We might view understanding as finely tuned capacities and abilities. As we've seen, these modifications occur through interaction with a concept from a variety of perspectives. It is not sufficient for information to flow from the environment to the mind. The mind must have the opportunity to act on that information, send a response back to the environment, and receive feedback about that response. This is what "tunes" the brain. Once tuned, the brain then generates behaviors of intelligent action, feeling, or thought consistent with understanding.

Teaching as Fostering Relationships

"I was asked to memorize what I did not understand; and, my memory being so good, it refused to be insulted in that manner." ~Aleister Crowley

It's not an easy task to shift a metaphor, particularly one that is as familiar as the *mind as container* metaphor. Despite the difficulty, when a metaphor has failed in its usefulness as often as this one, isn't it about time teachers looked for something better? The three metaphors of mind discussed in this chapter cast both teachers and students in three different roles.

- *Mind as container* forces teachers into the role of transferring knowledge objects into the container. The metaphor permits students little active participation in this process. Students are judged by the capacity of their file cabinets and their ability to keep their files in order and retrieve them on command.

- *Mind as food processor* also requires teachers to provide the knowledge objects in addition to the rules (disks and blades) needed to process the knowledge. The processing is recognized as internal to the student, but few solutions are offered when the blades don't work properly or when they process the mental food incorrectly. There is an insidious acceptance that the machine is "broken."

- *Mind as modifiable information processor* demands more. The key to this metaphor is interaction—development of *relationships* between knowledge objects and the learner. The role of the teacher is to foster those relationships. The teacher might play the role of matchmaker—introducing the parties, arranging meetings between them, and chaperoning what goes on during the meetings.

Because the nature of understanding has not been sufficiently explored in the educational context, educators settle for assessing it by requiring students to *state, explain,* or often, to simply pick an answer from a multiple-choice list. How can this be reconciled with the experience that one cannot always verbalize what one understands? Where is the "felt sense" that underlies true understanding assessed?

If tests truly assess understanding, why do we have Harvard graduates who get *As* on their astronomy tests yet explain that it's warmer in summer than winter because the sun is closer to the earth during the summer?[19] Why do we have students who get *As* on their tests of Newton's Laws of Motion but don't wear seatbelts? Why do we have elementary students who, when asked how old a person is if he has ten toes and five apples, will answer "fifteen?" Do they know how to manipulate numbers? Yes. Do they have number sense? Possibly? Do they understand? Hardly.

> "Understanding a thing is to arrive at a metaphor for that
> thing by substituting something more familiar to us. And the
> feeling of familiarity is the feeling of understanding."
> ~Lyall Watson

Kinds of Knowledge

Learning a skill requires a different approach than learning the formula for salt or the definition of *alliteration. Using* alliteration in writing requires a different thought process than simply defining the word. There is, however, a tendency to group these processes under two headings—declarative and procedural knowledge. Simplistically, knowing the rules of volleyball is declarative knowledge and being able to spike a ball is procedural.

Similarly, educators often divide knowledge into *content* and *process.* Content is the information in the file cabinet. "'Process' is all the cognitive skills that the curriculum activities are intended to develop that are supposed to enable the student to do something with the content."[20] Although arguments abound over which is more important (another limiting dichotomy), theorists are not very careful about distinguishing between them. For example, many so-called "content" standards are stated as processes—something a student must do to demonstrate "possession" of the content.

These knowledge categories are too broad to be particularly useful. Dr. Bereiter suggests a potentially more useful breakdown of knowledge.

Statable knowledge—This is knowledge the knower can pass on to others in some way, be it sentences, diagrams, formulas, or stories. Such knowledge can be observed by others, evaluated, and compared.

Implicit understanding—As described in the previous discussion on understanding, implicit knowledge refers to our relationships with things, people, or situations in the world. Understanding implies a deep enough relationship to produce intelligent action on the part of the knower. In Bereiter's words, "Implicit understanding is more like perception than like having propositions in the head."[21] The center fielder who, at the instant the bat strikes the baseball, begins to run to the exact spot where the ball will fall has implicit understanding—very different from someone who knows the equation for calculating projectile motion.

Episodic knowledge—This type of knowledge is related to a person's memories of things that happened to them personally. Episodic knowledge is something a person learned through experience that may be useful in some other context. Walking past a high-rise building under construction may remind a person of having a branch fall on his head in the woods. The recalled knowledge influences the person's behavior.

Impressionistic knowledge—Bereiter asserts all knowledge has an affective component. In fact, several neuroscientists propose that emotion is a necessary characteristic of human thought.[22] Neuroscientist Antonio Damasio[23] suggests that, in the absence of emotions, higher thought processes are impaired. In the case of impressionistic knowledge, the feeling is the knowledge. It is the hunch, the intuitive sense, the gut feeling that may not be accessible, nor expressible, at a conscious level, but that influences our behavior nonetheless.

Skill—Bereiter suggests there are two parts to any skill: a cognitive part—the "knowing how"—and a second part that can improve with practice. In school, much of the focus is on the first part, knowing how.

Students are taught "how" to do many different tasks, from solving a particular type of math problem to using reference materials. Unfortunately, with the proliferation of "hows" that students are now required to learn, there is little time for the practice that will improve those skills. Skills that remain at the level of "knowing how" are less likely to be used than skills in which the person feels some competence. I may know "how" to play bridge, but I rarely do it because I am painfully aware of how poorly I play.

Regulative knowledge—In the acquisition and use of knowledge, the issue of "self" as learner is typically ignored in education. In my experience, students become instantly alert when a teacher begins discussing how the brain/mind works. Suddenly, the information relates to them! They realize the more they know about how they process information, the more easily they can monitor and assess the products of their own thinking. Reflection on the beliefs that influence one's life or the biases that limit perceptions are just as valuable for students as they are for teachers. Done at an early age, self-reflection may make a profound different in a person's development.

Bereiter points out that schools place the greatest emphasis on *statable* knowledge and the "knowing how" portion of skills—the only two forms of knowledge that can be "explained" and transmitted. Neglect of the others comes partly from their variability from person to person. When educators are caught in the trap of group-think, there is no place for "knowledge" that varies among students, can't be easily *transmitted* to an entire group, and can't be objectively assessed.

The other forms of knowledge/understanding have not been adequately explored or even recognized as critical components of learning. However, they are all present in what most of us recognize as "intelligent behavior." "Competence in any domain will likely involve all six kinds of knowledge."[24]

Breaking knowledge down into its components is useful to educators to the extent that it helps to identify areas neglected in the teaching/learning environment. It is not useful if each component is broken off into a domain of its own and addressed as a separate part of instruction—as is often done with "thinking skills." In "real life," these forms of knowledge develop in parallel. They are interrelated parts of the system that encompasses the knower and the known. Dealing with the parts in isolation is likely to result in even more inert knowledge that is useful only in the context in which it is learned.

Are implicit understanding, episodic knowledge, impressionistic knowledge, regulative knowledge, or the practice of skills leading to mastery addressed in your school or classroom? Are any or all of them included, implicitly or explicitly, in your planning or instruction? If these types of knowledge are part of the competent behaviors that are the mark of the "educated" person, shouldn't they be explicitly included in the teaching/learning environment?

1 Callaway, R. (1979) Teachers' Beliefs Concerning Values and the Functions and Purposes of Schooling, Eric Document ED 177 110.
2 Manus, A. L. (1996, Summer). Procedural versus Constructivist Education" A Lesson From History. *The Educational Forum, Vol. 60*, 312–316.
3 Gazzaniga, M. (1992). *Nature's Mind.* New York: Basic Books. Edelman, Gerald. (1992) *Bright Air, Brilliant Fire.* New York: Basic Books.
4 Manus, A. L. (1996) Procedural…, 314
5 Ibid., 315.
6 Postman, N. (1995). *The End of Education: Redefining the Value of School.* New York: Alfred A. Knopf, 189
7 Abbott, J. (1999). Battery Hens, or Free Range Chickens: What Kind of Education for What Kind of World, published online by the 21st Century Learning Initiative, URL: http://www.21learn.org/publ/abbott_speech.html.
8 Fives, H., and Buehl, M. M. (2008.) What do teachers believe? Developing a framework for examining beliefs about teachers' knowledge and ability. *Contemporary Educational Psychology. 33*, 134-176.
9 Dewey, J. (1939). *Logic: The Theory of Inquiry.* New York: Holt Rhinehart and Winston, 8.
10 Palmer, P. J. (1998). *The Courage to Teach: Exploring the Inner Landscape of a Teacher's Life.* San Francisco: Jossey-Bass, 100–101. Adapted from Palmer's book with his kind permission.
11 Ibid., 101.
12 Noble, A. J.& Smith, M. L. (1994). Old and New Beliefs about Measurement-Driven Reform: "The More Things Change, the More They Stay the Same." National Center for Research on Evaluation, Standards, and Student Testing, Los Angeles, CA. (ERIC Document Reproduction Service No. ED 378 228)
13 Rogers, V. R.& Stevenson, C. (1988, February). How Do We Know What Kids Are Learning In School? *Educational Leadership.* 68-75.
14 Bereiter, C. (2000). *Education and Mind in the Knowledge Age*, Taylor and Francis, Inc. 21. In addition, the entire book can be read and downloaded at URL:

http://www.cocon.com/observetory/carlbereiter/ [Note: the spelling of "observetory" is the way it is spelled in the URL .a reference to Educational Technology.]

15 Hart, L. A. (1983). *Human Brain and Human Learning*. New York: Longman, 60.

16 Rao, V.& Hayagriva, R. (1995). *C++: Neural Networks & Fuzzy Logic*. 1–19

17 Bereiter, Education and Mind…, 15.

17 Ibid, pp. 9-10, 18-24

19 Marchese, T. The New conversations About Learning: Insights From Neuroscience and Anthropology, Cognitive Science and Work-Place Studies published by New Horizons for Learning Website, URL: http://www.newhorizons.org.

20 Bereiter, Education and Mind…, 2.

21 Ibid.

22 Edelman, G. (1992) *Bright Air, Brilliant Fire*. New York: Basic Books.

23 Damasio, A R. (1995) *Descartes' Error: Emotion, Reason, and the Human Brain*. New York: Avon Books, 43–45.

24 Bereiter, *Education and Mind…*, p 19.

Chapter 11 ~ Beliefs about Learning

"Now what I want is Facts. Teach these boys and
girls nothing but Facts. Facts alone are wanted in
life. Plant nothing else, and root out everything else.
You can only form the minds of
reasoning animals upon Facts:
nothing else will ever be of service to them."
Thomas Gradgrind in Charles Dickens's *Hard Times*

In an article in *Educational Leadership*, Paulette Wasserstein[1] quotes Dickens' schoolmaster and questions whether we have really evolved much beyond the factory model schools of the nineteenth century. Many of the assumptions under which the fictional Mr. Gradgrind taught are still present in our schools.

The Present Hierarchy

Classrooms involve complex interactions among information, students, and teachers. In traditional schools, that interaction is a hierarchy. The curriculum—*Knowledge*—is at the top of that hierarchy, while the student—the learner—is at the bottom of the pecking order.

Many fields have recognized the need to shift focus from inanimate objects and ideas to the people involved. Many medical professionals now treat *people* rather than just symptoms. By doing so, they have broadened and deepened their understanding of how and why people become ill and how they remain well. Companies that have shifted their primary focus from selling their *product* to identifying the needs of their *consumers* have seen remarkable increases in sales.

Once again, education remains firmly entrenched at the trailing edge of this new wisdom. Traditional educators still focus on the product they are trying to sell—knowledge—rather than on their consumer—the learner. When consumers complain and refuse to buy the product, they are criticized for their "lack of motivation" and forced to buy even more—with no change in the product itself.

Because education is compulsory, public education has a captive audience that has allowed them to largely ignore both consumer discontent and the volumes of research on what the consumer actually wants and needs. Public schools are, however, already feeling the pressure from "alternative" schools, private schools, and home-schooling. However, that pressure is met with indignant rhetoric, rather than a thoughtful reappraisal of why this exodus is occurring.

There's little doubt educational policymakers are worried. Confronted with the fascination many young people have with computer games, the Internet, and other electronic media, educators scramble to somehow incorporate those experiences into education—*without changing the fundamental approach to the transmission of knowledge objects.*[2] It's a sad commentary on education's failure to identify a purpose strong enough to stand on its own when teachers feel the need to compete with other sources of information. However, competing with the Internet, where students can access knowledge of their choice in a variety of appealing forms and at whatever rate they choose, is a losing battle.

A more productive question is "What can schools do for students that other information sources cannot do?" The answer to that question demands a shift of focus from product to consumer—from the transmission of knowledge to the needs of the learner. Those needs have been thoroughly researched and are available to anyone who wishes to understand them. Many thoughtful teachers, weary of the failure of conventional wisdom, now create learning environments consistent with those needs. They are entering uncharted territory, but have accepted their roles as leaders and as experts. They are the future of education if it is to remain a viable institution. If you are not already among their number, what will it take for you to join them?

Learning Is...

"Research shows that you begin learning in the womb and go right on learning until the moment you pass on. Your brain has a capacity for learning that is virtually limitless, which makes every human a potential genius." ~ Michael J. Gelb

There are dozens of learning theories, each viewing learning from a particular point of view—a single perspective. Each theory contains useful insights. It's interesting, however, that many of these theories fail to address the *process* of learning. How, specifically, does learning occur?

"[In] typical learning research…the continuing process of learning is never directly assessed. Usually, some hypothetical construct located inside the head, such as a schema or a trace is said to be built up or strengthened as a result of the learning process. …Learning, in this somewhat impotent view, is a covert process forever inaccessible to observation: only the effects of practice may be seen…. The general picture of learning curves that emerges is well known. Practice produces a directed drift of the response in the direction of the task requirement. In plain terms, the subject's performance improves and becomes less variable. Your grandmother could have told you that."[3]

Rather than discussing these theories, let's explore one aspect of learning that offers to shed some light on the process. That is the *organ* of learning—the brain. Few learning theorists consider the substrate in which learning occurs. Why is this a problem? It's possible for an architect to design a spectacular and innovative building that is impossible to construct with available materials and techniques. Similarly, theorizing about learning without considering the "wetware" that supports it can result in elegant, but meaningless theories.

In their book, *Wet Mind*,[4] neuroscientists Stephen Kosslyn and Oliver Koenig argue that cognitive models may *sound* reasonable and logical but the "machinery" of the brain does not support those models. For example, people are able to pick out curved objects within the environment and can distinguish among various degrees of curvature. Given that the brain contains neurons that respond to horizontal or vertical lines, an intuitive model might suggest that it also contains neurons that respond to various degrees of curvature.

"One could build a model of vision on this notion, explaining and predicting various behaviors in terms of 'curve sensitive neurons.' But until one actually finds neurons sensitive to curves, the model is useful only as a mental exercise. It has no validity in describing what 'really' happens.[5]

In actuality, brain structure doesn't support such a model. Instead, it appears neurons that are sensitive to the "ends of lines" may actually provide the input that allows the brain to identify a curved shape.

Because the brain is so tremendously complex, it's unlikely scientists or educators will ever understand some of its more involved processes. That is no excuse for ignoring the "wetware" in our theories of learning. Much is already known about what the brain can and cannot do. At the very least, we should be questioning whether there are structures in the brain that might accomplish the processes suggested in cognitive models. Or processes that would preclude them from happening![6]

"Brain-based learning" became a familiar battle cry for bringing education in line with current knowledge of the brain. Like "back to basics," it is a phrase used with little thought as to its actual meaning. *All* learning is "brain-based" so the term is relatively meaningless. However, making sure that schooling is *brain-compatible* is certainly of concern. What possible excuse can educators make for continuing to teach in ways that are *not* compatible with the brain's natural processes? With the information available from the "brain revolution" of the past several decades, continuing to teach in ways that "inhibit learning by discouraging, ignoring, or punishing the brain's natural learning processes"[7] is reprehensible.

> "We don't have to make human beings smart. They are born smart. All we have to do is stop doing the things that made them stupid." ~ John Holt

Education's Blind Spot

> "[In education]...the individual is just a statistic. Everybody is treated the same. Any differences due to experience, maturation, ancestry, or what the subject had for breakfast are canceled out. The organism, to put it bluntly, is treated like a machine whose task is to associate inputs and outputs. Any autonomously active, intrinsic organization within the organism or between organisms and their environment, although present, is swept under the rug." ~J. A. Scott Kelso[8]

Some early theories attributed an individual's ability to learn to his or her genetic inheritance. For others, the brain/mind was seen as a blank slate—John Locke's *tabula rasa*—upon which everything required to become a functioning human had to be "written." Today, despite ample evidence that infants in the womb are already learning and that intelligence is far from fixed, some persist in believing that some students are "born smart" and others are "born dumb."

There is an interesting "blind spot" in traditional education that permits time-honored group-think to continue. Consider the following four statements:

1. People look different. In fact, humans are surprised when they see two people who look alike. How likely is it that any rational person would suggest that all fourteen-year-old humans should be five-feet six-inches tall and able to bench press one hundred pounds?

2. According to the Human Genome Project, there are about *three billion* base pairs making up the genes and DNA in a human being. Only a portion of those are factors in a person's appearance and physical abilities. These genes remain relatively unchanged in their operation over the life of the individual. Although it's possible to change one's physical appearance through exercise, surgery, or cosmetic methods, physical appearance remains relatively constant throughout life.

3. The human brain is composed of about *ten billion* neurons, each of which has perhaps ten thousand connections to other neurons. This results in approximately one hundred *trillion* connections in the brain. Unlike genes, each of these connections, from the moment of formation, is subject to change by interactions with the environment— by experience. In other words, the brain *constantly changes* in response to experience.

4. No two people—even identical twins—have the same experiences as they grow and develop.

Taken together, what do these four statements mean? The number of genes and genetic variations that produce differences in *physical* appearance and ability are minuscule compared to the possible permutations in the way individual brains process information. Because no two individuals have lived through the same experiences— experiences that modify both the neurons and their connections—*the potential cognitive differences among human individuals is staggering*. Yet few people balk when reformers insist that all students of a certain age should be responsible for learning the same things—often, in the same way. The statement flies in the face of reason, science, and experience. *It is infinitely more irrational than insisting all fourteen-year-olds be the same height or be able to lift the same weight!*

Although many traditional educators would accept the four statements as true, they are somehow able to put that information in a corner and forget it when it comes to teaching. Perhaps they are hoping that, like so many reform efforts, it will eventually go away if they ignore it. This is simply not going to happen. The brains of students are not going to miraculously become alike for the convenience of education and the efficiency of assembly line transmission of knowledge objects.

In general, attempts to introduce brain-compatible teaching in schools often results in teachers adding a few activities for different learning "modalities", or giving students a "choice" of supplemental projects. These are apparently sufficient to salve the conscience and quiet that little voice that reminds us what really needs to happen. These changes make little or no difference in the fundamental metaphor that drives education—filling the mental containers with knowledge objects. As long as this remains the primary purpose of education, focusing on individual differences is literally "unthinkable" unless there is a teacher for every student. Schools will continue to operate in ways that are, at best, only marginally compatible with the brain's natural processes.

More About the Wetware

"BRAIN, n. An apparatus with which we think that we think."
~Ambrose Bierce, The Devil's Dictionary

There is little doubt that both genes and the environment play important roles in the development and variability of human capacities. Theories of nature and nurture are no longer seen in opposition to one another but rather as two parts of a whole. Arguments still exist, of course, about which is "more important," a little like arguing which side of a coin is more important.

The necessity of *both* processes is demonstrated in a theory of learning known as *selectionism*. This theory is based on substantial physiological data and supports other more established theories about how the brain makes sense of information, such as *constructivism*.

Selectionism supports what Socrates and other major philosophers throughout history have believed: Learning involves "drawing out" and modifying what is already in the mind. It's similar to the idea that a female infant already possesses all of the eggs she will ever produce.

Only those eggs that encounter the proper environment will develop into fetuses and later into fully developed humans.

According to selectionist theory, the brain contains a huge repertoire of potential cognitive processes at, and even before, birth. In the first step of learning, something in the environment "selects" certain of these processes. The process "switches on" in response to environmental cues, similar to a motion sensor switching on a light when something comes within its range. Subsequent learning then becomes the "fine tuning" of those processes, as a motion sensor that can be set to tell the difference between a moving leaf blown by the wind and a person.

The "template" for the development of a human infant has no way of knowing into which culture—nationality—the child will be born. The infant must, therefore, come equipped with the ability to hear, understand, and speak any of the world's thousands of languages and dialects. Those abilities are "turned on"—selected—by exposure to a particular language, even before birth.

Many people believe children learn language merely by listening and mimicking adults. Cognitive neuroscientist Steven Pinker[9] argues that the actual speech of young children suggests the "rules of grammar"—the basic structure of the language— may also be present at birth. How else can we explain why a three-year-old says "He hitted me" or "I eated all my food"? He's not mimicking the way an adult speaks. Parents don't "teach" the child to add "-ed" to make a word into a past tense. In fact, parents often think such language is cute and don't even correct the child. Yet, over time, the child "learns" the exceptions to the rules. Or more accurately, the processes involved in that action are "tuned."

Other research suggests that, when the neurons that are capable of some tasks, such as hearing the half-tones present in some eastern languages, are not "selected" early in life, they either shift to other purposes or are "pruned."[10] By adolescence, the number of connections in the brain has been reduced to about 60 percent of its original capacity. For example, adults who have not grown up in an environment where the Thai language is spoken can neither hear nor reproduce the half-tones present in that language—or they do it very poorly.

Which Processes Are Selected?

The term *selectionism* refers to the way the environment "selects" processes to be turned on, just as the environment into which a child is born "selects" the language neurons that will be activated and strengthened.[11] In any generation, some processes are perceived as more valuable than others. Environments likely to "turn on" the more valuable processes are readily available. In other cases, *people* make the decision about which processes are "more important."

Valued processes change from era to era. During the Renaissance, musical and artistic abilities were valued much more highly than they are today. Children were immersed in environments that encouraged the development of those abilities. In colonial America, hunting, raising crops, and the household arts were prized abilities. Children grew up in environments that "turned on" those capacities. It's important to recognize that those children may have also possessed the same latent musical and artistic talents of their Renaissance cousins—talents that were not "turned on" because of the difference in their environment.

In today's society, the valued processes seem to be the ability to collect and retain information from a variety of "basic" disciplines. It isn't sufficient that an individual exhibit remarkable abilities in one or two disciplines. To be truly "educated," they must exhibit those abilities in *all* of the disciplines.

But consider this: The great theoretical physicist and Nobel Prize winner Richard Feynman once decided to spend a year with the equally great biologist Max Delbruck. Feynman spent every day of that year in the lab, trying to "understand" the new field of molecular biology as he had so easily "understood" physics. Certainly, he gave himself sufficient time to develop the relationship with this new subject that leads to understanding. Feynman finished some experiments but at the end of the year announced he was going to leave biology to the biologists. His reason—he simply didn't think like biologists![12]

If a person of such obvious mental acuity is unable to develop understanding of a discipline outside his own, despite considerable effort, doesn't that suggest the insanity of defining intelligence in terms of the ability to know or understand *all* of the "required" disciplines? The selection and development of specific circuits in the mind of an individual are based on motivational, genetic, or cognitive dimensions of mind. The point is that each individual is *different*. The absence of a selected ability does *not* signify that a person is less intelligent.

The imprecision of meaning of such words as *educated* or *intelligent* traps educators in unwarranted beliefs. They are pressured by external decisions about which cognitive processes are important. Those decisions determine the environment in the classroom. And it is that environment that determines which of a student's innate processes have the opportunity to "turn on."

What the Brain Does Naturally

"The problem is fundamental. Put twenty or more children of roughly the same age in a little room, confine them to desks, make them wait in lines, make them behave. It is as if a secret committee, now lost to history, had made a study of children and, having figured out what the greatest number were least disposed to do, declared that all of them should do it."[13]~Tracy Kidder

Isn't it amazing how well suited humans are to the world in which they live? Not really! If humans had evolved on a different planet—in a different environment—they would have taken a much different form. The environment determines the behaviors necessary for survival and the structure of the organism.

Evolutionary psychologists Leda Cosmides and John Tooby[14] explain that the brain consists of a vast and complex collection of circuits. Each of those circuits evolved in response to some problem within the environment. It adapted to its environment. Originally, those adaptations had little to do with intellectual issues and everything to do with survival of both the individual and the species. Over time, as the environment demanded more complex functions, these same circuits have combined and been further "tuned" to do cognitive work.

What we do know is these circuits did *not* evolve to be repositories for isolated facts or "bodies of knowledge" that have been externally assembled as "basic concepts." The circuits evolved in response to actual situations that arose in the environment of the organism.. It wasn't necessary for early humans to be able to *name* a saber-toothed tiger and *identify* its genus and species. It *was* necessary for them to recognize a pattern against the background of the jungle, associate that pattern with large teeth and claws, and engage in the appropriate behavior to ensure their survival! The "natural" functions of the brain include the ability to detect patterns in a complex environment and to associate the patterns with appropriate behaviors.

After many years of trying to make computers *learn* like humans, researchers in artificial intelligence (AI) realized that learning is not the result of amassing huge quantities of information and related rules of processing. The successes that AI researchers have had in reproducing even the simplest tasks of which the human brain is capable have come when the "computer" was allowed to interact with the environment and create its own rules—"tune" its own circuits.[15]

Yes, schools have managed to stuff human brains full of information (input) and get corresponding output on tests. They've done this with sufficient success that they now demand even more information and more tests. The fact that many students have successfully adapted to this form of schooling is hardly a defense of the present system. It is, instead, an endorsement of the tremendous ability of the brain to adapt to unnatural conditions. A human can survive on a marginal, but that is hardly evidence that the diet is appropriate, or even acceptable.

What more might be achieved if students were permitted to interact with various environments in a "real world" context; to "turn on" and "tune" their innate abilities; in other words, to learn in ways that the brain does naturally?

The human brain has adapted to:

- interact with a complex environment;

- abstract patterns from the complexity in that environment;

- modify itself so that it functions more effectively in that environment;

- solve "real" problems it perceives in that environment; and

- attend to that which it finds personally interesting.[16] The adaptive value of that tendency is obvious. Noticing aspects of the environment that were a potential threat to self—or that might become a potential mate—ensured not only a creature's personal survival but also that of the species.

- As we examine today's schools, we find:

- brains that require complexity being bombarded with simplified basics;

- brains that require interaction with the environment to turn on their innate processes receiving their "experience" second hand through the words (and perceptions) of a teacher; and

- brains that have adapted to solve complex problems relevant to self being denied the opportunity to identify those problems and forced to solve predefined problems with predefined answers.

In a recent study, brain theorists were asked to identify the characteristics of brain-compatible instruction. The overarching idea put forth by the theorists was that an enriched environment was the most essential component. This environment must include:

- emotional involvement by both teacher and student;

- physical systems, such as movement and room arrangement;

- lowered stress and threat levels;

- experiences in the classroom, including trial and error, exploration, practice, creativity, and critical thinking; and

- challenge, problem-solving, and authentic work, in which the students do the work of learning and create their own meanings.[17]

To what extent do traditional classrooms resemble this "enriched environment?" Reforms too often address how educators can make the brains of students conform to what schools already do rather than asking the question that would truly transform schools. How can schools be made more compatible with the way humans learn? Answers are a function of the questions we ask. It's time to change our question. In the words of Albert Einstein, "The significant problems we face cannot be solved at the same level of thinking we were at when we created them."

How Real Students Learn

Theory is one thing. Real students are something else. If the statistics about neurons or the research on brain processes don't convince you that everyone is different, here are a few examples of how some real students learn.

1. A woman described how her eighteen-year-old son wanted so badly to go to college. But all through school, whenever he tried to read

anything, he had to fight for every word. Recalling a fascinating demonstration I'd seen some years earlier, I suggested she have her son stand with one foot in front of the other and read aloud as he shifted his weight from one foot to the other. If that didn't work, she should have him rock from side to side rather than front to back.

The next day, she sought me out to tell me what had happened. The simple act of rocking allowed her son to read smoothly and with ease. Why? It undoubtedly has something to do with the wiring of the young man's brain. But the bottom line is it that it worked in his case. Do we have to understand it before we use it?

2. Diane studied her spelling words prior to each test and spelled the words perfectly at home. However, she continually failed her spelling tests. Unpacking her learning strategies and how she used her senses to process information revealed that Diane recalled her spelling words by spelling them to herself internally. This inner voice is often called *internal dialogue*. Being an auditory learner, Diane was also extremely sensitive to external auditory sensations. Because internal auditory (sounds from inside) and external auditory (sounds from outside) share many of the same pathways in the brain, they necessarily compete for attention. Most of us know people who are so busy thinking about what they're going to say next they don't really hear what the other person is saying.

It turned out that Diane's spelling teacher pre-recorded the words for each spelling test on tape. He would say a word and then let the blank tape run for twenty seconds to give students time to write the word. Then he would say the next word. Diane's problem was that the tape was noisy. During the "blank" spaces, there was an audible hum or buzz that Diane found extremely annoying. It so focused her on "external auditory" that she was unable to "hear" herself spell the words. The annoying sound also changed Diane's emotional state to one of intense irritation, making it even more difficult for her to focus on cognitive processes.

In all likelihood, the teacher and many of the other students didn't even hear the noise, or if they did, it didn't bother them. A casual observer might have decided that Diane was a "poor speller" when, in fact, she was an excellent speller under most conditions.

3. Tim was distressed because he really loved science but couldn't seem to pass the tests. Like Diane, Tim seemed to understand everything when he studied at home. Yet when he took the tests, he

couldn't recall the information he needed. Tim was an active boy, which suggested movement might be an important factor in the problem. After Tim learned how to identify his internal sensory representations (what he sees, hears, feels, smells, or tastes in connection with a given "mental" process), his problem became clear.

While studying for the test, Tim was *associated* into his body. That is, he felt himself "doing" the experiment or in some way physically interacting with the information. When he took a test, rather than being in his body "doing," Tim was "watching himself" do. He was *dissociated* from the information his body provided. That was all it took to prevent him from accessing the information he needed. Tim somehow stored information in his body, so he had to *be in* that body to access the information. Once recognized, Tim consciously made it a point to "get into his body" on tests. His testing problems disappeared.

These are not "special" students. They are just like many other students you have sitting in your classroom—each of them processing information in unique ways. In the case of Diane and the spelling tests, the solution to the problem required a change on the part of the teacher. With Tim, it required only recognition on his part and a conscious change in his strategies.

If you're thinking something along the lines of, "Wow, I didn't realize it was that complicated," consider this. All students are engaging in various internal processes that are not only outside of the teacher's experience, but also outside of the students' awareness. To add to the confusion, the teacher is also engaging in similar unconscious processes. Perhaps the teacher always makes pictures of what she is talking about and assumes everyone else does the same thing. But not everyone "sees what you're saying."

It takes training to "unpack" a student's learning processes, but there is a growing movement toward having at least one person in a school who can work with students in this way. Problems aren't always the "fault" of the student. They can arise from a mismatch in how the student and teacher process information. At this point, it is simply important to recognize that such differences exist and be willing to explore them before deciding that students are in some way flawed.

---

1 Wasserstein, P. (2001). Putting Readers in the Driver's Seat. *Educational Leadership, Vol. 58, No. 4,* 74.

2 New technologies for the classroom, such as interactive whiteboards, continue to appear. However, entrenched in the "transmission of knowledge" paradigm, the programs being developed for these tools are largely updated versions of Power Point presentations or transparencies. Little or no thought is given to the potential of these tools to fundamentally change the way teachers, learners, and knowledge might interact.

3 Kelso, J. A. S. (1995). *Dynamic Patterns: The Self-Organization of Brain and Behavior*. Cambridge and London: A Bradford Book, MIT Press, 161.

4 Kosslyn, S. M. & Koenig, O. (1992). *Wet Mind—The New Cognitive Neuroscience*. New York: The Free Press.

5 Ibid., p 42.

6 John T. Bruer suggests that, because much of what we know about the brain comes from animal research, there is insufficient evidence to apply it to human learning. It is true that some have carried their conclusions too far. Although brain sciences may not yet know how learning does work, it can certainly contribute a lot to our knowledge of what does not work.

7 Quote in article "How Do People Learn?" at www.funderstanding.com/learning_theory_how5.htm. Based on the work of Renate Caine and Leslie Hart. See site for sources.

8 Kelso, *Dynamic Patterns...*, 161.

9 Pinker, S. (1994). *The Language Instinct: How the Mind Creates Language*. New York: William Morrow.

10 cf. Cowan, G. A. (1998). Concerning Relationships Between Cerebral Blood Flow, Synaptic Pruning, and Early Mental Development in Animals and Humans, Santa Fe Institute, www.santafe.edu/sfi/publications/Working-Papers/98-06-059.doc

11 Gazzaniga, M. S. (1992) *Nature's Mind*. New York: Basic Books.

12 Ibid., Epilogue.

13 Gardner, H. (1991). *The Unschooled Mind: How Children Think and How Schools Should Teach*. New York: Basic Books, 138.

14 Cosmides, L. and J. Tooby. (1992). From Function to Structure: The Role of Evolutionary Biology and Computational Theories. In M. Gazzaniga (Ed.). *Cognitive Neuroscience* (p 1199). New York: Oxford University Press.

15 Rao, V. and Hayagriva, R. (1995). *C++ Neural Networks and Fuzzy Logic*, 2nd ed. New York: MIT Press, 1–20.

16 Edelman, G. (1992). *Bright Air, Brilliant Fire*. New York: Basic Books, 143. Damasio, A. (1994). *Descartes' Error*. New York: Avon Books, 165.

17 Radin, Jean L. (2009)Brain-Compatible Teaching and Learning: Implications for Teacher Education *Educational Horizons, v88 n1* p 44 Fall 2009. Eric document number EJ868337

Chapter 12 ~ Beliefs about Teaching

"What we want is to see the child in pursuit of
knowledge, and not knowledge in pursuit
of the child." ~ George Bernard Shaw

It should be obvious by now that a teacher's behaviors are heavily influenced by fundamental beliefs about the purpose of education, the nature of knowledge, what learning means, and whether the focus in the classroom is on knowledge or students. Add to that the complexity of teaching itself, a complexity that is far from obvious to the student watching the teacher make assignments, hand out papers, and respond to questions. According to former Carnegie Institute President Lee Shulman,

"After some 30 years of doing such work, I have concluded that classroom teaching ... is perhaps the most complex, most challenging, and most demanding, subtle, nuanced and frightening activity that our species invented."[1]

In interviews with teachers, researcher Mary Kennedy found that

"...their practices reflect their concerns about six different things: (a) covering desirable content, (b) fostering student learning, (c) increasing students' willingness to participate, (d) maintaining lesson momentum, (e) creating a civil classroom community, and (f) attending to their own cognitive and emotional needs. At any given moment, one of these six areas of concern needs more attention than the others. If two students begin to quarrel, the teacher suddenly focuses on how to reinstate norms of courtesy and civility. If one student asks an imponderable, the teacher must think about the trade-off between maintaining lesson momentum and sustaining student willingness to participate."[2]

Kennedy suggests that one reason why professional development and research on "what works" fail to produce the expected outcomes because they rarely address more than one or two of the six concerns.

"For instance, a new approach to classroom management might address concerns about community norms but fail to address concerns about covering important content or fostering student learning. A new inquiry approach to science teaching may address concerns about content and student learning but fail to address concerns about lesson momentum or the teachers' own cognitive and emotional needs."[3]

Mary's story is typical of the quandary in which many teachers find themselves. Realizing that her current math curriculum didn't interest her sixth-grade students, Mary actively sought out interesting activities, even when they weren't related to the existing curriculum. A mathematics education professor suggested that Mary have her students approach "real world" problems, such as the batting averages of baseball players. She could first have students work in small groups to discuss and analyze how these averages could be determined by using available statistics such as the number of times a player had been at bat and his number of hits.

The professor suggested that Mary's role would be to ask appropriate questions to help the students "think through" the problem. However, Mary was obsessed with "finding a step-by-step computational rule that she could teach her students. 'It is important that I know exactly how to do it. I need to be able to show my students.'"[4]

Mary *believed* her students would be "learning" math if they learned to perform such a step-by-step computation and arrive at the "right" answer. Even more fundamental, Mary *believed* teaching mathematics involved providing students with a set of correct procedures rather than assisting them in engaging in "sense-making" activities that could be applied in many different contexts.

Mary's beliefs should not come as a surprise, given that most teachers were indoctrinated into just such a belief system when they were students. Why would we expect her to see mathematics as an approach to problem solving when the focus of her own education had been learning procedures and following those procedures to obtain single "correct" answers?

Even when teachers are willing to be flexible and open, to adjust their methods to the needs of the student, their hands are often tied by school reform efforts. Narrow and rigid application of knowledge is increasingly encouraged by policy mandates such as *Reading First* and *No Child Left Behind*. Teachers are left with minimal input or opportunities for flexibility. This trend is cited by Olsen and Sexton, who noted that current policy forces teachers into a "tightening of educational procedures, outcomes and teaching models."[5]

This is the dilemma many teachers face today—a dilemma of which they are largely unaware. The difficulty in ridding teachers of the belief that others control their fate and that of their students has been compared to overcoming the brainwashing that can occur in cults. Thus far, the "deprogrammers" have not been particularly successful in reducing the hold conventional wisdom has on teachers.

What is an Outstanding Teacher?

"When I don't have to know all the answers, I seem to have more answers than before when I tried to be the expert. The youngster who really made me understand this was Eddie. I asked him one day why he thought he was doing so much better than last year. He gave meaning to my whole new orientation. 'It's because I like myself now when I'm with you,' he said." ~Everett Shostrom in *Man, the Manipulator*

Although the beliefs of teachers are just now becoming a focus for research, a few studies have correlated beliefs with other factors such as teacher effectiveness and student "success." One such study identified three factors that were significant: teacher efficacy, locus of control, and pupil-control ideology.

Teacher Efficacy

Self-efficacy refers to a person's belief in his/her own capabilities to perform a given behavior in a specific situation.

"Efficacy beliefs help determine how much effort people will expend on an activity, how long they will persevere when confronting obstacles, and how resilient they will prove in the face of adverse situations—the higher the sense of efficacy, the greater the effort, persistence, and resilience. Efficacy beliefs also influence individuals' thought patterns and emotional reactions."[6]

For example, "...teachers with a high sense of efficacy were more likely than their low-efficacy counterparts to define low achieving students as reachable, teachable and worthy of teacher attention and effort...."[7]

A teacher's sense of self-efficacy is one of the most important factors in shaping that teacher's behavior. It is a critical factor in determining how easily a teacher will change. The less confident a teacher is, the less likely the teacher will be to attempt a change that puts him or her into an unfamiliar situation.

Locus of Control

Also called "outcome beliefs," this factor describes the degree to which people believe their actions affect their lives and the lives of others. People who believe that their own actions, rather than luck, fate, or the actions of someone more powerful, determine the outcome of events in their lives have an *internal* locus of control. People who believe their futures are "out of their hands" have an *external* locus of control. They prefer to assign responsibility to chance or to people more "in control" than themselves. An example of external locus of control is teachers who blame administrators for their inaction. There is a significant correlation between teacher burnout and external locus of control beliefs.[8]

Pupil-Control Ideology

A number of research studies have found that discipline—pupil control—is almost an obsession among some teachers. One researcher went so far as to say that control of pupil behavior is "...so pronounced that the goal of classroom order often displaces student learning as the definition of teaching effectiveness...."[9]

Control beliefs range from custodial to humanistic. Teachers with a custodial orientation:

- Are highly controlling.

- Employ punishment to achieve control.

- Act in a moralistic manner.

- Have impersonal relationships with students.

- Possess attitudes of general mistrust.

- Have, as their major focus, the maintenance of order. (One study found junior-high teachers have similar pupil-control ideologies to those who work in mental institutions!)

- By contrast, a teacher with a humanistic orientation

- Encourages active interaction and communication.

- Develops close personal relationships with students.

- Demonstrates mutual respect, positive attitudes and flexibility of rules.

- Fosters student self-discipline, self-determination, and independence.

These are, of course, the ends of the continuum. There are many teachers whose behaviors lie somewhere between these extremes. Where, on this continuum, do "outstanding" teachers lie?

Each year, several national organizations identify a "teacher of the year." State governments and many school districts have their version of the process, in which attempts are made to acknowledge and reward effective and exemplary teachers. Selection criteria vary, but for the National Teacher of the Year award, qualifications include "a.) superior teaching accomplishments; b.) evidence of exceptional teaching preparation;..."h.) evidence of superior and highly effective personal teaching style; and i.) esteemed recognition of colleagues, administrators, parents, students, and civic leaders for outstanding teaching."[10]

Given the massive standards-based reform efforts, one might assume that the selection of outstanding teachers would depend on how well their students did on standardized tests. Remarkably, this is not the case. Rather than adhering closely to a fixed curriculum, researchers found that expert teachers are "arational...following no detectible logic, but rather 'going with the flow' or 'becoming one with' their students...."[11]

Using the three factors listed above, researchers tested ninety state "teachers of the year" (TOYs) from 1987 to1990 and an equal number of practicing teachers who had not been identified as TOYs. Not surprisingly, the TOYs had a significantly higher level of self-efficacy and internal locus of control beliefs. However, these didn't predict teacher effectiveness as much as the pupil-control ideology. TOYs were *significantly more humanistic* in their approach to teaching than other teachers. Others describe them as *caring, trusting, accepting, friendly, respectful,* and *flexible.* They focus on a democratic climate of self-determination for students.

Another study of exemplary teachers[12] identified typical beliefs these teachers hold. These include the belief that:

"1. all children can learn and that it is the responsibility of the teacher to try various techniques and approaches to find out what will work for each child;

2. children do not all learn in the same ways since each is a unique individual;

3. a holistic approach to teaching improves learning;

4. knowledge is constructed, so care is taken in uncovering prior knowledge and building on it;

5. children, as learners, are teachers; teachers must also be learners;

6. teachers need to know each child very well in order to assist their intellectual, social, and emotional development;...

7. genuine understanding ... or generative knowledge... is a high priority, so continuity and connections in learning are emphasized;

8. teaching is guided by the child's strengths and interests;

9. learning is a continuous process, a 'continuum of growth';

10. self-reliance and independence of students is the ultimate goal;

11. time must be spent teaching children how to learn (learning about learning);

12. involvement of parents as teachers is crucial to learning; and

13. learning requires risk taking and mistakes"[13]

You may find it interesting to compare your own beliefs with those of the teachers in these two studies. Assuming you agree with the beliefs of these exemplary teachers, to what extent do your present classroom behaviors actually *support* the beliefs you claim to hold?

It's important to note that these teachers are *not* selected because they are "easy" or "popular." Many exemplary teachers have a reputation for being very tough—for having extremely high expectations and demanding that students live up to those expectations. Educators underestimate students when they believe students only want "easy" teachers. What they do want is teachers who listen to their ideas and their questions, treat them with respect, and demonstrate honest caring. For such teachers, students will work to the limits of their ability.

There is little or no mention in these studies of the number of knowledge objects that these teachers cram into their students and/or the subsequent test scores. How likely is it, however, that a teacher's peers, students, administration, and parents would praise a teacher whose students weren't demonstrating a high level of learning? At some fundamental level, it appears both educators and the public recognize what is important in teaching. Yet both continue to cave in to claims that increasing the number of standards and demanding that students "keep up" will ensure learning.

It is important to note that it is still possible for a teacher to demonstrate many or most of these qualities and still remain ineffective. It is imperative, then, that we don't give in to the temptation to create yet another checklist, and expect it to automatically improve the quality of teachers in our schools. For example, simply observing a teacher's behavior in the classroom without deeply analyzing the interaction between the teacher and students can be very misleading.

A study identified and described a number of observable characteristics and used them to identify differences among effective and ineffective teachers. The main categories included:

- Emotional Support, demonstrated by the level of positive climate, teacher sensitivity, and the teacher's regard for student perspectives.

- Classroom Organization, which includes behavior management, productivity, and instructional learning formats. To receive high marks for behavior management, a teacher would clearly and consistently communicate rules; be active, rather than reactive in management; and consistently praise students for meeting expectations.

- Instructional Support breaks into concept development, quality of feedback, and language modeling. A classroom with good instructional learning formats provides interesting materials and instruction, uses many modalities in instruction, and looks for opportunities that actively engage students. Teachers demonstrate a high regard for student perspectives by emphasizing student interests, motivations, and points of view, promoting students' autonomy; and encouraging them to talk and share ideas.[14]

How easy is it to identify these critical behaviors? Here is a description of the behaviors of a young high school trigonometry teacher taken from a video in the study.

He stands at the board, in jeans and a polo shirt, and says, "So let's see, special right triangles. We're going to do practice with this, just throwing out ideas." He drew two triangles." Label the length of the side if you can. If you can't, we'll all do it." Leaving the board, he moved quickly from student to student, asking for their ideas. Within two minutes, he was back at the board, taking the lesson a step further.

How would you judge the behaviors? Would you expect this teacher to be effective or ineffective? According to the researchers, moving about quickly might be interpreted as a bad thing because the subject was difficult. But for this teacher, his energy infected the class. Two and a half minutes into the lesson—the length of time it took a subpar teacher from another video to turn on the computer—this teacher had already laid out the problem and checked in with nearly every student in the class. He had established a non-threatening and positive climate, not only promising help, but giving individual feedback to his students.[15]

Another View of Teachers

"A teacher who can arouse a feeling for one single
good action, for one single good poem,
accomplishes more than he who fills our memory
with rows and rows of natural objects,
classified with name and form." ~ Goethe

In their book, *Education on the Edge of Possibility*[16], Renate and Geoffrey Caine describe three fundamental approaches they have observed among teachers. One might think of these as a teacher's stages of development.

- Instructional Approach 1 is consistent with the *knowledge as objects* and *mind-as-a-container* metaphors. It is the familiar "stand and deliver" model, wherein the teacher is in control of the information and transmits it to students. A Type 1 teacher tends to have a custodial, rather than humanistic view of teaching. The "top-down" model of teaching, from knowledge through the teacher to the student, prevails.

- Instructional Approach 2 contains some of the features of the first approach, but is more "complex and sophisticated." Although still driven by the "command and control" model of instruction, Type 2 teachers focus more on creating meaning rather than "just the facts, ma'am." They integrate more materials and engaging experiences into their teaching, while basically remaining in control.

* Instructional Approach 3, according to the Caines, is the most brain-compatible.

> "It differs radically from Instructional Approaches 1 and 2 because it is much more learner centered, with genuine student interest as its core. This kind of teaching is more fluid and open. It includes elements of self-organization as students focus individually or gather collectively around critical ideas, meaningful questions, and purposeful projects. Instructional Approach 3 teaching is also highly organic and dynamic, with educational experiences that approach the complexity of real life." [17]

Type 3 teachers perceive teaching and learning from the greatest number of perspectives. They have flexibility to include methods and approaches from all three categories. They adapt to moment-to-moment shifts in the present situation rather than arising from habit or limiting beliefs about teaching, learning, or students.

As with any other way of "sorting" people, these categories are merely steps on a continuum, but when one compares the description of Type 3 teachers to the characteristics of exemplary teachers, there is a definite correlation.

"Teaching is about everything human, and those who insist on looking only at intellectual abstractions, scorning getting themselves dusty with the rough-and-tumble of a child's reality, should not try it."
~Susan Ohanion

Knowing What and Knowing Why

Think of a practice that you use that has proven effective in facilitating learning. You know that it works because you see its effect on students. You know what you do. But do you know why it works? Do you have a research-based explanation for its effectiveness?

Even teachers who are highly effective can seldom explain why what they do works. Through trial and error, they have found that some things work and others don't. What's wrong with this, some may say. Master teachers are effective without knowledge of the brain or other educational research. What's wrong is that "many students with learning differences [normal variations] or learning disabilities [atypical variations] have not had their educational needs met."[18]

How many teachers can articulate their work based on a solid foundation of knowledge about how learning occurs? Yes, they may have learned a variety of theories in their teacher education classes. But are these theories what drive the day to day decisions in the classroom? Some suggest that this is one reason why teachers are not taken seriously as professionals. Ask a psychologist why he asks a particular question of a client and it's likely he can connect it to a particular theory or methodology. Ask a lawyer why he takes a particular direction in questioning witnesses, and it's likely she can provide case law related to her actions. Ask a teacher why he or she asks a particular question. How likely is it that the answer will relate to a particular learning theory?

A *profession* is often characterized by specialized training and knowledge. Can a field in which trial and error on the part of individuals is the most significant method of improvement be seen as a profession? Is the body of specialized knowledge changing in ways that show consistent improvement and adaptation to emerging paradigms? Would we consider medicine a profession if, after leaving school, each practitioner relied on trial and error to treat each person…or worse, used the same method to treat everyone?

I would be the first to agree that teachers in today's schools have little or no time to develop a theoretical background for their actions. As long as the focus remains on the transmission of more and more knowledge in less and less time, individual teachers must simply do the best they can with the resources they have.

221

What Makes Teachers Memorable?

Regardless of the beliefs other educators hold about learning and teaching, the most important beliefs are your own. In addition to analyzing the differences between your ideal and present classrooms, another way to reflect on teaching is to recall your "best" or favorite teachers. What qualities did they have that made them memorable?

Exemplary teachers are not easy to define. There are no simple rules about how to be an excellent teacher. In general, memorable teachers share a genuine concern for the development of individual students and are, through the force of their own interest and personality, able to motivate students to learn. Memorable teachers may share little in terms of personality but much in terms of the way they make their students feel about themselves and about learning.

The strengths of an exemplary teacher are apparent more in the faces and actions of their students than in watching the teacher, who may be laughing or stern, cajoling or demanding. Some would say choosing "outstanding" teachers is completely subjective. Yet, students often make that decision within moments of first encountering the teacher. Studies have demonstrated the personal characteristics of the teacher seem to be the defining factor. Exemplary teachers capitalize on their strengths and downplay their weaknesses, but are not afraid to admit their fallibility. In many cases, their willingness to learn along with their students teaches those students a most valuable lesson. Whatever the characteristics of the teacher, there is little doubt about the influence of those characteristics on the development of students—whether for better or worse.

---

1 Shulman, L. (2004). Professional development: Leaning from experience. In S. Wilson (Ed.), *The wisdom of practice: Essays on teaching, learning, and learning to teach.* p. 504. San Francisco: Jossey-Bass.
2 Kennedy, Mary M. "Knowledge and vision in teaching." *Journal of Teacher Education* 57.3 (2006): 205+. *General OneFile*. Web. 19 Aug. 2010.
3 Ibid.
4 Battista, Michael T. (1994, February). Teacher Beliefs and the Reform Movement in Mathematics Education. *Phi Delta Kappan,* 462–470.
5 Olsen, B.,& Sexton, D. (2009). Threat rigidity, school reform, and how teachers view their work inside current education policy contexts. *American Educational Research Journal,* 46, p. 25.

6 Pajares, F. (1996) Self-efficacy Beliefs in Academic Settings. *Review of Educational Research, Vol. 66, No. 4*, 543–578.

7 Agne, K J., Greenwood, G. E.& Miller, D. L. (1994). Relationships Between Teacher Belief Systems and Teacher Effectiveness. *The Journal of Research and Development in Education, Vol. 27, No. 3*, 142.

8 Ibid., 142

9 Ibid., 143.

10 Ibid., 144.

11 Ibid., 141.

12 Collinson, V. (1994). *Teachers as Learners: Exemplary Teachers' Perceptions of Personal and Professional Renewal.* San Francisco and London: Austin & Winfield. See also Collinson, V. (1999) Redefining Teacher Excellence. *Theory Into Practice, Vol. 38, No. 1*, 4–11.

13 Ibid., 86.

14 Pianta, Robert C., and Joseph P. Allen. "Building Capacity for Positive Youth Development in Secondary School Classrooms: Changing Teachers' Interactions with Students." In *Toward Positive Youth Development: Transforming Schools and Community Programs*, ed. Marybeth Shinn and Hirokazu Yoshikawa, 21-39. New York: Oxford University Press, 2008.

15 Bracey, Gerald W. (2009)"Identify and observe effective teacher behaviors." *Phi Delta Kappan* 90.10: 772+. General OneFile. Web. 19 Aug. 2010.

16 Caine, R. N. & Caine, G. (1997). *Education on the Edge of Possibility.* Arlington, VA: ASCD.

17 Ibid., 25.

18 Radin, Jean L. (2009)Brain-Compatible Teaching and Learning: Implications for Teacher Education *Educational Horizons, v88 n1* p 48 Fall 2009. Eric document number EJ868337

Chapter 13 ~ Beliefs about...
The Curriculum and Standards

Curriculum—from Latin meaning "a course for racing."

The Race—Where Is the Finish Line?

School mission statements often wax poetic in terms of the development of the "total child." However, what drives the everyday functioning of those schools is the *official* curriculum and the tests that hold teachers and students accountable to that curriculum. Curriculum designers are careful to mention that students should not be limited to the contents of the curriculum. They also acknowledge that "...we are all starting at different places, [so] we will take very different routes to arrive at our common goal." (I assume this is the royal "we" since students have had no input into the "common goal.")

Despite this tip of the hat to individual interests and abilities, tests at the end of the term are generally based on lists of knowledge objects identified in curriculum documents. Despite their acknowledged differences, students are typically tested on the same content in the same way. In only a relatively few schools do we find assessments that reflect the individual strengths of students. One obvious reason is such assessments can't be "standardized." Once again, group-think rears its ugly head and pushes the individual student into the background.

Components of a Curriculum

When people use the word *curriculum*, they are typically referring to the *content* of that curriculum. In schools that have adopted standards, the official curriculum reflects the strong emphasis on those standards. There is, however, more to a curriculum than the specific items listed in the "curriculum guide."

Explicit and Implicit Curricula

In Chapter 1, Larry Cuban's model of the *official, taught, learned,* and *tested* curricula was described. Educational theorist Elliot Eisner suggests the *explicit* curriculum, similar to Cuban's *official* and *taught* curricula, is a small part of what schools actually teach. Revising the content of this *explicit* curriculum does nothing to address the *implicit* curriculum.

> "...The implicit curriculum of the school is what it teaches because of the kind of place it is. And the school is that kind of place [because of] various approaches to teaching...the kind of reward system that it uses...the organizational structure it employs to sustain its existence...the physical characteristics of the school plant...the furniture it uses and the surroundings it creates. These characteristics constitute some of the dominant components of the school's implicit curriculum. ...These features are...intuitively recognized by parents, students, and teachers... because they are salient and pervasive features of schooling, *what they teach may be among the most important lessons a child learns.*"[1] (author's emphasis)

Eisner describes one of those lessons.

> "Most school rooms are designed as cubicles along corridors and have a kind of antiseptic quality to them. They tend to be repetitive and monotonous in the same way that some hospitals and factories are. They speak of efficiency more than they do of comfort.... Most of the furniture is designed for easy maintenance, is uncomfortable, and is visually sterile.... The point here is not so much to chastise school architects but to point out that the buildings that we build do at least two things: they express the values we cherish, and, once built, they reinforce those values. Schools are educational churches, and our gods, judging from the altars we build, are economy and efficiency. Hardly a nod is given to the spirit."[2]

Many caring teachers resist this sterile, impersonal environment. They find it as uncomfortable as do the students. These teachers do what they can to create an appealing environment. They form relationships with students. They do this in spite of the ever-present bells that trigger automatic movement from one class to the other much like the salivating of Pavlov's dogs. Despite the efforts of these teachers, the "kind of place school is" heavily influences the behavior of both teacher and student.

What do students learn? They learn their interest in a subject is less important than keeping to the class schedule or lesson plan. They learn social interaction is less important than the efficient functioning of passing periods. And they learn a consistent set of rules applied to everyone is more important than helping an individual student to understand the difference between appropriate and inappropriate behavior. Fundamentally, they learn that, as individuals, they are relatively unimportant in the scheme of things.

The Null Curriculum

"It is my thesis that what schools do not teach may be as important as what they do teach. Ignorance is not simply a neutral void; it has important effects on the kinds of options one is able to consider, the alternatives that one can examine, and the perspectives from which one can view a situation or problems. The absence of a set of considerations or perspectives or the inability to use certain processes for appraising a context biases the evidence one is able to take into account." ~Elliot Eisner

What curriculum designers and/or teachers choose to *leave out* of the curriculum is based on a number of factors.

- As demonstrated in Chapter 1, individual teachers have personal beliefs about the importance of various parts of the official curriculum. Given that they don't have time to "cover" everything, they automatically choose those concepts they consider more important or with which they feel more comfortable. It's not uncommon for teachers to choose topics simply because they find them more enjoyable or believe students will find them interesting.

- The same criteria for inclusion may apply for those who write the curriculum but in many cases, there is a more pervasive and unexamined motive. That is the current mindset, worldview, or paradigm of the culture or the individual. Because the Newtonian/mechanistic worldview still permeates traditional education, the universe of knowledge is consistently broken into parts. This mechanistic paradigm is "small chunk" as opposed to the systems paradigm, which is "large chunk."

The goals of the curriculum are stated in broad terms, but the actual content tends to be "small chunk"—specific bits of information and skills to be learned. The "big ideas," such as the paradigm shift that produced the Renaissance or the multitude of factors that converged to trigger the Civil War, may be *mentioned* at the beginning of each content section. However, the "small chunk" mentality is so deeply ingrained that these big ideas merely become handy titles for lists of specific facts to be learned. Little time is spent exploring these big ideas because there is no easy way to test students on them. Big ideas become part of the null curriculum.

The *null* curriculum supports the *implicit* curriculum. With economy and efficiency as the underlying societal values, big ideas are to be avoided. If big ideas became the reigning paradigm, curriculum developers and standards writers would find it difficult to identify specific concepts that *everyone* must know. There are simply too many perspectives when it comes to thinking of big ideas—too many connections and interactions, any and all of which might be "correct." This creates problems for standardized testing and data-driven assessment. The inability to "test" using multiple choice questions contributes to the null curriculum in unexpected ways. In an article in Education Week, Robert Leman and Arthur Packer describe the following incident. During a meeting, New York "...state's chief test-maker was asked why New York tested students' ability to factor a polynomial but not to speak standard English, even though good verbal skills matter far more on the job to far more people. The answer? 'Because we can test factoring but not speaking.'"[3]

In most schools, the prevailing worldview, such as mechanism or scientism, is taught. People in Western nations have adopted a relatively unquestioned worldview that the only valid way of solving problems of nature and man is science. This worldview is, therefore, the one that prevails in schools.[4]

> "...This is done covertly rather than overtly. That is, 'teacher talk' about the subject both presupposes the truth of these views and uses them to 'explain'. This is compounded by the fact that most popular textbooks also presuppose these views, presenting concepts in those frameworks without ever mentioning that there are other ways to explain them." [5]

It's unlikely that teachers are even aware of the worldview they hold because it is the only one to which *they've* been exposed. When someone suggests science may not be the best way to solve some problems, people react with shock, disbelief, or ridicule. Their indoctrination into this worldview is so complete that other possibilities are "unthinkable."

Students who question what the teacher says or express a different belief are seen as difficult or contrary.[6] Rather than taking time to help the student determine the strengths and weaknesses of his belief, the teacher often makes the student feel ignorant. As a student in one study put it, "If you ask a question he [the teacher] harasses you until you think you're stupid..."[7]

Interviews with the teacher in this study revealed that he truly didn't understand what the student was saying. His own worldview and beliefs were so "absolute" that he found the student's ideas "unthinkable" and concluded that the student was merely trying to be disruptive.

The lists of laws, rules, principles, definitions, and "steps" that make up so much of the official curriculum convey the implicit message that such knowledge is absolute. There is little or no discussion about how and why the knowledge came into being—what problems made new ideas necessary—what led to their acceptance. Many teachers who transmit these ideas believe that the "rules" of grammar or the "laws" of motion are sacrosanct—immutable and true in some absolute sense. And that's what they teach.

The kinds of knowledge mentioned in Chapter 10—*innate understanding, episodic knowledge, impressionistic knowledge*, and *reflective knowledge*—are ignored. This knowledge arises in the *knower* rather than in an external body of knowledge. Because the transmission of disembodied knowledge is the fundamental purpose of many schools, there is little reason to consider forms of knowing that arise in the mind. They are relegated to the null curriculum.

Once again, we encounter the foreground/background shift that must occur to make students, rather than knowledge, the primary focus of education. That shift will open a Pandora's Box that many traditional educators fear. The efficiency and economy that have been the rule in compulsory education will largely disappear. Authentic assessments will be needed to replace lists of factoids that can be machine-graded. Many tenets of conventional wisdom will shrivel in the light of research and honest, thoughtful appraisal rather than blind acceptance.

Beliefs about Standards

THE DIFFERENCES IN INDIVIDUAL DIFFERENCES
AUTHOR UNKNOWN

Once upon a time, the animals decided they must do something heroic to meet the problem of a "new world," so they organized a school. They adopted an activity curriculum consisting of running, climbing, swimming, and flying, and to make it easier to administer, all the animals took all the courses.

The duck was excellent in swimming, better in fact than his instructor. He made passing grades in flying, but he was poor in running. Since he was slow in running, he had to stay after school and also drop swimming to practice running. This was kept up until his web feet were badly worn and he was only average in swimming. But average was acceptable in school, and nobody worried about that except the duck.

The rabbit started at the top of the class in running, but had a nervous breakdown because of so much makeup work in swimming.

The squirrel was excellent in climbing until he developed frustration in the flying class where his teacher made him start from the ground up instead of from the treetop down. He also developed charley horses from over-exertion and then got a "C" in climbing and a "D" in running.

The eagle was a problem child and was disciplined severely. In the climbing class he beat all the others to the top of the tree, but insisted on using his own way to get there.

At the end of the year, an abnormal eel that could swim exceedingly well, and also run, climb, and fly a bit had the highest average and was valedictorian.

The prairie dogs stayed out of school and fought the tax levy because the administration would not add digging and burrowing to the curriculum. They apprenticed their child to a badger and later joined the groundhogs and gophers to start a successful private school.

Standards and Benchmarks

Although most teachers are affected by standards, some may not be familiar with the structure of standards documents. The Standards database created by the Mid-continent Regional Education Laboratory (McREL) identifies *standards*, the "big ideas" in each subject area, and *benchmarks*, the specific (and testable) items for which students are held accountable. Unfortunately, people often use the word *standards* when they are really referring to *benchmarks*.

The specificity of the standards themselves varies from subject to subject. There are only eight *standards* listed for language arts.

- Demonstrates competence in the general skills and strategies of the writing process.

- Demonstrates competence in the stylistic and rhetorical aspects of writing.

- Uses grammatical and mechanical conventions in written compositions.

- Gathers and uses information for research purposes.

- Demonstrates competence in the general skills and strategies of the reading process.

- Demonstrates competence in the general skills and strategies for reading a variety of literary texts.

- Demonstrates competence in the general skills and strategies for reading a variety of informational texts.

- Demonstrates competence in speaking and listening as tools for learning.

It would be difficult to find fault with any of these standards. However, because standards writers feared that teachers might interpret such terms as "demonstrates competence" in different ways, they broke down each standard into specific procedural statements—*benchmarks*. It's important to recognize that benchmarks were originally intended to be *examples* of topics that might be included in a standard. Over time, these "examples" have taken on a life of their own. In many states, they have *become* the content of the curriculum.[8]

There are different sets of benchmarks for primary, elementary, middle/junior high, and high school—when the Mid-Continent Regional Education Lab compiled all the standards documents in 2000, there were nearly four thousand benchmarks in fourteen subject areas. Here is one of several benchmarks for the first language arts standard listed previously:

Editing and publishing: Uses strategies to edit and publish written work (e.g., proofreads using a dictionary and other resources; edits for grammar, punctuation, capitalization, and spelling at a developmentally appropriate level; incorporates illustrations or photos; shares finished product).

Sounds reasonable—until you realize that this benchmark is listed for *Kindergarten to 2nd grade*! If this benchmark began with the words "for example," one might understand its value. But in many schools, benchmarks such as this are literally translated into tested behaviors that *all* students are expected to exhibit. Further, if the goal of the benchmark is to eliminate teacher variability in the interpretation of the standard, what guarantee is there that all teachers will interpret "developmentally appropriate level" in the same way?

In more content-heavy subjects, the standards multiply. For example, in world history, there are forty-six standards and although they are still "big ideas," they are at least an order of magnitude more specific than the language arts standards. Here is *one* of those forty-six standards, followed by *one* of the benchmarks for that standard—this one for elementary students in grades five and six.

Standard 19—Understands the maturation of an interregional system of communication, trade, and cultural exchange during a period of Chinese economic power and Islamic expansion.

Benchmark—Understands different elements of Japanese feudal society (e.g., Japanese government during the Kamakura and Ashikaga periods, and whether it was feudalism; the rise of the warrior class in feudal Japan and the values it prescribed; how the economic and social status of women and peasants changed in feudal Japanese society; how art and aesthetic values were cherished in the warrior culture in Japan and what this art reveals about Japanese values; how the Japanese successfully defended themselves against Mongol invasions in the 13th century).

Because world history deals with such a long period of time and so many different cultures, there are similar standards and benchmarks for each era and each culture. Rather than listing *general* knowledge and abilities as do the language arts standards, world history standards are already specific.

Textbook publishers take state standards documents very seriously, particularly in states with textbook adoption programs. If publishers want their textbooks adopted by a state, it is incumbent on them to make sure that every standard and benchmark listed in the state standards documents is "covered."[9] As an example, in 2009, Texas had a 125-page document just *listing* their history standards and benchmarks.[10] It's not uncommon for middle and junior high school history textbooks to run well over 1000 pages. Even at that length, there is barely enough room to *mention* each of the topics, much less develop it in any meaningful way. One analyst recently commented that today's textbooks belong in the reference section of a library…not in students' book bags.

A large percentage of benchmarks begin with or include the word *understands*. If understanding does, indeed, require the development of a relationship with an idea or concept, how can students conceivably develop those relationships given the number of specific ideas and concepts for which they are held accountable? Developing a relationship requires more than "touching on," reading about, or "discussing" an idea for twenty minutes. Until educators confront the time necessary to achieve true understanding, they will remain blind to the impossibility of *any* child, much less all of them, demonstrating true understanding of thousands of benchmarks in the time allotted.

The Case for Standards

> "Off the rack solutions, like bargain basement dresses, never fit anyone." ~ Francoise Giroud

Few words in education evoke as many heated arguments as the word *standards*. The word has taken on such negative connotations for many people that it may need to be replaced at some time. But this doesn't mean standards are "all bad." Let's begin by looking at why standards were proposed and why so many people feel they are needed.

Unfortunately, all teachers do not share high expectations for their students. Studies have shown that the expectations of teachers vary for students in different ability groups (so-called *remedial, average*, and *honors*), as well as for different cultural or socioeconomic groups. Many teachers adopt expectations about their students early in the school year, sometimes *before they even meet the students.*

In an article comparing the way experienced and beginning teachers think about their students, David Berliner[11] includes the following quotes from four "postulant" teachers.

> "I sorted the bad kids from the good kids from some of the ones that were just good natured, if they like to work, that type of thing.... I always wanted to have my eye out for the cause of the trouble, and I think that's natural."

> "I went through her [the previous teacher's] student cards and also went through the test scores and tried to divide the students into three groups, one group which I thought might be disruptive, one group which I thought would not be disruptive and that wouldn't need intense watching. The third group I really didn't know because the back of the card was blank. ...I decided to sort of rank cards from what I thought would be the best student from top to the obviously poorer students going down the stack just to get some sort of an idea of ranking."

> "Thirty some people I'm not going to remember right off the bat, but I'm going to try to identify who these people are. You know, your top side and your bottom side."

> "Kim Wong looks like an excellent student. He made an 89 on that test. And then the background sort of goes with that. His father is a scientist of some sort, and his mother does some kind of computer software. On the other hand, the other extreme is that Sue Gallegos. ...I think she made a 22 on the test; she was the low end of the score. She's going to be a real problem...."[12]

The beliefs that underlie such statements should, by now, be apparent. One thing is clear. Once a student has been "ranked," once a student has been labeled "bad" or "good," "top side or bottom side," the chances of that student changing the teacher's mind are greatly reduced. The teacher's expectations and beliefs about that student become a self-fulfilling prophecy, limiting the teacher to perceptions that support those preconceptions.

233

Teachers who hold low expectations for a student often spend less time and effort on that student than they do on students from whom they expect high achievement. Clearly unfair to the students, this is one of the main arguments for the creation of standards. According to an extensive study done by the McREL,

> "There appear to be three principle reasons advanced for the development for standards: standards serve to clarify and raise expectations, and standards provide a common set of expectations."[13]

Are these reasons valid? In government documents describing education policy, the word *standards* is frequently used synonymously with *expectations*. Rhetoric implies that *standards* will force teachers to *expect* the same achievement in all students, regardless of the child's background or previous educational experience. But this juxtaposition is not supported by experience. Standards are *external* criteria against which a product is evaluated. Expectations are much more complex. They are defined as something a person *looks for* or *anticipates*. Standards represent *minimum* criteria for a "product" to be acceptable. What a person *expects* may be anything from below minimum standards to well above standard. In practice, it is possible to have extremely high expectations without any standards at all, and to have extremely low expectations despite the imposition of standards.

I question whether there is a simple cause-and-effect relationship between the imposition of standards and a teacher's expectations. If you know that every student in your class will be held accountable for an externally generated list of concepts, does that really change what you believe about a particular student's ability to learn those concepts—what you *expect* of the student?

In theory, if all students are held to the same standards, the teachers will be forced to spend as much (or more) time with students for whom they hold lower expectations as they do with the "good" students. According to this reasoning, these students will get equal opportunities they didn't previously have. This is, without question, an admirable goal. If a teacher's livelihood depends on how well his students do on those high-stakes tests, he may feel compelled to work more with students he believes to be less capable. That's hardly the same thing as raising that teacher's expectations.

Equating standards with expectations fails to address the fundamental issue—the inappropriate and unfounded beliefs of teachers that create low expectations for some students. Although I despise the factory metaphor for schools, it may be of some limited use here. Does a manufacturer improve the quality of work of his employees by creating more specifications—finer tolerances—for the product? Isn't changing the work ethic of the employees themselves a more appropriate approach to improving their quality of work?

Another metaphor common in the standards movement—*raising the bar*—provokes a further question. Before a jumper can clear that bar, she must possess and refine the fundamental skills involved in jumping. The coach assists the jumper in learning and improving those skills. If the coach begins with the belief that the jumper has little natural ability, how does *raising the bar* change the way the coach treats the jumper?

Despite the worthy goals of standards—to give every student equal opportunity for an excellent education and to create high expectations for all—the standards movement may have put an ill-advised burden on students in the name of helping them. High expectations already exist in many classrooms. They are conveyed to students when teachers *believe in* those students. Recognizing that a student may not "have a mind" for geometry while acknowledging that same student's outstanding ability in literature is *not* a case of low expectations. Proclaiming that student incapable of "success" because he can't pass standardized tests in *every* subject is!

There is a critical difference between expecting *all* students to excel in *all* subjects and expecting *each* student to work to the absolute peak of his or her ability. It is no more reasonable to "raise the bar" to the same intellectual height for all students than it is to expect every student to be able to clear the same height physically. Why do teachers intuitively understand the message in stories like the one that began this section, yet continue to ignore it in their own teaching?

Standards and the Bell Curve

Some believe that standards eliminate the inequities produced by the Bell Curve.[14] Yet, the presupposition that, because a student is a certain age, he or she is ready to learn specific things is a holdover from Bell Curve thinking. The Bell Curve is an icon of group-think because it exists only when students are "measured" in groups.

Take any specific skill and compare the competency of a random sampling of the population on that skill. It comes as no surprise that some people are better at it than others! The Bell Curve has become such an important factor in educational decision-making, teachers have forgotten that it provides little information about any given student *except where that student stands within the group*—and then *only in terms of the measured characteristic*. If I know a student has average height, average speed in a hundred meter race, or average ability to fill in the correct bubbles on a math test, all I really know is how that student compares to others with whom he was measured. I know nothing about his other strengths or weaknesses and I certainly cannot justify extrapolating that information to judging his "intelligence" or his likelihood of "success" in life.

The Paradox of Standards Testing

The belief that standards can move education away from the Bell Curve, which assumes that a certain percentage of people are "below normal," is contradicted by actual events. Consider the following statements.

Standards recommend a *minimum* competency. According to the language of standards documents, schools are accountable to insure that all students can attain this minimum.

One would assume that questions on standards-based tests would assess student competency on those standards. There would be no question of what items to include—one would just include the items listed in the standards.

Given that, the best thing that could happen would be for every student to get all of the answers correct. Isn't that the stated goal of the standards movement?

Now consider what has happened in some states.

- "In North Carolina, state officials are saying that the passing score for the end-of-grade math tests was set too low because too many students passed...They need an even distribution of scores, passing and not passing (the Bell Curve), to show that the test is neither too easy nor too hard.

- "In California, officials are trying to decide where to set the passing score for their tests. They can't set it too low, because it will look like the test was too easy; and they can't set it too high, because it will look like it was too hard. They're not talking about which score will show that the students have learned the material—they're talking about comparing the students…so that there will be an expected number of passing and failing ones."[15]

How can a person "pass" a test of *minimums* without getting everything correct? It seems apparent that there is some confusion about the purpose of standards and their ability to force educators and the public to resist the Bell Curve mindset.

Standards aimed at the center of the Bell Curve effectively discriminate against those who don't fall at or near that center. Opportunities supposedly afforded to *all* students by rigorously worded standards are too much for some and too little for others. Students capable of more must plod along and stay with the class, making do with "extra credit projects" for stimulation. Those not yet ready fall farther and farther behind because all subsequent work depends on possession of basic skills that those students have not had the opportunity to learn. Ironically, some states are now thinking about using two sets of standards—one for the "higher ability" students and one for those with "lower ability." So much for eliminating the Bell Curve!

Standards for All—Literacy

"The teacher must not confuse Information with Education, otherwise the student may become a well-taught but wholly unlearning individual."
~S. E. Whitnall, in 1933

Are there any external standards that can and should be applied to all students? Literacy is, of course, something everyone agrees on as a fundamental goal of schooling. Unfortunately, it's difficult to get agreement from everyone about what *literacy* means. Is it simply the ability to read, write, and perform basic arithmetic operations? Or does it goes far beyond—to being a "well-educated" person? If so, what does *well-educated* mean?

Certainly, all healthy children should read, write, and develop an understanding of arithmetic sufficient to allow them to function effectively in society. Although these skills are spelled out in standards for early grades, there is simply no guarantee that every student can or will *develop* those skills *at the specified time*, any more than they will all be a certain height or weight at a specified time. The two factors that are ignored by these grade-specific standards are a student's individual readiness and a student's need to know.

Because communication skills and basic arithmetic are the fundamental "units" of literacy, doesn't it make sense to concentrate on those fundamentals at whatever level of readiness and need the student possesses? How can this happen in the present graded school system where content is neatly placed in grade level cubbyholes and where students proceed through grade levels at the same rate?[16]

There is little recourse for the child who "fails" to achieve all the externally mandated learning goals of a particular grade except the social stigma of being "held back." Or they may receive a "social promotion," falling even farther behind in the next grade. The effect of either of these choices on the child's inborn love of learning rarely enters the picture and is often the exact opposite of the stated goals of standards. Many students come to dread school and can't wait until they can legally leave it behind.

Cultural Literacy

Beyond the basic definition of literacy, the "essential" knowledge necessary for "cultural literacy" is another area of controversy. In 1988, E. D. Hirsch, Jr., and his colleagues wrote a book that addressed this issue. Called *Cultural Literacy*, the book listed 4,552 items *all* Americans *should* know to be culturally literate. These include:

- Who wrote Macbeth?

- What is a *nonsequitor*?

- What does *nouveau riche* mean?

- Who was Spiro Agnew?

Hirsch argues that "In an anthropological perspective (the name which Hirsch chooses for the Cultural Literacy point of view), the basic goal of education is acculturation, the *transmission to our children of the specific information* shared by the adults of the group or polis." [author's emphasis] Hirsch also states that, "... literate culture has become the common currency for social and economic exchange in our democracy, and is the only available ticket to full citizenship.... Membership is automatic if one learns the background information and the linguistic conventions that are needed to read, write, and speak effectively."

In *Engines for Education*, Roger Shank states that

> "The Cultural Literacy movement is gaining ground today as the public demands some assurance that schools are really teaching the 'right stuff' and that children are learning it. What better way to achieve these goals than to write down exactly what the right stuff is, tell it to students, then test them to make sure that they got it? Such a system seems to be rational.

> "The problem is that such a notion of the right stuff flies in the face of what we know about how the mind works. The Cultural Literacy movement, which purports to be founded on scientific findings concerning how people use knowledge, is actually based on a flawed notion of what people are and how they operate. ... it also faces a set of problems that stems from its rigid and faulty theories of what knowledge is, how people learn, and how teaching should be conducted."[17,18]

Other critics suggest that Mr. Hirsch's "...lists of core knowledge are flawed. They value *familiarity* of knowledge over the *significance* of what students *should* learn."[19] Further, in a country that is a much of a cultural patchwork as the United States, whose *culture* is to be chosen? Are the previous bits of knowledge any more significant than the following?

• Who wrote the Harry Potter series?

• What is Kwanzaa?

• What does *cloud computing* mean?

• Who is Sonia Sotomayer?

Lists such as these are the ultimate example of the *knowledge as objects* and *mind as file cabinet* metaphors. First, the items are context-free and, therefore, meaningless in and of themselves. They are subject to the problem of how and why one might retrieve them from the file cabinet for any reason other than a game of *Trivial Pursuit*® or *Jeopardy*®. Further, the choice of which knowledge objects are "essential" clearly reflects the age, interest, culture, and yes, the education, of the person identifying those objects, not to mention the passage of time. Some might say they represent an elitist view of what makes an educated person, preventing those whose strengths lie in other areas from being valued for their gifts.

The obsession with the possession of knowledge ignores the exponential proliferation of information. More and more "stuff" becomes "essential" as determined by people who work within a given discipline. As the number of disciplines also increases, the amount of essential information becomes prohibitively large. The race to "collect" these bits of information effectively eliminates any time to truly "understand" any of it.

What Is Essential Knowledge?

"What learners need is not, in the last analysis, finite bundles of ...competence properly describable as 'skills', but the vision to see what is appropriate in a given situation. They especially need the vision to see which tiny drop of an almost infinite ocean of ...accessible knowledge is needed to solve a given problem." ~ Christopher Ormell[20]

The word *essential* means *containing the essence of something*. Those who make up lists of "essential knowledge" apparently perceive *essence* as a collection of isolated bits of information. What is the *essence* of language? Is it a list of grammar and syntax rules? Is it punctuation and spelling? Is it a list of books and authors? Or is it a method of communication between members of a species? What is more essential—knowing the definition of *simile* or the ability to explain oneself more effectively to someone else?

Although there may be little agreement on what specific knowledge within a discipline is actually essential, agreement is more readily reached when people "chunk up" to the big ideas—ideas that are more representative of the "essence" of the discipline. What is the essence of science, of mathematics, of history? What are the pervasive principles that a practitioner in each of these disciplines uses to understand and effectively operate in the world? I would suggest that, whatever they are, they are orders of magnitude different from today's benchmarks.

What is the *essence* of historical understanding? What does an historian look for when first studying an era or a culture? Isn't it more "essential" for students to know how to "unpack" the volumes of information available on a subject—to find patterns and meaning within it—than to memorize isolated bits of that information? Once possessed of that ability, all eras—all cultures—are open to study as the need arises.

This is not to say specifics are unimportant. However, when the need for those specifics arises from the big ideas, the learner acquires them much more readily and willingly. If one has the picture on the cover of a jigsaw puzzle box as a template when putting together the puzzle, one can see where the piece fits. Learning the specifics without the big idea is simply collecting puzzle pieces.

The call for accountability remains. Certainly, schools should be accountable—but accountable for what? Presently, the answer to that question seems to be "accountable for high test scores." All too often, the rigidity of the present system and the focus on the accumulation of isolated bits of information has left students with an aversion to books and learning. In this rapidly changing world, where what one learns today may be obsolete tomorrow, wouldn't it be more effective if schools were held accountable for developing students who 1.) possess the tools they will need for future learning; and 2.) exhibit a love of learning? Students who will continue to grow in wisdom and in their ability to function effectively (and happily) in a changing world?

There are ways to assess those qualities despite the claims of some that such goals are "wishy-washy," ill-defined, or ambiguous. Creating such assessments requires starting at the beginning in terms of the behaviors we really want students to exhibit. It also requires rethinking the idea that "standards" (and standardized tests) are the only, or even the most effective or appropriate, measure of accountability.

A switch to standards that focus on pervasive principles rather than isolated facts is unlikely to occur until students become more important than efficiency, economy, and standardized data. This is no small change, no isolated reform. It requires that education *transform* into a very different process.

World-Class Schools

Another argument for standards is the poor showing of American students on international tests. Some have argued that reformers have "cooked" the statistics to make a point, but let's assume that, at least in some subjects, American students do indeed score lower than students from other countries. Let's also assume, as many do, that the tests reflect the quality of our educational system. (Think about the presuppositions in that belief.)

In 1994-95, The Third International Mathematics and Science Study (TIMSS) was conducted with millions of students at five grade levels in more than forty countries.[21] In addition to testing students in mathematics and science, extensive data were collected from students, teachers, and school principals. TIMSS may well be "the largest and most ambitious study of international student achievement ever conducted."[22] In 1995, researchers did an extensive analysis of the data they collected and, not surprisingly, found a direct correlation between test scores and how subjects were taught.

The recommendations they proposed for mathematics educators speak to teachers of all disciplines and grade levels.

- Focus on powerful, central ideas and capacities.

- Pursue greater depth, so that content has a chance to be meaningful, organized, and linked to the student's other ideas, and to produce insight and intuition rather than rote performance.

- Provide rigorous, powerful, meaningful content-producing learning that lasts.[23]

Compare these recommendations to the present standards and benchmarks in math and science. Why, when standards documents demand that *all* students use research findings to support their ideas, do the writers of those documents ignore this highly significant research?

Mathematics educator Seymour Papert argues the "...deep structure of our educational system is linked to our models of knowledge and cannot change until they do."[24] Changing that structure is challenging.

> "...any such shift threatens the stability of the entire system [because] so many things are tied to the existing paradigm—textbooks, journals, equipment, research labs, university departments, and a great number of individuals who fear the profound effects of such a profound change."[25]

Are those reasons sufficient to justify the mindless adherence to practices that are known to have a negative influence on so many students?

Perspectives on Standards

The issue of standards has been widely discussed in educational journals as well as in recent books by authors such as Susan Ohanion[26], Diane Ravitch[27], and Alfie Kohn.[28] Rather than restating the arguments, I'd like to raise several questions.

1. The first issue relates to the McREL study concluding that:

> "Even the brightest students would need *nine additional years of schooling* to master the nearly 4,000 benchmarks experts have set in 14 subject areas."[29](author's emphasis)

According to researcher Robert Marzano and his colleagues,

> "Subject-matter specialists and policymakers who have sought to clarify what students should learn have not considered the curriculum as a whole. The net result is a curriculum that is overwhelming to teachers and students."[30]

Experts from each discipline have amassed the "essential" information from their fields. Too often, rather than beginning with the fundamental question of what is really important for people to know, many standards are simply a restatement of what textbooks already contained or what had been traditionally taught.[31]

Even more fundamental is the issue of the disciplines themselves. The subject areas traditionally taught in schools are artificial and arbitrary categories created in order to efficiently manage the universe of knowledge. Those categories do not exist in the real world. A simple experience such as driving a car encompasses physics, math, chemistry, technology, driver education, law and government, reading, communication, psychology, and a host of cognitive thinking skills. Yet a person doesn't need to take classes in all those subjects before driving. Isolating one of those disciplines at the expense of the others gives students a skewed understanding of mental processing.

Are the categories presently used appropriate in the twenty-first century? Are they consistent with the emerging systems view of the world? Do they place artificial barriers on teaching about the effects of chemical pollution on biological systems, or how enhanced communication through the Internet can influence the practices of tuna fisherman? Wouldn't a thematic, rather than a discipline-oriented, approach to content be more appropriate? If so, what are those themes and what essential knowledge arises from them?

2. Standards-based reformers claim that all "normal" students are capable of achieving the goals set in the standards. What evidence do they offer that this is true? How do they define "normal"? If a Nobel Prize winner in one branch of science didn't "think" the way colleagues in another branch did, can we really expect "all" students to achieve the same level of understanding in such diverse fields as science, history, technology, and mathematics?

Does every student need to *know the date of the Council of Trent* or do they need a sense of how religion may influence the history of the times? Does every student need to *know about the growth of the Maurya Empire and the political and moral achievements of the emperor Asoka*, or do they need an understanding of how the past influences the present? How do these two benchmarks contribute to a student's "understanding" of history when there is time to do little more than memorize a few names, dates, places, and "major points"?

3. In many cases, the people who wrote the standards and benchmarks are recognized experts in their disciplines. It is unlikely they would have been asked to work on such an important project if they weren't deemed successful. I would challenge those writers to take the same tests on the standards that *all students* must know—*not in the discipline for which they wrote the standards, but in all the other disciplines*. If the standards and benchmarks are truly *essential* for a person to be successful—to be "educated"—then the standards writers should have no problem with those tests. Isn't it fair that, before setting out the lists of "essential knowledge" by which the success of teachers and their students shall be judged, those engaged in the development of those lists should subject themselves to that same judgment?

4. "To expect all of our educational aspirations to be either verbally describable or measurable is to expect too little."[32] With these words, Elliot Eisner addresses another flaw in the system of standards—they are simply too limiting in what they require. But, you may say, standards don't limit students from going farther, from thinking more deeply. In a number of ways, they do.

First, they rarely allow either teachers or students the time to think more deeply. Second, they teach—through the implicit and null curricula—that thinking more deeply is not as important as possessing and reproducing specific facts. Eisner asks how one can describe the qualities of a Beethoven quartet in precise, unambiguous, measurable terms. Of course, that won't be a problem when the "less important" subjects such as music and art are dropped from the curriculum because there is no longer time to include them.[33]

> "Standards are crisp, unambiguous, and precise. A person can swim five lengths of the pool or cannot. Someone can spell *aardvark* or cannot. Someone knows who the 27th president of the United States was or does not. ...But what about the rhetorical force of a student's essay? What about the aesthetic quality of her painting? What about the cogency of his verbal argumentation? What about her intellectual style, the ways she interprets the evidence in a science experiment, the way in which historical material is analyzed. Are these subject to standards? I think not."[34]

Standards proponents counter questions such as this with words like "fuzzy," "wishy-washy," or "touchy-feely." Here is a classic example. In November 1996, then-Texas Governor George W. Bush harshly criticized some of the standards in the Texas Essential Knowledge and Skills (TEKS). He was especially upset about one standard in particular.

> "I don't know what that means. Moreover, I don't know how you test a child on that sentence. We must state plainly what we want students to know and when we want them to know it. No touchy-feely essays or learning by osmosis. No holding hands until the karma is right. Just straightforward lists of state expectations.

> "I intend to make sure that the TEKS is fundamental education. If it ends up with mush in there, I won't be satisfied."[35]

Here is the "mush," the "touchy-feely" standard, about which then-Governor Bush was so upset.

> Students will be expected to analyze "the influence of the speaker's verbal and nonverbal behaviors on the listener's perception and acceptance or rejection of the message."

Unlike many of the benchmarks, this statement actually requires students to "analyze" rather than simply *state, explain,* or *understand.* Because it is a higher level thinking skill, analysis isn't as easily tested in multiple-choice questions. However, consider this.

- Research suggests that 80 percent of communication may be nonverbal.

- "Spin doctors" are now essential members of business and political teams. Their jobs? To influence the perception of others!

- Billions of dollars are spent each year researching people's reactions to various words, colors, or behaviors. The results of this research are used in advertising, business, and politics—with the obvious intent of influencing the minds and thoughts of the population.

Shouldn't "essential knowledge" include the ability to recognize when one is being manipulated? To identify and protect oneself against the verbal and nonverbal "tricks" used to influence opinions and purchasing? In fact, the skills mentioned in this very standard were used to analyze why Governor Bush "won" the nationally televised presidential debates. Are educators so obsessed with easily tested "facts" that higher-level thinking skills such as analysis have become "mush"?

5. Finally, let's assume the standards and benchmarks are right on the money. Let's assume they are exactly what every student should know and be able to do. Let's also assume E. D. Hirsch's list of "things" every cultured person must know is correct. Finally, let's say that every student in every school aces every test of every standard and benchmark as well as tests on Hirsch's list. What would we have? Would insightful conversations arise whenever people met? Would society have fewer problems—or more people who could solve those problems? How would this marvelous community of "educated, culturally literate, successful" people serve civilization?

If we are to believe the words of the standards documents, achievement in all of the disciplines will allow everyone to be successful. That success, either implied or directly stated in many of those documents, means having a productive job in a well-paying profession. Does this mean people will no longer *choose* to wait tables, repair cars, play a guitar in a coffee house, or sit in Jackson Square in New Orleans and draw portraits of passersby?

The definition of success described in standards documents is both limited and limiting. Certainly every student should have the right and the opportunity to go as far or as high in academia as they wish. However, the assumption that this is the only measure of success is both inaccurate and elitist. Despite the tremendous abilities that students demonstrate in areas not included in the standards, the implicit curriculum sends the message that they are failures because they don't remember Hammurabi's Code or can't balance a chemical equation.

What if teachers went into the classroom with the belief that, metaphorically, every child has within him or her a great work of art? A Peter Max print is not a Michelangelo. Rembrandt is very different from Van Gogh or Grandma Moses. Nevertheless, there is value in the work of each of these artists.

If expectations are truly the concern, let's look once again at exemplary teachers. These teachers hold the highest expectations for their students—just not the same ones for all! In their classrooms, each individual student is given the opportunity to achieve—and is *expected* to achieve—as much as that student is capable of achieving. The teachers worry less about "leaving no child behind" than about "moving every child ahead." Their expectations arise, not from external standards, but from the beliefs they have in and about their students.

Even without the belief that all students can learn, many teachers fail to support either the philosophy or the goals of standards-driven programs such as NCLB. In one study, teachers overwhelmingly expressed their belief that NCLB will not live up to its expectation for universal proficiency for all students by 2013-14. They believed that the goal was completely unrealistic given existing inequities in resources, teachers, and student background between and among school districts.

In the same study,

> "Many teachers also commented that NCLB went against their personal teaching philosophies and felt extreme pressure to 'perform and conform' to scripted curricula and standards. One teacher commented: 'The reality is that all children are different and should be educated differently to best meet their individual needs. As a nation of different people, we must envision a future where those differences ARE important. No two children are the same, so why do we insist on closing our

eyes to those differences? It is those nuances of culture, language and tradition that we must build upon in order for true national success."[36]

Unfortunately, those who support standards accuse teachers who oppose them of being lazy…of not wanting to be "exposed" as poor teachers by high stakes tests. This is yet one more example of the low esteem in which the teaching profession is held. Even with added criticism from other knowledgeable stakeholders, discontent in standards has not yet reached critical mass sufficient to force a reexamination of the fundamental concepts.

For example, early in the history of NCLB, Robert Reich, a former U.S. Secretary of Labor, said,

> "…[W]e're embracing standardized tests just when the new economy is eliminating standardized jobs. If there's one certainty about what today's schoolchildren will be doing a decade or two from now, it's that they won't all be doing the same things, and they certainly won't be drawing on the same body of knowledge.
>
> "…[I]n the old mass-production economy…most people spent most of their working lives performing the same operations over and over…. A standardized education was appropriate because jobs were standardized. In general, the largest pedagogical challenge was to train young people to sit still for long periods of time, be patient, follow directions, and be punctual."

Reich points out that the new economy requires much different skills.

> "Many of the new jobs depend on creativity—on out-of-the-box thinking, originality, and flair. …Other jobs…depend on the ability to listen and to discern what other people are feeling or what they're needing."
>
> "…Tests can help measure whether children have achieved an adequate level of communication skills and numeracy, and even help pinpoint where children need more guidance. But in many other ways, our new obsession with standardized tests runs exactly counter to the new demands of the modern economy."[37]

As the emphasis on standards have largely failed to fulfill its promise, increasing numbers of people are speaking out against the unreasonable toll that standards and high-stakes testing have placed on students and teachers.[38]Criticism of the latest incarnation of standards—the Common Core State Standards Initiative—are no less harsh, attacking the project on many levels. Here are a few examples from an article by Sara Bernard entitled *National Education Standards Initiative Draws Criticism.*

- The Gesell Institute calls the K-3 standards "inappropriate and unrealistic," claiming that they completely ignore early child development research showing that early readers do not have an advantage over later readers.

- The NCLB-induced 'push-down' effect asks younger and younger children to do more and more. "Once, schools gave youngsters a chance to learn how to read according to their own development. Now, a child who still can't read by the end of first grade is in deep trouble from which it can be hard to emerge."

- The Center for Elementary Mathematics and Science Education claim that the proposed standards are not up to par for the 21st century since they limit students to a "back-to-basics curriculum that has ignored the profound changes in the last 50 years."[39]

Debates about what students should be taught and how that learning should be assessed are ongoing. Once again, teachers must stand up and make their voices heard rather than allowing themselves (and more important, their students) to be victims of a system that is too often driven by political and economic expediency rather than honest concerns for individual students.

---

1 Eisner, E. (1994). *The Educational Imagination: On the Design and Evaluation of School Programs*, 3rd ed. New York: Macmillan College Publishing.
2 Ibid, pp. 96–97.
3 Leman, Robert I., and Packer, Arnold. Will We Ever Learn? What's Wrong With the Common-Standards Project. *Education Week*, April 21, 2010, accessed at http://www.urban.org/publications/901345.html on August 14, 2010.
4 Lest you decide that I am "anti-science," I taught chemistry, physics, and physical science for twenty years and chaired the science department of a large high school. I feel qualified to comment on science because of my familiarity with it and the way it is taught. I do recognize the contributions it has made to society. However, it is

not the only way to expand human knowledge. Because students are not presented with other alternatives, they are led to believe that science is the only valid approach to "truth." Worse, they are taught that any idea that cannot be "proven" by science is not worth considering.

5 Proper, H., Wideen, M. F., & Ivany, G. (1988). World View Projected by Science Teachers: A Study of Classroom Dialogue. *Science Education, Vol. 72, No. 5*, 547–560.

6 Yerrick, R. K., Pedersen, J. E., & Arnason, J. (1998) We're Just Spectators: A Case Study of Science Teaching, Epistemology, and Classroom Management. *Science Education, Vol. 82*, 619–648.

7 Ibid.

8 If you find yourself responding emotionally to material in this chapter, I would invite you to examine the beliefs you hold about standards. I've spoken to some educators who become very defensive when standards are challenged. If the meaning that every educator assigned to the word standards was based on the same beliefs about expectations and the value of standards, the controversy would not exist. It's not a question of whether standards are good or bad. It's a question of clearly defining and assessing the beliefs and presuppositions underlying their use, as well as examining whether research supports those beliefs and presuppositions.

9 Major textbook publishers include correlation charts when they submit their books to state adoption committees. On these charts, each standard and benchmark is accompanied by the page or pages of the book on which the item is addressed. It is not uncommon for adoption committees to look first at these charts and immediately dismiss any book that does not have a completely filled correlation chart, even if that book is of a much higher quality!

10 In May of 2010, a conservative school board instituted new standards and benchmarks to address what they saw as "liberal" curriculum content. The content of the "new" standards is so different that teachers will have to undergo training on how to implement them. The passage of these new standards also means that many textbooks no longer "cover" included material, or "cover" it in what are now considered unacceptable ways.

11 Berliner, D. C. (1987). Ways of Thinking About Students and Classrooms by More and Less Experienced Teachers. In J. Calderhead (Ed.). *Exploring Teachers' Thinking* (pp. 60–84) London: Cassell Educational Limited

12 Ibid., pp. 65–66.

13 The Call for Standards. (1999) McREL URL:www.mcrel.org/standards-benchmarks/docs/chapter1.html.

14 Reeves, D. B. (2001). "If You Hate Standards, Learn To Love the Bell Curve." *Education Week. Vol. XX, No. 39*, 52.

15 Sauer, A. (2001). Standards vs. Bell Curve: It's Not an Either-Or Proposition. *Education Week, Vol. XX, No. 41*, 49

16 Some ungraded schools where students are grouped by readiness and need rather than by age and grade are addressing developmental issues based on individual students rather than Bell Curve "averages." Time is apportioned in terms of what is going on in the learning process rather than by some rigid external schedule designed for convenience rather than learning. Students enter the "flow" of learning and stay there until their need to know is satisfied for the time being. Unfortunately, other schools see "ungraded" classes as depositories for "difficult" students rather than as a fundamentally sound way to structure schools.

17 http://www.engines4ed.org/hyperbook/nodes/NODE-93-pg.html. Accessed on August 25, 2010

18 Hirsch's "lists" of items required for Cultural Literacy are now published by the "Core Knowledge Foundation" in a series of books, such as "What Every First Grader Should Know." The books are available from Preschool through high school.

19 Marzano, R. J., Kendall, J. S., & Gaddy, B. B. (1999, April 21). Deciding on 'Essential Knowledge.' *Education Week.*

20 Ormell, C. (1996). Eight Metaphors of Education. *Educational Research. Vol. 38, No. 1,* 67–75.

21 TIMMS is an ongoing project. Tests are conducted every four years. See http://nces.ed.gov/timss/ for more information.

22 URL: http://www.timss.bc.edu. Accessed on August 14, 2010

23 Schmidt, W. H., McKnight, C. C., & Raizen, S. A. (1996). Splintered Vision: An Investigation of U.S. Science and Mathematics Education: Executive Summary. Lansing, MI: U.S. National Research Center for the Third International Mathematics and Science Study, Michigan State University.

24 Harel, I. and Papert, S. (Eds.) (1991). *Constructionism.* Norwood, NJ: Ablex.

25 This quote came from a paper entitled Privileging Generalizations Creates Problems, originally published on the ILT web. It is no longer available at that site. Check ILT at Columbia University for similar documents. www.ilt.columbia.edu

26 Ohanion, S. (1999) *One Size Fits Few.* Portsmouth, NH: Heinemann.

27 Ravitch, D. (2000). *Left Back: A Century of Failed School Reforms.* New York: Simon and Schuster.

28 Kohn, A. (2000). *The Case Against Standardized Testing: Raising the Scores, Ruining the Schools.* Portsmouth, NH: Heinemann.

29 Marzano et al. (1999). Deciding…

30 Ibid.

31 The reliance on textbooks for "essential" information is often a case of a dog chasing its own tail. As a writer of textbook materials, I can testify to the way publishers select concepts for a new book. In many cases, it's a matter of surveying many of the other "best-selling" textbooks at that grade level and making sure that the same concepts are "covered" in the new book.

32 Eisner, E. (1994). *The Educational Imagination: On the Design and Evaluation of School Programs*, 3rd ed. New York: Macmillan College Publishing, 113.

33 This is not an exaggeration. There are already schools where "frills" such as art or music have been dropped. In at least one school district, recess has been dropped because it took away time from learning. "A five-year-old in Atlanta confided to a Times reporter, 'I'd like to sit on the grass and look for ladybugs.' But the Atlanta public schools, like a growing number of districts across the country, have eliminated recess from the school day. Who can read this without weeping? The standards mania has brought us to the point of making children too busy for ladybugs." Ohanion, S. (1999). *One Size Fits Few*. Portsmouth, NH: Heinemann, 13.

34 Eisner, E. (1994). *The Educational Imagination*...p 114.

35 Lindsay, D. (1997, November 12) Double Standards. *Education Week*. URL: http://www.edweek.org/ew/1997/12texas.h17

36 Fingon, Joan C. "What teachers say about school reform does matter." *Reading Today* 27.2 (2009): 18. General OneFile. Web. 19 Aug. 2010.

37 Reich, R. B. (2001). Standards For What? *Education Week, Vol. XX, No. 41*, 64, 48.

38 cf. Greenberger, S. S. (2000, November 2). Schools Group Opposes MCAS As Requirement. *Boston Globe*. National Survey Gauges Parent Perceptions of State-Mandated, Standardized Tests (2000, June 13). Alexandria, VA. ASCD. Rotberg, I. C. (2000, November 1). What Are We Doing To Our Schools? *Education Week*, 44.

39 Bernard, Sara. (2010, April 6) National Education Standards Initiative Draws Criticism. Accessed at http://education.change.org/blog/view/national_education_standards_initiative_draws_criticismAugust 14, 2010

Chapter 14 ~ The Future Begins Now

"Morpheus: I'm trying to free your mind, Neo. But I can only show you the door. You're the one that has to walk through it." ~The Matrix

"All truly wise thoughts have been thought already thousands of times; but to make them truly ours, we must think them over again honestly, till they take root in our personal experience.
~Johann Wolfgang von Goethe

The previous quotations are from two very different sources, but both carry the same message. When it comes to a "makeover" for the mind, no one can do the job for you. It must be your choice. Personal growth and development arise from the willingness and determination to examine your life and figure out what, if anything, you would like to change.

Barbara Marx Hubbard speaks of "conscious evolution." We now understand enough about how and why we act to be able to alter our behavior in many different ways. Until we recognize and utilize our ability to *choose* our worldview, to *choose* our beliefs, to *choose* the reality in which we wish to live, behavior remains habitual and unexamined. We *must not* entrust the future of our children to habit!

I once had a mathematics teacher who began the class by saying, "Calculus is easy. You just take a pie, divide it into an infinite number of pieces, and then measure the pieces." Unfortunately, my mind went into an "infinite" loop because the statement conflicts with my fundamental understanding of the word *infinite*. To this day, I'm still cutting the pie into an infinite number of pieces. I doubt I will ever get to the actual measurement.

It occurs to me that, in pointing out the tremendous variability in the minds of individuals, I may have created a similar monster. "Teaching is easy. You just take hundreds of thousands of students; divide them into an infinite number of possibilities for teaching, learning, and thinking; and then teach them." Perhaps the task that confronts teachers is not unlike the leap of faith required of Neo in the movie *The Matrix*.

If I didn't think that this task was possible, I wouldn't waste your time or my own. The task *is* possible once educators recognize and break free of the conventional mindset. That mindset is the true monster—one that has gobbled up the enthusiasm of too many teachers and the love of learning of too many students. Your vision of the ideal classroom is not a dream. It is a viable possibility—but one that will require effort to realize.

Making a Difference

Early one evening, an old man was walking alone along the edge of the seashore. From a distance, the old man could see a young boy busily tossing objects into the sea. As the old man drew closer, he could see the young boy was picking up starfish from the sand. One by one, the boy was tossing each starfish back into the ocean. As the old man looked about, he could see the shoreline was covered with many thousands of starfish that had been washed ashore by the tide.

"What is it you are doing?" asked the old man.

"I'm throwing these starfish back into the sea so that they may live," said the boy.

"But there are so many of them lying on shore," said the old man. "Do you really believe your time and effort will make any difference?"

As the young boy tossed the next starfish he was holding into the sea, he looked up at the old man and said:

"It made a difference to that one."[1]

One person *can* make a difference. *You* can make a difference. Many teachers feel that the problems of education are so great that nothing they do matters. Because teachers are rarely aware of what happens "down the line" when they make a difference in the life of a single child, it sometimes seems as if their efforts are wasted. Nothing you do for a child is ever wasted!

Teachers often use the constraining power of the larger system to excuse their failure to act. When confronted by the call for change, high school teachers insist that until the demands for university admissions shift, they are bound to use teaching methods that enhance potential performance on standardized tests. This thinking backs up all the way to

Kindergarten where teachers contend they must "get the kids ready" for first grade. Often, that means cutting back "play time" to "cover" more and more required information. Never mind the fact that much of what these students have learned prior to entering school has been achieved through that same "play." After all, school is a deadly serious business!

In 1991, John Gatto was named New York State's Teacher of the Year. In a recent article, Gatto was described in this way:

"For 30 years, he taught English in some of New York City's toughest schools—and became the East Coast's answer to Jaime Escalante, the East Los Angeles teacher immortalized in the film *Stand and Deliver*. Gatto was the kind of once-in-a-lifetime teacher who changed lives (hundreds of former students remain in touch with him), even as he outraged administrators."[2]

Gatto tells of two events that made him begin questioning "conventional wisdom." The first occurred early in his career when he was hired as a substitute teacher in a Spanish class. Rather than "baby-sitting" as is expected of many substitutes, Gatto decided to do what he could to teach the students. He asked them if they knew how to tell time in Spanish, figuring he'd review it with them. When they said they didn't, he spent the period teaching them. At the end of the third period of the day (out of five identical classes), he was called to the principal's office where an assistant principal began screaming at him. "How dare you do this! You have destroyed the entire curriculum for the month of June. You will never be hired at this school again!"

Sounds impossible, but Gatto recognized that this attitude was not uncommon. "They expected so little of these kids that it was easy to communicate the whole curriculum for the month of June in 15 minutes."[3]

Another experience brought the message home even more clearly, driving Mr. Gatto into full-time teaching. While subbing in a third grade "remedial" reading class, he had dutifully given the students their assignment and settled back to wait out the period when a little girl approached him.

"I don't need to do this. I already know how to read."

Gatto at first tried to explain that adults who were looking out for her best interest believed she needed to do the assigned reading. When she insisted she could already read anything, he opened a book to "The Devil and Daniel Webster" and handed the little girl the book. She read it perfectly. Gatto told the little girl older people sometimes make mistakes and promised to talk to the principal.

When he followed through on his promise, the principal replied she was not in the habit of taking instruction from a substitute teacher. She went on to tell Gatto, "...You have no idea how clever these low-achieving children are. They will memorize a story so it looks as if they know how to read it." Apparently not realizing the remarkable ability she'd identified as trickery, the principal reluctantly tested the girl herself. Although the results left the principal no alternative but to transfer the girl out of remedial reading, her last words to Gatto were, "You will never be hired at this school again."[4]

The sad thing is these stories are not isolated incidents. Too often, a few experiences like this early in a teacher's career can reverse a lifetime of high ideals and make that teacher downshift into survival mode. How much emotional abuse must students suffer before someone challenges conventional wisdom on their behalf?

Educational Soma

If the young people of today are to be saved from a future resembling that of Aldous Huxley's *Brave New World*, it is time for teachers to break free from the Pavlovian conditioning of conventional wisdom. Otherwise, we will continue to see a mindless adherence to the mechanistic worldview that places information before people and bows at the altar of efficiency and productivity. Society is already reaping the "rewards" of that thinking.

The belief that there is an objective way to "measure" learning in the same way in which manufacturers can assess the quality of a product is one of the most damaging unexamined presuppositions of the mechanistic metaphor. It is so pervasive that concern over grades has become more important to parents than what a student is learning, to say nothing about what sort of person the student is becoming.

The acceptance of this mindset—this belief that "smartness" can be objectively measured—reached its most absurd, but predictable height (depth?) in a network television show purporting to identify "The Smartest Kid in America."

In a commentary in *Education Week*[5], education professor James R. Delisle stated,

> "I'm not sure what upset me more: the fact that a contest could qualify as the sole indicator of finding America's most gifted child, or the willingness of viewers to believe this was possible."

Delisle questioned the meaning of the word *smart*. Recalling the students who had made the greatest impact on him in twenty-two years of teaching experience, he remarked they were often students who had more questions than answers. Delisle told of the five-year-old who asked, "If butter melts yellow, and chocolate melts brown, why doesn't snow melt white?" Where is the kind of thinking that goes into formulating such questions recognized and rewarded?

Delisle also recalled Brian, a sixth-grader who undertook a project to furnish an entire household for a family of seven who had lost their possessions in a house fire.

> "Brian corralled his classmates and made them care as deeply about these strangers as he did—and he did so without ever opening a social studies book...what he opened, instead, was his heart."

How does one objectively assess the size of the heart?

The first step in re-humanizing the educational process is to adopt a new paradigm, one that focuses on the often unpredictable nature of living systems. Someone once said people are more comfortable with old problems than with new solutions. Isn't the future of the next generation and the potential for a quantum leap in education worth a little discomfort?

Shift Happens[6]

"Things do not change; we change."
~Henry David Thoreau

It's no longer acceptable to blame one's inaction on society. A culture changes when its people change. Where better to bring about change in people than when they are children, first developing their views of the world? Who better to do this than the teachers to whom those children's futures are entrusted?

Make no mistake. Every teacher does make a difference in the lives of children. Whether that difference results in disenchanted or energized minds is the issue. Teachers must recognize they teach infinitely more than content. They must accept the responsibility for the future and rebel against an education system that, by design or by accident, focuses on *turning out* students who are "easily managed." In the words of Mahatma Gandhi, "You must *be* the change you wish to see in the world."

Candace Pert points out that major shifts in paradigm, such as the shift from the Ptolemy's earth-centered theory of the universe to the Copernican sun-centered theory, don't happen without major resistance from the establishment. Pert, a researcher in the field of endocrinology, had the audacity to combine data from several medical disciplines that had previously been studied as virtually closed systems. In doing so, she incurred the wrath of established researchers. But in her persistence, she was among the first to identify endorphins—molecules in the body that mediate emotions. Her belief that the health and well-being of humans took priority over bowing to the old paradigms of medical research made such breakthroughs possible.

Such will almost certainly be the case for a major shift in the paradigm that dominates education. Those at the forefront of meaningful change will take considerable heat from others within the establishment who feel threatened. Pert offers these words of encouragement:

"It may take a good decade, or…it may take much longer.
But, eventually, the new view becomes the status quo, and
ideas that were rejected as madness will appear in the popular
press, often touted by the very critics who did so much to
impede their acceptance."[7]

People have long understood how "little things" can transform a situation. In a metaphor of yesteryear, we learned that "for want of a nail…the kingdom was lost." Today, the metaphors have changed, but the idea remains. Even seemingly insignificant choices and actions can have a profound influence on the future through interactions within the system. Whatever the metaphor, individual teachers can no longer downplay their importance in the development of their students.

If transformation is to take place, educators must change their metaphors from static one-way transmission to a fluid "mind dance" between teacher and student. This cannot occur until educators call into question the "truths" under which they have been operating for so long.

We must replace those "truths" with principles more attuned to human beings than to machines.

> "Our scientific power has outrun our spiritual power.
> We have guided missiles and misguided men."
> ~Martin Luther King, Jr.

Re-examining Conventional Wisdom

> "Advice is like snow; the softer it falls the longer it
> dwells upon, and the deeper it sinks into the mind."
> ~Samuel Taylor Coleridge

Coleridge's words are equally true of any idea to which people are exposed repeatedly and without examination. Many myths of education—the tenets of conventional wisdom—are long overdue for re-evaluation.

Myths are socially or culturally accepted stories about "reality" that people have constructed over time. Psychologist Arthur Combs points out the dangers accompanying any myth.

- Myths contain a "germ" of truth. Because partial truth yields partial solutions to existing problems, people continue to do research based on the myth for a long time, even when no overall solutions are forthcoming.

- Myths are often expressed as dichotomies, thus limiting the use of a wide range of strategies. Either objectivism or constructivism; either individualized learning or standards; either strong discipline or concern for self-esteem.

- Myths justify our preferred behaviors and constrain others. People can always find good reasons in their myths for the things they'd rather do (or not do).

- Myths become institutionalized and therefore exempt from question. When someone says, "Everyone knows that…" what follows is often a myth. Questioning such statements opens a person to ridicule. Once a culture or social institution has adopted a myth, it is very robust and difficult to dislodge.[8]

Myths are based on "truths" that, as we have seen, are true only in some contexts. As the culture or social institution changes, the contexts change. Through the accretion of new information, the mythical stories become inappropriate or outdated. They produce contradictions and inconsistencies that seem beyond resolution—and they are, *as long as the institution retains the myth.* Such is the case with education. *Education needs new storytellers who will write the stories for the future.*

Educational theorists such as Arthur Combs[9], Ellen Langer[10], Neil Postman[11], Larry Cuban[12], and others[13] have identified a number of educational myths that are worthy of examination. Their writings are a place to begin in exploring fruitful alternatives to conventional wisdom.

Conventional wisdom forms the *foundation* in the *edifice* of traditional education. *Education as a structure* is a strong and pervasive metaphor. It is not, however, without its own limitations. Our experience of structures, particularly those with solid foundations, is one of stability and permanence. A call to begin hacking away at the foundations of those structures is unthinkable. Therefore, such heresy is met with horror and disdain. What about the presupposition that those foundations are solid? Is it correct?

Mindful change, based on determined self-examination and regard for what *is* rather than what experts say *should* be, offers great promise. Before shaking their heads at the failure of today's youth to live up to educator's expectations, it is imperative that educators look to themselves. As Carl Jung said, "If there is anything we wish to change in the child, we should first examine it and see whether it is not something that could better be changed in ourselves."

The Re-humanization of Education

Retired education professor Seymour Sarason tells of an experience he had in a first-grade classroom:

> "The new school year had begun a week earlier. One child was sitting in her seat, head down, crying silently. Occasionally, the child would slowly approach the teacher and nestle against her. The teacher would then take the child back to her seat, saying sympathetically: 'When school is over, your mother will come for you. Stay in your seat and try to do what the other students are doing.' Later the teacher told me that each day the

child cried when the mother brought her to school. What the child wanted, the teacher said, was to be held, cuddled, and soothed. My conversation with the teacher went something like this:

SBS: The girl asked to be held?
T: Yes. She would raise her hands for me to pick her up.
SBS: Did you?
T: No.
SBS: Why not?
T: (with a surprised look) If I picked her up and cuddled her, then that is what other children would want me to do for them."[14]

The story is sad for several reasons. Even at the tender age of five or six, children are capable of understanding the needs of others. For the teacher to ignore those needs teaches the rest of the students a profound lesson. It is the kind of lesson that is prevalent in the implicit curriculum and that, in all likelihood, remains with the students much longer than the explicit lessons to which they were exposed that day.

The story is also sad because it illustrates how some teachers have suppressed their natural empathy in deference to time and content. For this teacher, the worst-case scenario involved taking time away from "teaching" to hug every child in the class!

Does this mean what goes on in classrooms should be based on what makes every child happy? Of course not. What it does suggest is that the prevailing focus on content, efficiency, and productivity at the expense of individual human beings has effectively dehumanized education.

George Leonard states, "Education, at best, is ecstatic."[15] If educators truly wishes to create lifelong learners then, according to Leonard, the purpose of education becomes "...the achievement of moments of ecstasy." By this he means, not the libido ecstasy of Freud, but the joy and delight we have all experienced when we are caught up in the flow of learning.

Some resist the thought of too much joy in the classroom. Their philosophical roots are showing! There is a lingering, if unconscious, belief that anything of value must be acquired through hard work and suffering. Pain and disappointment are necessary to strengthen the mind and heart. Enjoyment is something that comes after the work is done—or never. Delayed gratification is the ultimate virtue. Have you ever felt guilty for reading a book or doing something else you enjoyed when you "should" have been working—doing something "productive"?

Future generations will reap what today's teachers sow. The lessons you teach will pass to future generations just as the lessons our grandparents taught have passed to us and our children. The world created by our students will spring from the resources that adults give them today. The cooperation or competition, the love or the hate, the mutual respect or lack thereof, and the ability to confront and solve problems that are unimaginable in today's world will rest at least in part on the choices teachers make during their lives in the classroom. Those choices are the source of your legacy to the future.

Realism or Miracles?

"Never doubt that a small group of thoughtful citizens can change the world. Indeed, it is the only thing that ever has." ~Margaret Mead

There is a story about an educational reformer who holds a séance so he can speak to John Dewey. When the great philosopher appears, the reformer asks how to bring about real change in American schools. Dewey asks if the man wants the realistic way or the miraculous way.

"Well, the realistic way, of course," says the reformer.

"A million angels would come down from heaven and visit every classroom in America, wave their hands, and education reform would immediately become established," Dewey replies.

"Then what would be the miraculous way?" asks the reformer.

"Educators would do it themselves."[16]

The time for miracles is upon us. Teachers need not wait for some signal that every educator is prepared to change. Throughout the world, especially since the advent of the Internet, there are many examples of small groups of people creating major changes in the world.

Some teachers no longer find it "unthinkable" to question conventional wisdom. They are no longer willing to accept a "wisdom" that has taken such a toll on young people. Many are eager to reclaim their vision of the ideal classroom and to midwife its birth into the "real world." Revolutions need not be noisy. When a relatively few teachers around the country—around the world—accept their power and exercise it mindfully, education *will* change.

Parents will be among the first to let an administrator know when their sons or daughters come home talking about school in a positive way—when they can't wait to tell what they did in class that day, rather than answering "nothing" when asked what they learned. How many administrators would force compliance to external mandates on a teacher whose classroom is filled with students eagerly engaged in learning? This is one way to place subtle pressure on the system.

The profound influence of an individual teacher's beliefs, values, and metaphors dictates that the most pervasive change *must* come from within. Certainly, we should consider the trends and tendencies identified in research. But unless individual teachers are factored into the equation, there can be no valid extrapolation to results in the classroom.

Many years ago, a scoutmaster taught his troop of young men how to make a tiny magnifying glass from a bent blade of grass and a drop of water. Years later, while serving in the military, one of the young men from the troop was shot down over enemy territory. He started a signal fire—using a blade of grass and a drop of water! There was no way the scoutmaster—my father—could ever have anticipated that what he had taught that day would eventually save a life.

No teacher can know how the things he or she says or does will play out on the stage of life. Make no mistake. It does play out in some fashion. Whether your words or actions make a positive or negative impact on the life of a single child, you *will* have changed the world.

The Ultimate Challenge for Teachers

"It is not necessary to change.
Survival is not mandatory."
~W. Edwards Deming

New technologies, better understanding of how humans interact with their environment, and emerging sensibilities among some segments of society have threatened a number of professions, such as logging and mining. People who made their living clear-cutting huge sections of forest were once secure in the knowledge that construction trades would always have a need for lumber. Their top priority was providing lumber with little regard for the impact of logging on the environment.

Those days are gone. Public pressure has forced the logging industry to change its practices—to put the environment, rather than the bottom line, in the foreground. Loggers who lost their jobs have reacted in several ways. Some accepted the change and set about retraining themselves in other professions. Others still fight for a return to the old ways—arguing that jobs are more important than a few owls or an unattractive view. Their energy is directed at *trying to preserve a way of life that is unlikely to return* rather than moving into an inevitable future.

When humans find themselves at such a crossroads, it is those who are willing to break free of the old way of thinking and accept the challenge who thrive. They accept that, in the short-term, things may get worse or things may get better. But of greater importance, they accept that things will change—regardless of what they do. They actively *choose* to lead the way in that change rather than being pushed by external forces, kicking and screaming all the way.

Current reform efforts attempt to preserve the old way of life while pacifying those who criticize the institution. Because this "old way" is based on beliefs and metaphors that are contradicted by present knowledge and experience, shuffling those beliefs and metaphors around, tacking on bits and pieces to appease critics is ineffective.

> "...Now, in the space age, the reformers are offering the
> nation an educational horse and buggy. They would improve
> the buggy, keep the passengers in it longer, and pay the driver
> more. But it would still be a horse and buggy."[17]

What is needed now is not *re*-formation, but *trans*-formation—a metamorphosis into something very different. Such a change in form often requires a long period of growth—like the birth of a child after nine months of development or the emergence of a butterfly after a period of time spent in the chrysalis. At times it requires an effortful and potentially painful shedding of the old skin. In the world of the teacher, this transformation may require the shedding of many old beliefs of conventional wisdom.

Caterpillars do not change into butterflies when someone tells them to. The change occurs when the organism can no longer continue as it has in the past. When the new form into which the caterpillar has developed becomes cramped and uncomfortable within its cocoon, it *must* break free.

Although humans encounter this type of change at birth, much of life is spent rebuilding comfortable cocoons—familiar maps of the world that offer consistency and stability. Venturing beyond those maps into the unknown may be frightening, but there are tremendous possibilities in the world outside for those who have the courage to step beyond their present edges.

The world of the caterpillar or the world of the butterfly is the choice teachers face today. To carry this metaphor a bit further, consider that many students have already emerged into the world of the butterfly— the world of complex questions rather than simple answers. That is why they so strongly resist being forced back into the cocoon every morning and can't wait until the final bell of the day when they can return to that larger world.

Your vision of the ideal classroom can be the first crack in your cocoon. The care and feeding of that vision is one way to move toward the transformation—to go beyond your limited map. By teaching mindfully and reflecting on the choices you make, the day will come when you will look at the old ways of teaching—at your old ways of behaving—and realize that they no longer fit your new form. Would a butterfly creep along a branch like the caterpillar when it can fly?

When a sufficient number of teachers experience this transformation—when they step into the new beliefs and metaphors supported by both research and experience—the institution of education cannot help but undergo radical change.

What Now??

"There comes a time in the affairs of man when he must take the bull by the tail and face the situation." ~W. C. Fields

I began this book describing the power of teachers—not power *over* but power *to*. Now you face a choice with regard to your own power.

- You can deny it—turning your back on the influence you wield every hour of every day.

- You can reject it—handing it over to others and like Pilate, washing your hands of the responsibility.

- You can ignore it—as so many have throughout the history of education.

- You can embrace it—mindfully reflecting on the way in which you use that power to influence the students in your charge.

- You can use that power to teach authentically—so students will learn problem solving by solving real problems, clarity of thought by thinking, understanding by developing relationships with knowledge, and humanity by observation of and participation in authentic human endeavors.

- You can use that power by asking "Why?" and demanding answers that are more than platitudes and time-worn myths.

- You can use that power to help yourself and your students break free from the traditionally sanctified prison many schools have become.

- You can use that power to create a haven wherein students are encouraged to explore limitless possibilities, to ask questions for which there are no easy answers, to seek paths that are "less traveled," and to know *this* teacher is in *this* room to make learning happen.

The future of each teacher is irrevocably bound to the future of that teacher's students and ultimately, to the future of society. Your future, along with some of the actions you can take to reach that future, are now present before you in the ideal classroom you have created. Because you have created that template—have actually experienced what it is like to inhabit that future—that vision will unconsciously direct your actions. There is nothing to prevent you from changing your mind along the way—nothing to keep you from re-visioning the future and planning new and different ways to reach it. The important thing is to continue moving—whether in small steps or giant leaps. Begin now to change the face of education.

1Making a Difference. (2000, July 30). Tri-Development Center/Aiken County Board of Disabilities, URL:
http://www.aikentdc.org/resources/inspirational/difference.htm
2 Pink, D. H. (2000, October 28) I'm a Saboteur." *Fast Company*, October 28, 2000. URL: http://www.fastcompany.com/online/40/wf_gatto.html.
3 Ibid.
4 Ibid.

5 Delisle, J. R. (2000, June 21). The Smartest Kid In America. *Education Week, 49,* 52–53.

6 Pert, C. (1997). *Molecules of Emotion: Why You Feel the Way You Feel.* New York: Scribner, 19

7 Ibid., 20

8 Combs, A. W. (1979). *Myths in Education—Beliefs that Hinder Progress and their Alternatives.* Boston: Allyn and Bacon.

9 Ibid.

10 Langer, E. J. (1997). *The Power of Mindful Learning.* A Merloyd Lawrence Book. Reading, PA: Addison-Wesley.

11 Postman, N. (1995). *The End of Education: Redefining the Value of School.* New York: Alfred A. Knopf.

12 Cuban, L. (1992, October). The Corporate Myth of Reforming Public Schools. *Phi Delta Kappan,* 157–159.

13 See also Illich, I. (1971) Deschooling Society. *World Perspectives, Vol. 44,* New York: Harper & Row. Smith, F. (1995, April). Let's Declare Education a Disaster and Get On With Our Lives. *Phi Delta Kappan,* 584–590. Tobin, K.& McRobbie, C. J. (1996). Cultural Myths As Constraints to the Enacted Science Curriculum. *Science Education, Vol. 80, No. 2,* 223–241. Britzman, D. (1986). Cultural Myths in the Making of a Teacher: biography and Social Structure in Teacher Education. Harvard *Educational Review, Vol. 56,* 442–456.

14 Sarason, S. B. (1991). *The Predictable Failure of Educational Reform: Can We Change Course Before It's Too Late?* San Francisco: Jossey-Bass.

15 Leonard, G. (1987). *Education and Ecstasy.* Berkeley, CA: North Atlantic Books, 17.

16 Boles, K. C.& Troen, V. (2000, February 2). America's New Teachers: How Good and For How Long? *Education Week,* 39.

17 Leonard, G. (1987). *The Great School Reform Hoax. Education and Ecstasy.* Berkeley, CA: North Atlantic Books, 245.

Appendix A
Self-Inventory

The items in this Self-Inventory are intended to help you identify patterns of thought you have overlooked or forgotten. The information is about you and for you. No one will see your responses unless you choose to share them. The items are far from exhaustive, but represent the kinds of questions you might ask yourself in probing your unconscious beliefs about education and teaching.

Don't worry about making your answers socially or politically acceptable because no one else will know. The goal is for *you* to know—for *you* to bring into consciousness some of the beliefs, values, and meanings that form the foundation of your teaching.

An inventory is an interesting metaphor. When people in business "take inventory," they literally take stock of the resources they have on hand. That is what you will do as you answer these questions. Taking an inventory doesn't imply anything about the value of present resources—about whether they should be retained, modified, or gotten rid of. It merely provides a baseline—a starting point for future decisions.

Businesses often find items during an inventory they didn't recall having or resources that had been hidden in some dusty corner. As they deal with the complex world of the classroom, educators sometimes forget the reasons they had for entering the profession. The inventory gives you the opportunity to revisit some of those reasons. Inventories can also help people identify items that are outdated or no longer useful.

Knowing where you stand at present helps you decide what you need to do to reach your goals. Before taking tennis lessons, you begin by assessing how well you already play the game—what you already do well. Then you seek the level of coaching that will take you from that place and move you ahead.

We all start somewhere. There's not much point in going back to the beginning if you're already three-fourths of the way to your goal. As you compare your responses with some of the ideas in *Teaching in Mind*, the inventory will help you clarify what you want to accomplish and why you behave as you do. Are you digging that hole because someone told you to, because you need the hole to plant a tree, or because you have a vision of the gorgeous landscape that will someday grace the site?

There are no right or wrong responses to any of the questions. There's nothing sacred about the items themselves. If something in the wording of the item troubles you, change it. Use the items to help you access your own ideas, not to force you into irrelevant channels of thought. This is particularly true for those who teach very young children or children with special needs, or for those who have yet to begin teaching. After you get a sense of the item, feel free to modify it to address similar content in your own setting.

If you wish, write comments next to any item. You may wish to qualify your answers or to clarify your own perceptions. The closer your responses are to your true experience and perceptions, the more useful they will be later.

Some of you are already experienced in introspection—self-reflection. For others, it may be a somewhat unfamiliar process. The only advice I might offer is to focus on what you really think rather than on what conventional wisdom might say—except where you firmly believe in that conventional wisdom. Some suggest you should accept the first thing that "pops into your head." However, when you're in a profession heavily dominated by tradition, the first thing that "pops" may be what you hear all the time rather than what you really think. You may have become accustomed to suppressing your own thoughts in order to function in your environment. Only you can sense whether the answers are your own or those of the culture.

Organize your answers in the most useful way for you. You may choose to use a journal. If a particular item triggers more in-depth thoughts or musings, spend a few moments jotting down those thoughts. Some people may enjoy discussing these questions with others. You don't need to complete the inventory in a single sitting. Do what's right for you, remembering that your purpose is to explore your inner landscape—a world that is often out of consciousness. Only you have the map to that landscape.

As with most things of value, completing the inventory will take time. For those of you who really don't have the patience to complete the whole thing, just do the items that seem to be the most important to you in your present situation. However, I do encourage you to explore as deeply as you are able. You will find it time well spent.

Section A

Read each of the statements. Then place an X on the line indicating whether you **SA**=Strongly agree; **A**=Agree somewhat; **N**=Are neutral; **D**=Disagree somewhat; **SD**=Strongly disagree

1. A student's intelligence is innate—determined by genetics.
    SA   A   N   D   SD

2. A student's intelligence is influenced by the environment.
    SA   A   N   D   SD

3. Student ability is more fixed than variable.
    SA   A   N   D   SD

4. Students from disadvantaged backgrounds are generally less capable than other students.
    SA   A   N   D   SD

5. Success in learning is directly related to the amount of effort a student is willing to expend.
    SA   A   N   D   SD

6. Students should be required to solve problems in the accepted way to demonstrate their understanding.
    SA   A   N   D   SD

7. Students must learn the basics before they can tackle more complex problems.
    SA   A   N   D   SD

8. It's more important for students to learn the right answers than to figure out why their previous answer was wrong.
    SA   A   N   D   SD

9. Most children find it difficult to pay attention.
    SA   A   N   D   SD

10. Students who have done poorly in early grades are less likely to succeed in later grades.
    SA   A   N   D   SD

11. There is a generally appropriate level of instruction (body of knowledge and depth of processing) for every grade/age level.
    SA   A   N   D   SD
12. Students are motivated by grades or other external rewards.
    SA   A   N   D   SD
13. There are more similarities than differences in the ways in which students process and store information.
    SA   A   N   D   SD
14. A student's learning style is the same for all or most contexts.
    SA   A   N   D   SD
15. A child's level of accomplishment is most accurately assessed when they are compared with other children in their own age, grade, and/or socioeconomic background.
    SA   A   N   D   SD
16. In order to insure success, all children should be taught a fundamental set of "thinking skills"—strategies or sequences of thinking that have been identified as effective.
    SA   A   N   D   SD
17. A good objective test measures how well a student understands a subject.
    SA   A   N   D   SD
18. It would be unfair to give individual students different types of tests.
    SA   A   N   D   SD
19. Teachers should have a consistent set of rules all students must obey.
    SA   A   N   D   SD
20. Good discipline is at the heart of good teaching.
    SA   A   N   D   SD
21. The primary role of the teacher is to transmit knowledge.
    SA   A   N   D   SD

22. There is a body of knowledge every successful person should possess.
    SA   A   N   D   SD
23. In general, knowledge flows from experts down to the less informed.
    SA   A   N   D   SD
24. Standards insure students are given an equal opportunity for success.
    SA   A   N   D   SD
25. Standards insure equally high expectations for all students.
    SA   A   N   D   SD
26. Standards effectively identify the concepts that all successful students should know.
    SA   A   N   D   SD
27. There is an optimal (best) way to solve any problem.
    SA   A   N   D   SD
28. A quiet classroom is more conducive to learning than a noisy classroom.
    SA   A   N   D   SD
29. For the most part, our school/district is guided by a single set of uniform goals.
    SA   A   N   D   SD
30. In general, the most important content is what is spelled out in the school/district curriculum guide.
    SA   A   N   D   SD
31. The arrangement of knowledge by disciplines is the most effective way to transmit that knowledge.
    SA   A   N   D   SD
32. Change is difficult and requires considerable effort.
    SA   A   N   D   SD
33. It's important to keep students from failing at a given task.
    SA   A   N   D   SD

34. Students should take more responsibility for their own learning.

SA   A   N   D   SD

Section B

Read each of the statements. Then place an X on the line indicating whether you **SA**=Strongly agree; **A**=Agree somewhat; **N**=Are neutral; **D**=Disagree somewhat; **SD**=Strongly disagree

1. I follow a similar plan from day to day so students will know what to expect.

SA   A   N   D   SD

2. When I grade papers, I mark the incorrect answers.

SA   A   N   D   SD

3. I believe I can influence a student's learning.

SA   A   N   D   SD

4. What goes on in my classroom is based largely on my own decisions.

SA   A   N   D   SD

5. I often ask divergent, open-ended questions that require reflection, analysis, and evaluation by the students.

SA   A   N   D   SD

6. I ask questions for which I may not already know the answers.

SA   A   N   D   SD

7. When I ask a question, I always wait until some student provides an answer before going on.

SA   A   N   D   SD

8. When a student answers a question incorrectly, I ask the student how he/she arrived at that answer.

SA   A   N   D   SD

9. I allow students to work together on assignments.

SA   A   N   D   SD

10. I vary my teaching methods from student to student.

    SA   A   N   D   SD

11. I teach more for what students will need in the future than what they may need at the present.

    SA   A   N   D   SD

12. I spend more time with those students who really want to learn.

    SA   A   N   D   SD

13. District/school policies prevent me from teaching in the ways that I want.

    SA   A   N   D   SD

14. Most of what I teach is proven knowledge rather than knowledge that is likely to change.

    SA   A   N   D   SD

15. There are some concepts I don't enjoy teaching.

    SA   A   N   D   SD

16. The amount of time I spend on a concept depends on how important the concept is.

    SA   A   N   D   SD

17. The amount of time I spend on a concept depends on how much I know about it.

    SA   A   N   D   SD

18. I know I've done a good job when someone compliments me.

    SA   A   N   D   SD

19. I know I've done a good job because of my own internal sense of accomplishment.

    SA   A   N   D   SD

20. I am satisfied with the condition of public education as a whole.

    SA   A   N   D   SD

21. I have occasionally felt dissatisfied with my own teaching.

    SA   A   N   D   SD

22. I keep up with major theories and research in education.

   SA   A   N   D   SD

23. I am satisfied I am achieving the goals I set for myself as a teacher.

   SA   A   N   D   SD

24. For the most part, I am an effective teacher.

   SA   A   N   D   SD

Section C

1. When you are deciding what to teach, how important is each of the following factors?

   1=Very important; 2=Somewhat important; 3=Neutral; 4=Somewhat unimportant; 5=Unimportant

   _____a. curriculum guide   _____f. textbook content

   _____b. student motivation   _____g. my past experiences

   _____c. student interest   _____h. my preferences

   _____d. current affairs   _____i. other (specify)

   _____e. students' questions

2. How important is each of the following classroom practices to teaching and/or learning?

   1=Very important; 2=Somewhat important; 3=Neutral; 4=Somewhat unimportant; 5=Unimportant

   _____a. lectures   _____g. teacher-generated activities

   _____b. discussions

   _____c. student questions   _____h. student-generated activities

   _____d. note-taking

   _____e. homework   _____i. group work

   _____f. tests/assessments   _____j. cooperative learning

   _____k. other (specify)

3. When you are deciding *how* to teach, how important is each of the following factors?

1=Very important; 2=Somewhat important; 3=Neutral; 4=Somewhat unimportant; 5=Unimportant

_____a. the responses of individual students

_____b. the responses of the class

_____c. the interests of individual students

_____d. the interests of the class

_____e. what I learned in teacher training

_____f. research on learning theory

_____g. what seems right at the moment

_____h. my school's goals and objectives

_____i. my personal goals and objectives

_____j. the way my peers teach

_____k. requirements of my job

_____l. other (specify)

4. In terms of discipline, where does your classroom tend to fall on the continuum? (Place an X on the line.)

Total teacher control_____Total student control

5. I seek advice about teaching-related problems. (Circle one.)

Often   Sometimes   Never

If your answer to question 5 is *Never*, skip to question 7.

6. If your answer to question 5 is *Often* or *Sometimes*, from whom do you get advice that you've used?

7. If your answer to question 5 was *Never*, why do you choose to not seek advice?

a. I don't have any problems with my teaching.

b. I don't want others to know I have problems.

c. I don't know anyone whose advice I'd take.

d. I take pride in solving my own problems.

e. Other (specify)

Section D

Answer the following questions in whatever detail you find useful.

1. Given the opportunity, what would you stop doing in your teaching you presently do?

2. Given the opportunity, what would you do that you are presently not doing?

3. What prevents you from having the opportunities mentioned in the two previous questions?

4. What would need to happen in order to create these opportunities?

5. What is your definition of *education*? In other words, what do you believe is/are the primary purpose(s) of education? List as many as you wish, and then prioritize them from most to least important.

6. To what extent, if any, have your perceptions of teaching changed since you began teaching?

7. If your perceptions have changed, what caused these changes?

8. To what extent, if any, have your teaching methods changed since you began teaching?

9. If your methods have changed, what caused these changes?

10. Are you satisfied with your role as a teacher? If not, why not? What would have to happen to increase your satisfaction? What do you need to do to bring those events about?

Section E

Complete each of the following sentences.

1. Teaching means....

2. As a teacher, I'm very good at....

3. As a teacher, I'm not very good at....

4. The part of teaching I enjoy the least is....

5. The part of teaching I enjoy the most is....

6. The most important responsibilities of a teacher are...

7. Teachers should always....

8. Teachers should never....

9. Students should always....

10. Students should never....

11. My *most* important goal *for the students* is....

12. My *most* important goal *for myself* (in teaching) is...

13. When a student answers a question incorrectly, I generally....

14. When a student asks a question for which I don't know the answer, I generally....

15. I am really impressed with a student who....

16. The most important thing I do as a teacher is....

17. Something I need to do better is....

18. A good teacher is one who....

19. A poor teacher is one who....

20. I'm most comfortable when my students are....

21. I'm least comfortable when my students are....

22. The most important thing I teach my students is....

23. If a student doesn't learn what I'm teaching, it's usually because....

24. When students do poorly on a test, it's usually because....

25. When students do well on a test, it's usually because....

26. A good student is one who...

27. A poor student is one who...

28. I know learning is taking place when...

29. The most important reward I get from teaching is...

Section F

This section is about the metaphors teachers use to describe their work, their students, or other aspects of their teaching experience. For example, some teachers say they are *like gardeners, performers, police officers, zookeepers, coaches,* or *weavers.* They may describe their students as *clay to be molded, sponges that absorb information,* or *plants to be nurtured.* On separate paper, complete each of the following metaphors (actually similes) in whatever way seems appropriate. Here is an example.

Students are like sponges because they absorb information and wring it out on the test.

It's important for you to fill in the second part of the metaphor (after the word *because*). This illuminates your interpretation of the metaphor. It identifies the characteristics of the two categories in the metaphor on which you tend to focus. The more detailed you can make this section, the more you'll understand how your metaphors influence your behaviors in the classroom. If you feel more than one metaphor fits your experience, list them all.

1. Teaching is like...because....

2. Discipline is like...because....

3. Learning is like...because....

4. My classroom is like...because.....

5. Testing is like...because....

6. Planning a lesson is like...because....

7. Students are like...because....

8. The curriculum is like...because....

9. My school is like...because....

10. My principal/supervisor is like...because...

11. Knowledge is like...because....

12. When I'm at my worst in the classroom, I'm like...because...

13. When I am teaching at my best, I am like...because....

Section G

Answer the questions on a separate sheet of paper.

1. Imagine the following situation.

A student comes up to you with a request to do something different from the task you assigned to the rest of the class. The subject area on which the student wants to work is generally the same as that studied by the rest of the class, but s/he wishes to study it in a different way. The student would do the work independently of you and independent of the work the rest of the class will be doing at that time. What would you tell the student? Why?

2. Think of one or two memorable teachers you've had. What, specifically, made them memorable?

3. What is the mission statement of your school or district? Do you agree with what it says? If you were to rewrite a mission statement of your own, what would it include?

4. How do you feel about being "wrong"? If you have believed something because of incomplete information, how open are you to getting more information that may challenge that belief? Does being wrong mean you have failed in some way?

5. What is the most important thing you would like your students to remember about you?

6. Think of one or two memorable learning experiences you have had in your life. Describe them. Think about what it was that made them memorable. You may wish to ask a few other people about their memorable learning experiences. To what extent are the characteristics people identify with memorable learning present in your present teaching/learning environment?

This concludes the formal part of the Self-Inventory. If there are any aspects of teaching that haven't been explored in the inventory and about which you have strong feelings, you may wish write your thoughts about that subject.

Obviously, these items haven't begun to address specific subject matter issues and many other factors that are unique to your role as a teacher. Hopefully, they have given you a sense of how you might explore these other issues.

Interpreting Your Responses

Although your responses to the inventory are interesting in and of themselves, what you have discovered is unlikely to make any meaningful change in your behavior unless you take the time to analyze your responses. That can only be accomplished by recognizing the role your beliefs, values, and metaphors play in the choices you make.

Section A deals with your beliefs…yes, beliefs…about students and knowledge. Section B asks about your own behavior and choices in the classroom. Those are also based on beliefs, so it is useful to ask yourself *why* you make those choices rather than others. Some of the items in Section A and Section B are used as examples in a number of chapters of *Teaching in Mind*. As you see how influential they are in shaping your perceptions and behaviors, you will learn how to analyze other beliefs with which you strongly agreed or disagreed.

As an example, how did you answer items A34 and B4? If you *strongly agreed* that students should take more responsibility for their own learning, and also *agreed* that most of what goes on in your classroom is determined by you, can you see the problem? How can take responsibility for something over which they have no control?

Section C helps you to understand what you value and how those values influence your choices of content and teaching methods.

Section F helps you to identify your operating metaphors. However, if you don't read the chapters on metaphors and their entailments in *Teaching in Mind*, you won't understand how those metaphors shape your classroom and the experience of your students.

In short, the Self-Inventory was designed to be used in conjunction with the explanations and processes in the book. Without that background, its usefulness will be limited.

Appendix B
Dispositions

In 2000, the National Council for Accreditation of Teacher Education (NCATE) made a significant change in their Professional Standards for the Accreditation of Schools, Colleges, and Departments of Education. Historically, the standards had focused on assessing the knowledge and skills of teacher candidates. Recognizing that the possession of excellent knowledge of a subject area and the skills to teach that subject does not automatically make a person a good teacher, NCATE added a third component to the standards, something they called "professional dispositions."

Following the description of the standards regarding Knowledge and Skills, NCATE describes this component as follows:

> **3. Professional Dispositions** Candidates are familiar with the professional dispositions delineated in professional, state, and institutional standards. Candidates demonstrate classroom behaviors that are consistent with the ideal of fairness and the belief that all students can learn. Their work with students, families, colleagues and communities reflects these professional dispositions.[1]

While this sounds basic enough on the surface, once schools of education began thinking about how they would assess this standard in prospective teachers, they realized that it was not as easy as it might sound. What, specifically, are dispositions? How does one recognize them in others? NCATE's description suggests that they can be observed in classroom behaviors. What behaviors suggest that a teacher is "fair?" What behaviors insure a belief that all students can learn?

It is relatively easy to "assess" content knowledge and knowledge of instructional strategies with pencil and paper tests. Assessment of skills is more difficult because the application of knowledge (skills) must be assessed based on the observer's interpretation of the candidates' actions. Still, it is relatively easy to observe whether prospective teachers do or don't use appropriate methodology. By the time we get to dispositions, not only does the "standard" become vague, but it fails to define "professional dispositions" in any meaningful way. How does one assess something that is so vague?

Few would argue that a teacher's unseen mental processes profoundly influence the effectiveness of that teacher in the classroom. But that doesn't mean that developing and assessing "appropriate" mental process in prospective teachers is easily accomplished. The issue quickly evolved into a lively, and sometimes contentious, debate that continues today.[2]

While some teacher education institutions immediately set about defining professional dispositions and generating checklists to "assess" their presence, others called on NCATE to further define what they were looking for. The NCATE Glossary presently defines professional dispositions as *"…attitudes, values, and beliefs demonstrated through both verbal and non-verbal behaviors as educators interact with students, families, colleagues, and communities. These positive behaviors support student learning and development."*

The two dispositions that NCATE specifically included were "fairness and the belief that all students can learn." They further state that *"… 'all students' includes students with exceptionalities and of different ethnic, racial, gender, sexual orientation, language, religious, socioeconomic, and regional/geographic origins."*[3]

While NCATE's goals are undoubtedly noble, their attempts to "define" dispositions are no more successful today than they were in 2000. What, specifically, is "fairness?" Is it possible to assess the disposition of "fairness" by observing a candidate's actions? For example, one might choose to assess fairness in terms of the time a teacher spends with each student. But that would imply that "all students" would have equal needs, which is a clearly invalid assumption.

Stating a couple of examples of dispositions is vastly different from *defining* a disposition. Does telling me that a dog, a cow, and a whale are all mammals help me understand what a mammal is? Many educators continue to believe that "professional dispositions" can be identified and defined. Studies produce endless descriptive data and endless lists of "qualities." Despite these efforts, researchers are no closer to agreeing on 1.) what professional dispositions effective teachers should be expected to have; and 2.) how each of these dispositions can be defined. If, after 10 years, there is still a lack of consensus about what dispositions are, moving to the step of assessing them seems fruitless…yet NCATE dictates that it must be done for accreditation.

What Are Dispositions?

As Shakespeare said, "Ay, there's the rub." Here are some responses from a variety of educational sources:

1. As previously stated, NCATE (2006) described dispositions as "values, commitments, and professional ethics that influence a teacher's behavior toward his/her students, families, colleagues, and communities."

2. In 1993, Lillian Katz stated that "a disposition is a tendency to exhibit frequently, consciously, and voluntarily a pattern of behavior that is directed to a broad goal. Katz has also referred to dispositions as "the trend of a teacher's actions in particular contexts," and "patterns of behavior that are exhibited frequently and intentionally in the absence of coercion, representing a habit of mind."[4]

3. Various researchers in the field have used terms such as *tendencies, values, habits of mind, attitudes, behaviors, ethics, ethos, social justice, kindness, sense of integrity, moral will, character,* and *virtue.*

4. Many descriptors are not so much definitions as lists of qualities to be assessed by observing external behaviors. These include *initiative, fairness, decency, service, pro-social behavior, honesty, humility, trust, empathy,* and *a sense of community.*

As Ritchhart states, "Undoubtedly, all of these are 'part' of what make a teacher effective, but failure to actually define dispositions makes it difficult to establish the usefulness of dispositions as a concept and to build on one another's research."[5]

The search for specific definitions for dispositions brings to mind an argument before the United States Supreme Court. In 1964, after years of debate on what constitutes "obscenity," Justice Potter Stewart explained "hard-core" pornography, or what is obscene, by saying, "I shall not today attempt further to define the kinds of material I understand to be embraced . . . [b]ut I know it when I see it..."[6] After 50 years of discussion, the question has still not been resolved. One wonders if the same will be true for dispositions.

The Case For Assessing Dispositions

Those advocating the inclusion of dispositions in NCATE Standards base their arguments on the belief that certain dispositions are essential to effective teaching. Because dispositions are assumed to represent an individual's tendencies to act in a particular manner, they are predictive of whether teachers are likely to apply the knowledge and skills they learn in teacher preparation programs to their own classroom teaching. Wilkerson argues that "dispositions are, in the long run, more important than knowledge and skills."[7]

Wasicsko puts it this way. "It is not so much what the teacher knows or does; rather, it is who the person is that makes all the difference. It is particular human qualities or dispositions in combination with, and shining through, their knowledge and skills that allow some teachers to transform many students' lives.[8]

The Case Against Assessing Dispositions

The titles of this section and the previous one are misleading because they suggest that there is a dichotomy—for and against positions, only one of which is correct. Clearly, most of the arguments for the inclusion of dispositions in teaching standards are based on common sense and experience. At issue, then, is not whether dispositions are important in shaping an effective teacher, but whether those characteristics can be 1.) identified; and 2.) defined sufficiently to be assessed fairly.

At the heart of the argument against including dispositions in the NCATE Standards is the fact that there is no agreed-upon definition of the construct. Some critics go farther, suggesting that the dispositions construct is inherently fuzzy and difficult, if not impossible, to define operationally.[9] Without clarity, dispositions cannot be measured reliably and validly. And without an operational definition or psychometrically sound measures, it is difficult, if not impossible, to gather empirical evidence to determine the impact of teacher dispositions on student achievement.

In fact, in 1999, James Raths, a supporter of NCATE who argues strongly for the importance of attention to values and beliefs in education, described his own research in a letter to the chair of AACTE accreditation.

> "I have been unable to scale dispositions reliably--and my research program is essentially a failure. I have searched the literature and appealed to measurement specialists on a national scale for help, but there is little out there. So much of what is written in these standards calls on our colleagues to measure dispositions and their strengths. Can it be done? I consider it a

strategic and grave error to include this language.... This language requires [teacher education institutions] to do something that cannot be done. Please take this technical problem into account when considering a revision of the document."[10]

In addition to these methodological issues, opponents warn that by including dispositions in the NCATE Standards, the educational community becomes vulnerable to the danger of ideological bias. William Damon, a professor of education at Stanford University, wrote that NCATE "intended the term 'dispositions' to signify 'beliefs and attitudes' that reflect a particular stance toward moral issues large and small." Damon warned that "unless assessment for accreditation was based on clearly defined principles rather than 'the fuzzy intuitions of whoever happens to be in charge of the process at any one time,' the assessment process could be used to eliminate anyone who didn't pass certain political litmus tests and to indoctrinate those who were afraid of being eliminated."[11]

Describing problems in implementing the assessment of dispositions, Payne and Summers acknowledged a sense of responsibility to ensure that only teacher candidates "...who were knowledgeable in their content and skilled in and disposed toward creating safe learning environments for all students could obtain teaching credentials." However, they admitted that, because there were no objective criteria measuring "appropriate" dispositions, "dismissing unsuitable candidates was nearly impossible, in part because the faculty's judgment of the candidates' suitability was typically based on the answer to one question: "Would I want this person teaching my child?"[12]

Let's return to the question of whether, as NCATE suggests, dispositions can be verified by observation. As an example, we'll use one of the dispositions that NCATE has identified—that a teacher should have high expectations for the achievement of all students. Murray[13] points out how difficult it is to draw valid conclusions about the presence or absence of a particular quality by observation alone. We observe a behavior—"the teacher seats certain pupils further away and outside the classroom zone of frequent teacher-pupil interaction, looks at them less, asks them low-level questions, calls on them less often, and gives them less time to respond, offers them fewer hints when they are called on, and gives them less praise and more blame than other pupils."[14] We also observe that these pupils perform at lower levels than the pupils who are "seated inside the zone of frequent interaction and receive more teacher attention, more higher level questions, more hints, more time to respond, more praise, etc.)"[15] Aha, you might say...proof of the correlation between teacher behavior and student achievement *and* the absence of high expectations on the part of the teacher.

Murray says that there is a strong temptation to assume that a "disposition" caused the teacher to behave as she did. However, he points out that "the evidence is consistent with a teacher disposition of insensitivity or with the dispositions of low expectation, prejudice, or meanness. On the other hand, the evidence is equally consistent with the opposite dispositions of kindness and caring. The kind and caring teacher, believing the pupil does not know very much, will not want to embarrass the pupil by calling on the pupil often, will ask appropriately easy questions when the pupil is called on, will give fewer hints, and will offer less time when the pupil fails to respond, as it would be unkind to prolong the pupil's embarrassment and so on."[16]

The factors involved in this interaction and conclusion are extremely complex. First, the teacher apparently does not have similar expectations for all students. And yes, her treatment of students for whom she has lower expectations is likely to contribute to their lack of achievement. However, her behavior could very well be the result of a misconception, rather than a disposition of prejudice or intolerance. Many prospective teachers are exposed to research studies that conclude that students from particular ethnic or economic backgrounds tend to do poorly in comparison with to other students. (Think about the validity of such studies in terms of anything outside of the statistics. Yet many use these studies to infer a cause and effect relationship between these factors and achievement.) Ignorant of other data suggesting that many students with these same backgrounds excel, the teacher acquires expectations in line with the original study. So yes, it is clear that the teacher has "low expectations," but not because that teacher is prejudiced or intolerant.

Second, observing the behaviors themselves tells us nothing about the *why*. In fact, as Murray points out, the teacher may well be exhibiting empathy and kindness in attempting to shelter the student from embarrassment. As you can see, the complex interaction of "dispositions" is not at all amenable to being assessed by observation.

In such as case, "I know it when I see it" is wholly dependent on the observer's dispositions, experiences, and beliefs in cause and effect. What goes on in the mind of the teacher is not, and never will be observable, even to the teacher. It is doubtful that the teacher made a conscious decision where to place these students. Rather, the behavior was driven by a set of unconscious presuppositions, beliefs, and values working together to generate a complex and unstated "reason."

Models of Assessment

In their most recent attempt to explain dispositions, NCATE states that they expect them to be assessed based on a candidate's behavior. Clearly, they recognize that one can't directly assess a belief, an attitude, or a value. Some institutions respond by having groups of educators make up lists of qualities they expect to see in an effective teacher. A second group then ranks the behaviors in terms of importance. Using this list as a rubric, teams of evaluators decide whether a particular teacher does or does not demonstrate these behaviors sufficiently to suggest the existence of the characteristic. One might think of this approach as assessment by consensus. While it does minimize the role of individual preferences, it is still highly subjective.

Thornton[17] summarizes several other models used by institutions to assess dispositions.

Standards Language: Such models focus on checklists, rating scales, and rubrics, which are correlated with the language of state and national standards...[however,] the descriptors provided, and the criteria for assessing these dispositions look more like pedagogical practices or teaching behaviors than dispositions. Many restate pedagogical competencies and expectations with the words "value," "believe", or "committed to" in front of them."[18]

"Professional" Behaviors: These assessments focus on behaviors such as attendance, work ethic, preparation, punctuality, sense of humor, and appropriate dress. Such checklists avoid the pitfalls of assessing thought, relying solely on easy to document behaviors. But do they capture the essence of what makes a teacher effective? It's possible that at least some of these institutions, recognizing the impossibility of actually assessing teacher thinking, came up with a solution that would satisfy NCATE without becoming bogged down in unanswerable questions and risking lawsuits!

Self-Perceptions: An increasingly popular method of assessment is "self-perceptions." For example, the teacher candidate may be asked to respond in writing to a description of a typical classroom incident. Thornton points out that, "Although the model gives insight into how the candidate sees him or herself in relation to others and the greater world, it is limited to the candidate's self-awareness and ability to express their self-reflection." Earlier in this book, we saw examples of how we can express the highest ideals, yet behave in very different ways depending on the complex context in which we find ourselves.

Another application of the self-perception model is a questionnaire utilizing a Likert Scale. In one study, teacher candidates were given a list of qualities, such as "Teachers should be responsive and thoughtful listeners." 100% of the participants "strongly agreed" with the statement. 97% agreed or strongly agreed that "Teachers should engage in reflection to understand themselves and to understand their impact on student learning and well-being."[19]

Only 84.9% of the candidates agreed or strongly agreed with the statement that "Teachers should have high expectations for all students." This statistic is particularly interesting because in his defense of NCATE's inclusion of dispositions as a standard to be evaluated, Arthur Wise, the president of NCATE, specifically named two professional dispositions—fairness and *belief that all students can learn*. These are expected in candidates graduating from teacher education programs meeting accreditation standards. Yet despite more than 15% of their students who clearly did not possess that belief, the researchers concluded that "... generally speaking, [the candidates who took part in the study] appear to have dispositions of effective teachers."

Perhaps I'm a bit cynical, but I would hesitate to correlate teacher education students' response to such questions as indicative of their actual behavior...or even a "disposition" to behave in such a manner. How likely are students to "disagree" or "strongly disagree" with statements that they have undoubtedly heard or read about as qualities of a teacher that are prized?

Morals and Ethics: Some proponents focus on the moral and ethical aspects of teaching, such as the teacher's beliefs about students with diverse backgrounds. Citing the inequities in the traditional treatment of minorities in schools, Villegas argues that assessment of "social justice" dispositions is critical in the training of teachers. "The overriding goal of the social justice agenda in teacher education is to prepare teachers who can teach all students well, not just those traditionally well served by schools, so that, as adults, all are able to participate equitably in the economic and political life of the country." [20]

Others have an even more profound goal, focusing on the "moral character" and "virtue" of teacher candidates. For example, Osguthorpe argues that teacher educators must prepare "teachers of good disposition and moral character simply for the sake of teaching that accords with what is good, right, and virtuous."[21] The ability of the teacher to act as a role model is critical to others. They go so far as to say that teachers must be able to transfer key dispositions to their students and teach them ethics and "virtues."[22]

It would be difficult to contradict these positions, but agreeing does little to answer the question of how, specifically one assesses such dispositions. Who defines what is good, right, or virtuous?

Context: One assumption in assessing the existence of dispositions is that they are stable, rather than context-dependent or subject to change. This assumption fails to take into account the role of context in the tremendously complex interaction of values, beliefs, and external pressures present. For example, what disposition motivates a teacher to call on a particular student at a particular time? What factors would motivate the teacher to *not* call on that particular student? Would the behavior change if the teacher were being observed? If the teacher felt rushed to cover a lot of material in a little time? If there was a test coming up?

The Role of Dispositions in Defining and Assessing Dispositions

The various ways in which people approach dispositions, define them, and identify essential dispositions from among them are largely shaped by the dispositions of the definer. Attempts to define appropriate dispositions lead to an even larger group of abstract and essentially indefinable terms. For example, the dispositions required by a faith-based institution may be very different from those valued by an institution that focuses on "out of the box" thinking.

In choosing to observe behaviors as indicators of the possession of appropriate dispositions, there remains the problem of the observer's interpretation. What does it mean to "treat students with respect"? What behaviors definitively prove the existence of respect? Is a teacher respectful if he speaks kindly to a student? Is she disrespectful if she corrects a student's misunderstanding of a concept? Is a teacher respectful if he firmly demands the student's best efforts? The meaning of respect in these behaviors is in the eye of the beholder.

Can Dispositions Be Taught?

A basic assumption is that teacher education programs change the students in some meaningful way, increasing their knowledge and skills to make them exemplary teachers. A prospective teacher comes into the program unfamiliar with various theories of learning. During the course of the program, the teacher learns. In theory, this results in a change of behavior that makes the candidate more likely to succeed in the classroom. Is this same thing true of "dispositions." Can they be taught or developed? And if so, how?

In his book *Being and Becoming: A Field Approach to Psychology*, psychologist Arthur Combs discussed five beliefs held by effective helpers. At the First Annual Symposium on Educator Dispositions in 2002, Professor Emeritus Dick Usher reformulated the five as dispositions of teacher effectiveness. This list of dispositions for effective teachers included: empathy, positive view of self and others, authenticity, and meaningful purpose and vision. Usher then elaborated on these dispositions.

> "Dispositions are not behaviors. They do not exist as distinct entities of actions or thoughts, or traits. Rather, they represent the ways in which an individual has stocked, structured and ordered his or her psyche or mind; or, in the language of the theoretical underpinnings of Combs and this associate, his or her perceptual field.

> "Dispositions are determiners of behavior though not in a one-to-one way. They are constellations of personal meanings from which behaviors spring and thus they do determine the probability of effectiveness for one's professional choices and behaviors. As such dispositions are not open to direct measurement, however, dispositions can be inferred and

inferences can be subjected to standards of validity and reliability for use in research and other measurement tasks.

"Dispositions are also not open to direct change from or by the environment though they can change in the same ways that all human changes occur: through changes in one's physical, spiritual, emotional, and cognitive functioning that necessitates dispositional reconstruction."[23]

Whether dispositions can or cannot be changed from or by the environment, teacher education is still left with the problem of NCATE's Standard. Like many of the tasks that teachers are "required" to do, such as "cover" 24 years of content in 12 or less years, the standard stems from good intentions, but doesn't concern itself with the question of how the goal can be reached.

The Debate Goes On

Many schools of education and researchers have dutifully responded with studies that enabled them to produce a list of dispositions that satisfied themselves and NCATE.[24] Yet some fundamental issues related to the role of dispositions in teacher education remain unresolved. For example, Hess[25] argues that there is no rigorous empirical evidence demonstrating that certain beliefs or dispositions improve teacher effectiveness. Yet six years earlier,

"…Taylor and Wasicsko claimed that 'there is a significant body of research indicating that teachers' attitudes, values, and beliefs about students, about teaching, and about themselves, strongly influence the impact they will have on student learning and development.' Similarly, whereas the National Network for the Study of Educator Dispositions (NNSED) (2004) offers a research-based, pilot-tested instrument with which prospective teachers can self-assess their disposition to teach (http://www.educatordispositions.org/moodle/moodle/), Johnson, Johnson, Farenga, and Ness (2005) wrote that 'nowhere in the literature can one find a reliable and valid measure of a candidate's (or anyone's) dispositions'."[26] With such disparity in perception, a quick end to the debate does not seem realistic.

William Damon of Stanford University warns that only rigorously defined standards can adequately protect prospective teacher candidates from subjective whims. He goes on to list what can and cannot be fairly assessed.

"1. It is acceptable to assess skills, knowledge, and understandings… that derive from the established knowledge base of education.

2. It is not acceptable to assess attitudes and beliefs related to religious preference or political ideologies.

3. Beliefs that are directly related to a candidate's capacity and motivation to teach are appropriate to examine. For example, it reasonable to ask candidates whether they believe that all children can learn. (Author's note: If the candidate says "Yes," does this prove the presence of that belief? Consider the pressures on the candidate to give the "acceptable" answer.)

4. It is reasonable to assess personal characteristics that are essential to the job of teaching, including character virtues such as honesty, responsibility, and diligence. (Once again, one must be careful not to make assumptions about the existence or lack thereof based solely on behavior.)

5. It is not acceptable to assess personal characteristics that have only a speculative relationship with teaching ability. For example, some teachers are shy, while others are gregarious."[27]

This description of the dispositions debate is in no way intended to be exhaustive, nor is it intended to take a position. It is merely an exploration of a current issue in education that addresses the qualities that make teachers effective.

Those involved with teacher education…and its accompanying problems of accreditation…have a vested interest in dealing with this debate. The results will certainly influence what does or doesn't happen in the training of prospective teachers. But what of the millions of teachers who are already in the classroom. Will a solution to the problem change anything about the way they presently teach? Unlikely…unless someone decides that every teacher needs to "take a test" or go back to school to be "trained" in the "correct" dispositions.

Even when studies generate a series of behaviors that they have mathematically confirmed reliable and valid, the listed behaviors still focus on *what* the prospective teacher does. They universally fail to question the actual beliefs and values that underlie those qualities. *Why* did the candidate choose to act in that way? Each person's *why* is different, based on the complex interactions of the realms of conscious and unconscious thought.

Some insist that effective teacher education can bring about significant changes that may turn an otherwise ineffective teacher into an effective teacher. We don't have to wait until educational professionals "agree" on what dispositions are, whether or not they can be taught or changed, or how to assess whether a person has the "correct" dispositions for teaching. We can begin today to utilize the one method that has been shown to yield results—self-reflection.

Teaching in Mind offers many processes to mine your own thinking, as well as to understand how your thinking profoundly influences not only what you do in the classroom, but what you perceive and how you interpret the behavior of others. By establishing a cause and effect relationship between your thoughts and behaviors, you then have the choice of whether to change. You can analyze whether your beliefs are valid in the light of research and/or the experience of others. Then you can decide what you can or should change to bring your experience in line with your vision of education.

If theorists feel the need to continue the debate about "essential dispositions," so be it. But you need not wait for their conclusions. You have it within your power today to identify and assess your own thinking, and to shape it in ways that bring you closer to your vision of an effective, successful, and memorable teacher.

---

[1] http://www.ncate.org/public/unitStandardsRubrics.asp?ch=4#stnd1. Accessed August 26, 2010

2 Borko, Hilda, Dan Liston, and Jennifer A. Whitcomb. "Apples and fishes: the debate over dispositions in teacher education." *Journal of Teacher Education 58.5* (2007): 359+. General OneFile. Web. 14 June 2010.

3 http://www.ncate.org/public/glossary.asp?ch=155#P. Accesses on August 26, 2010

4 Katz, L. (1993). Dispositions as educational goals. Urbana, IL: ERIC Clearinghouse on Elementary and Early Childhood Education. [ED363454] Accessed from http://www.edpsycinteractive.org/files/edoutcomes.html on August 26, 2010

5 Ritchhart, R. (2001). From IQ to IC: A dispositional view of intelligence. *Roeper Review, 23(3)*, 143-50.

6 JACOBELLIS v. OHIO, 378 U.S. 184 (1964)

7 Wilkerson, J. R. (2006). Measuring teacher dispositions: Standards-based or morality-based? *Teachers College Record*, published April 20, 2006

8 Wasicsko, M. M. (2007). The perceptual approach to teacher dispositions: The effective teacher as an effective person. In M. E. Diez & J. Raths (Eds.), *Dispositions in teacher education* (pp. 55-91). Charlotte, NC: Information Age.

9 Johnson, D. D., Johnson, B., Farenga, S. J., & Ness, D. (2005). *Trivializing teacher education: The accreditation squeeze.* Lanham, MD: Rowman & Littlefield.

10 Raths, J. (1999, November 15). Letter to John Oehler, chair of the AACTE committee on accreditation. Retrieved July 9, 2004, from http://udel.edu/educ/raths/ncatecomments.html

11 Honawar, Vaishali. "Teacher Ed. Community Is Striving to Interpret Candidate 'Dispositions'." *Education Week 27.28* (2008): 1. Academic OneFile. Web. 14 June 2010.

12 Payne, Maggie, and Deborah G. Summers. "From thought police to thoughtful practice: the evolution of dispositions assessment in a teacher education program." *Teaching and Learning 23.1* (2008): 40+. General OneFile. Web. 14 June 2010.

13 Murray, Frank B. "Disposition: a superfluous construct in teacher education." *Journal of Teacher Education 58.5* (2007): 381+. General OneFile. Web. 14 June 2010.

14 Ibid.

15 Ibid.

16 Ibid.

17 Thornton, Holly. "Dispositions in action: do dispositions make a difference in practice?" *Teacher Education Quarterly 33.2* (2006): 53. General OneFile. Web. 14 June 2010.

18 Ibid

19 Singh, Delar K., and David L. Stoloff. "Assessment of teacher dispositions." *College Student Journal 42.4* (2008): 1169+. General OneFile. Web. 16 Aug. 2010.

20 Villegas, Ana Maria. "Dispositions in teacher education: a look at social justice." *Journal of Teacher Education 58.5* (2007): 370+. General OneFile. Web. 16 Aug. 2010.

21 Osguthorpe, Richard D. "On the reasons we want teachers of good disposition and moral character." *Journal of Teacher Education 59.4* (2008): 288+. General OneFile. Web. 14 June 2010.

22 Helm, Carroll M. (2009) The Assessment of Teacher Dispositions, *The Journal of Experimental Education, 77(4),* 367-407

23 Usher, D. (2002, November). Arthur Combs' five dimensions of helper belief reformulated as five dispositions of teacher effectiveness. Paper presented at the meeting of the First Annual Symposium on Educator Dispositions: Effective Teacher--Effective Person. Eastern Kentucky University.

24 See for example, Richardson, Dianne, and Anthony J. Onwuegbuzie. "Attitudes toward dispositions of teachers." *Academic Exchange Quarterly 8.3* (2004): 31+. General OneFile. Web. 14 June 2010. Payne, Maggie, and Deborah G. Summers. "From thought police to thoughtful practice: the evolution of dispositions assessment in a teacher education program." *Teaching and Learning 23.1* (2008): 40+. General OneFile. Web. 14 June 2010.

25 Hess, F. (2006, February 7). Schools of reeducation? *Daily Camera.* (Reprinted from *The Washington Post*, February 5, 2006)

26 Borko, Hilda, Dan Liston, and Jennifer A. Whitcomb. "Apples and fishes: the debate over dispositions in teacher education." *Journal of Teacher Education 58.5* (2007): 359+. General OneFile. Web. 14 June 2010.

27 Damon, William. 2007. Dispositions and Teacher Assessment: The Need for a More Rigorous Definition. *Journal of Teacher Education, Vol. 58. No. 4*, Nov/Dec 2007, pp. 365-369

Index

CPSIA information can be obtained
at www.ICGtesting.com
Printed in the USA
JSHW020912141219
2950JS00001B/26